In all my years of ministry, .
the Spirit combined with such sound biblical theology. I've seen
the anointing and I've heard good teaching, but I've never seen
them combined like this!

—Pastor Peter Cochrane
Former Superintendent, Scotland's Assemblies of God

The message in this book got my heart so pierced that my
ministry took a turn. It rekindled fire on the inside of me, left
my heart burning for lost souls, and burned a desire to preach
the gospel that the Lamb of God may get the reward of His
suffering. Now I am back on the highways, bypaths, streets,
and the markets, preaching the gospel with a new zeal and fire!
Thank you, Lord Jesus, and thank you, Doc, for bringing the
message of your book to Africa!

—Pastor Robert Kingstone, Pastor
Agape-Calvary Church, Mawego, Kenya, East Africa

Dr. Sandy's book powerfully captures the incredible love of Jesus
that led Him to the cross for me. She describes how He looked
into the cup of God's wrath and saw my face, and I was undone
by this, forever changed.

—Pastors Rod and Michelle Smith
Heartbeat Ministries, Norwich, England

The message of the Lamb and the cup He drank for us is
essential to experiencing the pure love of God and the softening
of the heart. Dr. Kirk's book radiates with passion for Jesus, and
it gives an extremely necessary revelation.

—Pastor Greg Violi
Hutte David's Church, Bielefeld, Germany

My wife, Cathy, and I are pastors with many ministerial
responsibilities and at times we have found it difficult to stay
focused in our personal relationship with the Lord. Dr. Sandy's
book changed my life and gave me understanding on how to stay
on fire for God, even with a very heavy schedule. If you desire

to really know the true meaning of the cross or to carry a revival fire that can never be put out, Dr. Sandy's book is a must for you.

—PASTOR MARK A. KUNTZ, FOUNDER
GREATER WORKS MINISTRIES, WASHINGTON STATE, USA

UNDONE
BY A REVELATION OF THE LAMB

UNDONE

By a REVELATION
OF THE LAMB

SANDY DAVIS KIRK, PH.D.

Undone: By a Revelation of the Lamb by Sandy Davis Kirk PhD
Published by Creation House
A Charisma Media Company
600 Rinehart Road
Lake Mary, Florida 32746
www.charismamedia.com

Unless otherwise noted, all Scripture quotations are from the Holy Bible, New International Version. Copyright © 1973, 1978, 1984, 2010, 2011, International Bible Society. Used by permission.

Scripture quotations marked AMP are from the Amplified Bible. Old Testament copyright © 1965, 1987 by the Zondervan Corporation. The Amplified New Testament copyright © 1954, 1958, 1987 by the Lockman Foundation. Used by permission.

Scripture quotations marked KJV are from the King James Version of the Bible.

Scripture quotations marked MT are from the Masoretic Text. The Masoretic Text is considered the authoritative Hebrew text of the Jewish Bible and is widely used as the basis for translations of the Old Testament in Protestant Bibles.

Scripture quotations marked NAS are from the New American Standard Bible © Updated Edition, Copyright © 1960, 1962, 1963, 1968, 1971, 1972, 1973, 1975, 1977, 1995 by The Lockman Foundation. Used by permission. (www.Lockman.org)

Scripture quotations marked NKJV are from the New King James Version of the Bible. Copyright © 1979, 1980, 1982 by Thomas Nelson, Inc., publishers. Used by permission.

Scripture quotations marked TCNT are from The Twentieth Century New Testament. T.C.N.T.: Brooke Foss Westcott and Fenton J. A.

Hort, The Twentieth Century New Testament (New York: F.H. Revell,1904).

Design Director: Bill Johnson
Cover design by Nathan Morgan

Visit the author's website: www.gloryofthelamb.com

Events and conversations herein are recounted from the author's memory, and the author has sought permission, when possible, from individuals named. Some names have been changed to protect individuals' privacy.

Library of Congress Cataloging-in-Publication Data: 2013930877
International Standard Book Number: 978-1-62136-354-5
E-book International Standard Book Number: 978-1-62136-355-2

While the author has made every effort to provide accurate telephone numbers and Internet addresses at the time of publication, neither the publisher nor the author assumes any responsibility for errors or for changes that occur after publication.

First edition

13 14 15 16 17 — 9 8 7 6 5 4 3 2 1
Printed in the United States of America

*I saw the Lord sitting on a throne,
high and lifted up…So I said,
"Woe is me, for I am undone!"*

—Isaiah 6:1, 5, NKJV

DEDICATION

I dedicate this book to the memory of my dear parents, Bill and Suzanne Davis.

TABLE *of* CONTENTS

Introduction

A HEART UNDONE

A Transforming Revelation of the Cross

How long has it been since you've shed a tear over the cross of Jesus Christ? I'm sure you love the cross, but have you ever looked into the Father's cup and received such a stunning revelation of the Lamb that you were left trembling in repentance and passion and fire? If you're like me, I had cried more tears over the death of my dog than over the death of my Lord.[1]

Rarely had I thought about the cross, except perhaps once a year at Easter. Even then I only scratched the surface, glancing at the wounds but overlooking the depths of the Father's cup. Jonathan Edwards said that Jesus' primary reason for coming to earth was to drink that cup[2]; but I had never read a book, never heard a sermon, and as a Bible teacher, never taught a class on this highest purpose of Christ on earth.

Then I gazed with all my heart into the contents of the Father's cup, and everything changed. Like Paul, I saw the risen Lamb and I fell to my face, blinded by the brilliance of His glory. Suddenly I could see, really see, what I had missed for all of my Christian life. Like Isaiah, I saw the Lamb "high and lifted up," and I was undone! (Isa. 6:1, 5). Like the Jews at Pentecost, I was "cut to the heart" (Acts 2:37) by a breathtaking revelation of the gospel. That's what I believe will happen to you as you gaze at the Lamb of God in this book.

Through the years, I've watched students and pastors weeping at the foot of the cross on the floor of our chapel in Alabama, on the carpets of England or Germany or Canada, on the dirt floors of Africa, on cement floors in Peru, on the plush rugs of Hong Kong or Taiwan. Their hearts were utterly astonished, ravished, electrified by a revelation of what Jesus

1

did when He drank the Father's cup. They didn't know that they didn't know. But once they saw the magnitude of what Christ did, their hearts were undone. And when they stepped out and began to preach the message of the cross, people everywhere were also undone by a revelation of the Lamb.

This book cries for depth and truth. It is actually my systematic theology course made into warm fresh bread, as well as a revised and expanded version of my little book *The Glory of the Lamb*.[3] It implores the church to once again honor the blood of the Lamb and return to the pure gospel of Christ. It trumpets a call for strong scriptural doctrine to undergird our experience of revival.[4] But it also pleads for theology ablaze—an earnest appeal for passion and fire to burn in the midst of sound biblical teaching.[5]

Solomon said, "Where there is no vision [no redemptive revelation of God] the people perish" (Prov. 29:18, AMP). The word "revelation" in Greek is *apokalyptō*, meaning to remove a veil or a covering, "exposing to open view what was before hidden."[6] I'm not calling for a new revelation but a *new emphasis*. As Pastor Peter Cochrane, former superintendent of the Assemblies of God of Scotland, said to me, "Lass, this message seems new, but it is not newfangled. It's a *new focus!*"[7]

Of course the message of the cross and the Father's cup is not a new revelation. It's as old as the Bible, but because we've covered it over with every other subject, it has been overlooked. The time has come now for the veil to be removed as our hearts are undone by a fresh revelation of the full radiant glory of the Lamb.

Historically every great revival has uncovered a forgotten biblical truth. I believe the final great revival will unveil a revelation of the Lamb, even as the final book of the Bible unveils a Revelation of Jesus as the Lamb of God. A fresh revelation of the glory of the cross will be the energizing truth that drives the final great revival. That's why, as darkness sweeps over the nations, the glory of the Lamb is rising. The time at last has come to restore the plumb line of the cross to the center of His church. Even as the Lamb is the center of the throne in heaven (Rev. 5:6), He must become the center of His church on earth.

A. W. Tozer, in his classic book *The Knowledge of the Holy*, said, "To regain her lost power, the church must see heaven opened and have a transforming vision of God."[8] I invite you now through these pages to gaze upon Jesus until you experience your own transforming vision of the Lamb of God.

Now, as we begin this first chapter, let's go back to a time before time when the Father asked the Son a penetrating question. The story opens somewhere in timeless, spaceless eternity, where the preexistent glory of the Son filled the realms of God.[9] I beckon you into this story now; but first, please ask the Holy Spirit to prepare your heart to be undone by a piercing revelation of the Lamb.

INTRODUCTION ENDNOTES

1. J. C. Ryle asks this searing question: "Will you not wonder that any can hear of the cross and remain unmoved? I declare I know no greater proof of man's depravity, than the fact that thousands of so-called Christians see nothing in the cross. Well may our hearts be called stony, well may the eyes of our mind be called blind, well may our whole nature be called diseased, well may we all be called dead, when the cross of Christ is heard of and yet neglected...Christ was crucified for sinners, and yet many Christians live as if He was never crucified at all!" (J. C. Ryle, "The Cross," www.biblebb.com).
2. Jonathan Edwards, "Christ's Agony," *The Works of Jonathan Edwards*, vol. 2 (Edinburgh: The Banner of Truth Trust, 1995), 587.
3. *The Glory of the Lamb* (Hagerstown, MD: McDougal Publishers, 2004). This time, however, we will not include John's narrative; but we will dig much deeper, going straight to the heart of the story. As I love to do, I'll weave in current stories of Bible students and pastors who have been gripped and transformed by a revelation of the Lamb.
4. John Piper, in *The Supremacy of God in Preaching*, says, "Our people are starving for God....Most of our people have no one, no one in all the world, to tell them, week in and week out, about the supreme beauty and majesty of God." He continues, "My guess is that one great reason why people sometimes doubt the value of God-centered preaching, is because they have never heard any" (John Piper, *The Supremacy of God in Preaching* [Grand Rapids, MI: Baker Book House, 2004], 14–15). Never heard any? Is Piper right? In most of our churches in the West, rarely do we hear a sermon about God the Son, God the Father, God the Holy Spirit, the attributes of God, the Lamb of God, or about "Christ and him crucified" (1 Cor. 1:23; 2:2), which was Paul's central message.

5. Sadly, I've often heard people scoff at the idea of "theology." Even the very word *theology* is often mocked, when actually theology simply means a study of God (*Theos*: God; *ology*: study of). But isn't this what we need? We don't need dry intellectualism, but we do need theology that burns. Indeed, this is what feeds the soul, grounds our doctrine, gives us a true understanding of the Bible, and anchors our precious experiences with God. Theology ablaze can be thrilling and deeply fulfilling. This is what we crave—a study of *God* Himself. What could be more wonderful than learning more about Him? As Frederick Faber wrote, "Only to sit and think of God—Oh what a joy it is! To think the thought, to breathe the name—earth has no higher bliss" (Frederick W. Faber, cited in A. W. Tozer, *The Knowledge of the Holy: The Attributes of God* [San Francisco, CA: Harper Collins Publishing, 1961], 12).

6. Spiros Zodhiates, compiler and editor, Lexical Aids to the New Testament.

7. Pastor Peter Cochrane from Edinburgh, Scotland, on November 13, 2011.

8. Tozer, *The Knowledge of the Holy*, 121.

9. The term "pre-incarnate" speaks of the Son's existence before He came in human flesh. Similarly, Christ's "preexistence" speaks of the eternal existence of the Son before the existence of the world. Speaking of His eternal existence, the Psalmist wrote, "Before the mountains were brought forth, Or ever you had formed the earth and the world, Even from everlasting to everlasting you are God" (Ps. 90:2, NKJV). Jesus explained, "Before Abraham was, I am" (John 8:58, NKJV). He said, "I am the Alpha and Omega...who is and who was and who is to come, the Almighty" (Rev. 1:8). When Jesus described Himself as "the Alpha and the Omega," which are the first and last letters of the Greek alphabet, "He implies," says Wayne Grudem in *Systematic Theology*, "that he is before everything else; he is the beginning and will always be the end (or goal) of everything" (Wayne Grudem, *Systematic Theology* [Grand Rapids, MI: Zondervan, 1994], 169).

SECTION ONE

THE ETERNAL GLORY
of the LAMB

Chapter 1

THE ETERNAL LAMB

Unveiling the Covenant Between God and God

LONG BEFORE GOD tumbled galaxies into space and sprinkled the universe with starry constellations, the Father turned to His Son. As He looked at His Beloved, it must have stirred Him deeply.

Light poured from this beautiful, preexistent, uncreated Son of God.[1] Joy exuded from His being and His smile drenched infinity with love. On and on, endlessly, boundlessly, brilliantly, the glory of Christ flooded out through the realms of God.[2]

While gazing at His lovely Son, with love bursting in His heart, the Father began to unveil His plan of redemption: "My Beloved, I want Us to have a family. Son, I want to give You a bride!"

I believe He must have paused at this point, choking back deep emotion. "But this will require a fathomless sacrifice. Son, You must lay down Your life as a lamb!"

This divine transaction in the Godhead is known as the eternal covenant, described in the Bible: "The God of peace, who through the blood of the eternal covenant brought back from the dead our Lord Jesus" (Heb. 13:20). This sacred covenant, "which God devised and decreed before the ages" (1 Cor. 2:7, AMP), was not between God and man, as were His covenants with Adam, Noah, Abram, Moses, and David. This covenant was between *God* and *God*.[3]

THE ETERNAL COVENANT OF REDEMPTION

We are touching a raw nerve in the heart of God as we look into the mystery of this grand covenant. This is when the Father first disclosed the horrific suffering His Son would endure as the Lamb of God, for Christ was "a lamb without blemish or defect...chosen before the creation of the world" (1 Pet. 1:19–20).

May we tremble with reverence as we pause to look into this sacred covenant between God and God, for "the secret [of the sweet satisfying companionship] of the Lord have they who fear (revere and worship) Him, and He will show them His covenant and reveal to them its [deep, inner] meaning" (Ps. 25:14, AMP).

We don't have an exact account of the words, but we know the biblical background; so let's consider what that holy conversation could have been like as the Father revealed His heart to His Son:

> *Oh, My Son, My beloved, I want to create for You a bride, but it will cost you everything. It will mean You must tear Yourself from My side and step down into a fallen world of sin and pain. You must lay aside Your robes of eternal glory, robe Yourself in human flesh, and then allow Your flesh to be torn to bloody shreds on a cross.*

The Father wanted His Son to know what He would endure if He agreed to this covenant, so He showed Him the savage scourging that would leave Him flayed in pieces like a lamb for the burnt offering.[4] He revealed to Him the thorns that would pierce into His skull and the massive spikes that would drive through His hands and feet. Then the Father told His Beloved Son about the filthy mass of human sin that would plunge down upon Him, causing God to withdraw His presence and leave Him all alone on a cross.

At this point I can envision the Father taking a deep breath and looking straight into the eyes of His Son. With love tears streaming from His eyes and grief swelling in His heart, He told His Beloved the most painful and monumental part of the plan:

> *Then, My Son, You must open wide and drink down every drop of My cup of wrath! You must drink it all alone, for I will open the heavens and roar down upon You my undiluted wrath against sin. Over and over again, with pounding fury, You will be punished with My severe judgment, taking upon Yourself the*

punishment which they deserve for sin.[5] *My Son, this is what*
You must endure if You agree to become a lamb.

WHEN I SAW THE LAMB

Let me pause here to share with you now what happened that opened my
eyes to this covenant between God and God. As a young Bible teacher,
I had been hungrily reading the works of Jonathan Edwards, preparing
for an "Old Testament Survey" course I was teaching. My pastor had
suggested that I read Edwards, so I had been plowing through Edwards'
The History of the Work of Redemption, where I first learned about the
covenant of redemption, about which I knew nothing. As I read, my
heart began to race.

Edwards described, "Some things were done before the world was created, yea from eternity. The persons of the Trinity were, as it were, con-
federated in a design and a *covenant of redemption.* In this covenant the
Father had appointed the Son and the Son had undertaken the work, and
all things to be accomplished were stipulated and agreed."[6]

I began studying this covenant and teaching about it in my classes. I
realized that it is foundational to God's grand plan for the human race. It
dawned on me later that one reason the cross has been so slighted in our
day is because we don't know about this covenant. I read John Flavel's
description of the conversation between the Father and the Son in the
councils of the Godhead before the creation of the world, and my heart
began to pound even more.[7]

Then one day, while preparing for a "Life of Christ" course I was
teaching, I discovered a sermon by Jonathan Edwards called "Christ's
Agony." When I read it, I can honestly say I had an experience much like
Martin Luther's encounter with the cross. It was like lightning striking
my heart and transforming my whole Christian life.[8]

Edwards graphically described the agony of the Father's cup of wrath
which Jesus must engulf on the cross. As I read, I was thoroughly
and forever undone. If you've read my *Glory of the Lamb* book or *The
Unquenchable Flame,* you've already heard bits of this story. But I must
tell it again, for on this day, over twenty-five years ago, a theological revolution exploded in my own heart.

I knew vaguely about the wrath of God which Jesus endured on the cross, but I had never been impacted by it. I had never let it touch my heart so deeply. Now it began to rush over me like a tidal wave crashing over the shore of my heart and drenching me with passion for the Lamb like I'd never known. I realized that the reason I had little passion for the cross is because I had never looked into the covenant of redemption, primarily the Father's cup. Edwards wrote:

> A sense of that wrath that was to be poured out upon him, and of those amazing sufferings that he was to undergo, was strongly impressed on his mind by the immediate power of God.[9]

As I read these words about the Father's cup, I thought to myself, *This is the most important work of God ever accomplished on this earth!* Indeed, Edwards said, "His principal errand for coming to earth was to drink that cup."[10] That God's own innocent Son would drink down every drop of His eternal wrath, taking my punishment for sin, stunned my senses and filled me with a burning passion to tell others.

A few days later I visited a Methodist Sunday school class and poured out my heart about the cup. The class had been discussing the purpose of the cross. "Lots of people have died on crosses and we don't worship them," one man said. "So what's the big deal about Jesus' cross?" The class rushed to Jesus' defense, telling about the rejection of His people, the pain of whip and thorns, the agony of spikes hammered through hands and feet, the bearing of our sin and the abandonment of His Father.

I listened, my heart in my throat. I was only a visitor so I hesitated to express myself as passionately as I felt. But finally I could hold back no longer. I opened my mouth and began to pour out my heart about the Father's cup of eternal wrath. My voice trembled and tears flowed down my reddened cheeks as I said, "It wasn't just the pain of nails and scourge and spear! It wasn't only the dread of rejection and the terror of bearing our sin! Above all else, it was the horror of enduring floods and floods of God's wrath and punishment against our sin! This is what the Father showed Him in the great covenant of redemption before the creation of the world! This is what caused Him to bellow that cry, "My God, my God, why have you forsaken me?" on the cross.

As I spoke, my heart shook, and I could feel fire burning down upon me. It was like nothing I had experienced in my whole life! I had been baptized in the Holy Spirit for years and had attended countless Pentecostal services and Charismatic conferences, but this was a fire like I had never encountered. The class asked me to come back and teach a series on the cross, which I did. But what most amazed me was the rush of fire burning down from heaven which I felt as I spoke about the covenant of redemption and the Father's cup. I honestly felt like a baptism of fire had descended upon me, and I can tell you today—this flame has lasted for a lifetime. Years later I have discovered that this is a fire that attends a revelation of the Lamb.

As I sat in church that day, still trembling and feeling the heat, I silently wept before God, repenting for all the other subjects, the other messages and topics I had taught through the years. These subjects were good, but in comparison to what Jesus did when He drank the Father's cup, it was like trying to hold the light of a match up to the fiery brilliance of the sun. They were peripheral subjects, not central, and they didn't carry the fire from heaven upon them.

That day I made a promise to God. Like Paul who said, "I resolved to know nothing while I was among you except Jesus Christ and him crucified" (1 Cor. 2:2), I resolved to God that for the rest of my life I would teach and preach and write about the cross of the risen Christ. That was almost thirty years ago, and I have dedicated my whole life to teaching this message. The fire that I experienced that day has never dimmed, and I've seen it burn in many other lives.

Through the years, as I've taught this course in Bible schools around the world, I've seen the same fire fall on those who catch the message. Not only this, but pastors and Bible students have told me over and over again that when they preach about the Father's cup, the spirit of revival sweeps in. One pastor said, "Whenever I preach the cross, especially the Father's cup, the fire of God comes down and miracles happen!" Another pastor said, "Now that I've understood the Father's cup, the cross has become my only message!" One pastor told me that the weeping was so intense when He preached about the cup and the cry of Jesus, he had to stop and wait for the people to stop sobbing. When he finally resumed, revival flooded the whole church.

Oh, this is what we need! We need a passionate, heart-burning revelation of the Lamb of God to transform us. We need a theological revolution, which brings the gospel of Jesus Christ back to the center of the church. But it has to begin with you and me. We cannot call others to the cross until the cross has marked our lives. We cannot call others to Calvary until Calvary has melted us within. Such a view will pierce to the depths of our hearts; as Spurgeon said, "The piercing of the heart begins when we look upon the pierced One."[11]

That's why I'm asking you now to look with me into this great covenant between God and God which was planned before the creation of the world. This is where that piercing begins.

THE SON'S RESPONSE

Looking back on this eternal covenant of redemption, I can imagine the Father telling His Son what will happen after He fully drains this cup of wrath. Indeed, His heart would rupture and pour out a flood of blood and water. The power of this blood would be immeasurable, for it would be the blood of God. This blood would be for cleansing, saving, and preparing a bride for the Son. The water would be the first release of the pent-up river of life which will flow from the side of the Lamb (John 19:34; Rev. 22:1).

Then I believe the Father would have explained to His Beloved:

> *Son, I want You to have a bride who chooses to love You as I love you—with an infinite and unquenchable love. This is why We must create people with a free will. They must be able to choose whether or not they will love You.*

Now I see the Father, with searching eyes, asking the eternal question, the one on which the redemption of His bride would hinge:

> *Son, will You go? Will You lay down Your life as a lamb?*

I can imagine the tender emotion that must have ravished the Father's own heart as He waited for His Son's response. Not only the Father, but also the Holy Spirit must have held His breath, shaken by such a divine request. Through timeless eternity the Spirit of God had always loved the Son. He could not imagine the agony of parting from Him and leaving Him to suffer alone as a Lamb.

Now from this eternal vantage point, I picture the Son as He slowly closed His eyes and bowed His head. I see tears slipping down His face as He pondered this monumental request of His Father.

Silence must have filled the halls of infinitude. If angelic hosts were created yet, I'm sure no seraph in eternity breathed a sound. Angels stood aghast. Timeless moments passed as the Son looked ahead and saw what He would endure.

He saw Himself flung up on two stakes of wood, stripped of His robe of glory, draped instead in naked, bleeding flesh. He saw Himself crushed with human sin and cast into the raging flames of God's wrath and punishment. But He also saw something else. He saw a bride, taken from His wounded side and washed in His own blood. He saw Himself rising and ascending to the throne and receiving a bride covered with His resurrection glory. He saw a bride who would love Him and would live only to bring Him the reward of His sacrifice for her.

In fact, *He saw you,* and He loved you even then; for the Bible says, "He chose us in him before the creation of the world" (Eph. 1:4). Oh, please take this in because it's so vital to understand. Before you were ever born, Christ looked into the Father's cup of wrath and saw what would happen to you if He refused to drink it. The Bible says that all who reject Christ "will drink of the wine of God's fury, which has been poured full strength into the cup of his wrath" (Rev. 14:10). But the Son could not bear to see you have to drink the Father's cup of wrath for your sin. He could not endure living without you in His presence.

This is why "for the joy set before him" (Heb. 12:2), He lifted up His head and looked into His Father's eyes. I can envision Him, with tears spilling from His eyes and love gushing from His heart, crying with all His might:

"Yes, Father, I will go! I will offer Myself as Your Lamb!"

At this point, I can imagine the Son of God collapsing into His Father's arms. Together they wept, the Holy Spirit sobbing with them, for each of them knew the magnitude of this costly sacrifice.

Surely angelic hosts fell prostrate before the One who offered to pay such a price. They didn't fully understand this eternal covenant of redemption, for "angels long to look into these things" (1 Pet. 1:12). Heavenly beings could not imagine how One so revered by angels could be so "despised and rejected by men" (Isa. 53:3).

How could One so honored in heaven, where seraphim hide their eyes from the shining of His face, have the beard plucked out of His face with human spit dripping down His cheeks? How could One whose head is crowned with splendor have His lovely head crammed with piercing thorns? How could One before whom elders fall down in worship, casting their crowns at His feet, experience spikes pounded through His hands and feet? How could One around whom adoring hosts cry, "Glorify!" encounter angry mobs, screaming, "Crucify"?

Surely they must have wondered, *How could Majesty stoop to such misery? How could the crowned Prince become the crushed worm? How could the honored King become a humiliated criminal? How could the triumphant Lord become the tortured Lamb?* They didn't know, so all they could do was tremble on their faces as God embraced God.

Finally, after the emotion in the Godhead settled, I envision the Father straightening, lifting His mighty arm, pointing to the Son, and proclaiming: "Behold the Lamb, slain from the creation of the world!" (See Revelation 13:8; 1 Peter 1:19–20.)

At that moment all heaven must have exploded with glorious praise. Seraphim—the fiery ones—flamed more brightly as they fervently proclaimed, "Holy, holy, holy!" (Isa. 6:3). Awe and adoration flooded the limitless realms of infinitude. Worship from the tongues of angels streamed through boundless, timeless eternity.

THE FATHER LOOKS DOWN TODAY

Yet angels are not recipients of this redemptive work of the Lamb. We are! Jesus never bled for them. He bled for us!

Today the Father looks down on His people and sees how we have neglected the blood of His Son. He sees how the power has drained from our gospel because we've failed to keep His Son's sacrifice central as it was in the early church. He sees how this has weakened our message.

He sees how we have forgotten to keep the Lamb on the altar; and though revivals come from God Himself, the fire cannot be maintained for we've ignored the secret of the burnt offering.[12]

Sadly, because we've overlooked the cross and the blood of the Lamb, I believe He sees how the church has almost slipped into cardiac arrest. This gripping story of a young man on a far flung battlefield in Vietnam helps illustrate what I'm trying to say.

> A young soldier lay face down in the mud, his heart barely beating, blood draining out and pooling around his head. His friend found him and lifted his body to rush him to a medivac. But suddenly the wounded soldier stopped breathing. His eyes fixed and his body went limp in his friend's arms. "Oh, no!" gasped his friend. "I think he's dead," he moaned as he placed his body into the arms of the medic.
>
> The medic grabbed electrodes of a defibrillator and thrust the paddles to the soldier's chest. "Stand back!" he shouted as bolts of electricity jolted the soldier's body, but he didn't respond. Trying again, the medic yelled, "One, two, three!" Suddenly, a monitor picked up a heartbeat. Immediately, the medic slipped a needle into the soldier's vein, and in moments color returned to his ashen face. He was rushed to the nearest hospital where he received an emergency blood transfusion, and a dead young man was brought back to life.

The church is like that dying soldier. The blood has drained from her gospel and she has almost slipped into cardiac arrest. She's been riddled with subtle forms of materialism, humanism, and mysticism until her senses have dulled and the life has slowly and imperceptibly ebbed out. The church needs electrodes applied to her heart. She needs her soul defibrillated. She needs her veins infused with a fresh transfusion of the blood of Christ.[13] She needs a heart-jolting revelation of the Lamb.

I only know that's what I needed. I had never studied or taught on the cross. I had never felt any emotion or passion over the blood of the Lamb. I had never let it touch the deepest feelings of my heart. I thought the gospel message was only for evangelists, not teachers. By neglecting the gospel and failing to honor the blood, I had trampled over the blood of Christ.

Though I loved God dearly, I had never wept over the cross. I was oblivious to what really happened when Jesus gave Himself as a Lamb. Most of all, I was sound asleep to the magnitude of the Father's cup. As I said before, I had cried more tears over the death of a pet than over the death of my Savior.

That is, until my heart was utterly undone by a revelation of the Lamb. When I looked into the great covenant of redemption and then gazed into the Father's cup of punishment pouring down on Jesus, it broke me in a million pieces. I wept and wept in repentance, spilling tears of godly sorrow and, like the apostle Paul, resolving to know only "Christ and Him crucified" (1 Cor. 2:2).

Now, after almost thirty years of pouring out this message in books and schools around the world, I feel the Father's tender devotion to His Son pounding in my heart. I sense His powerful yearning to see His Son glorified in the church on earth. Deep in my spirit I hear Him thundering these words:

> *This is My Son! He will be honored for His sacrifice on the cross!*
> *His blood will be honored on earth as it is honored in heaven.*
> *My Son will receive the reward of His suffering as a lamb!*

If your heart is hungry for a deeper revelation of the cross, before you read on, please join me in this prayer of repentance for neglecting His sacrifice.

> *Oh, Father, I am so sorry for overlooking the sacrifice of Your Son! I repent with all my heart for trampling His blood with my indifference. I didn't mean to. I just didn't know about the eternal covenant of redemption. I didn't understand the Father's cup. Please forgive me and wash me with His precious blood. Right now, I open my heart and choose to earnestly behold the Lamb until I am completely undone!*

CHAPTER 1 ENDNOTES

1. His preexistence is His eternal existence before time and space (see note #9 in the introduction). There in the glory of the Godhead, the Son lived in face-to-face communion in the arms of His loving Father. "The Second Person is forever in the embrace of the Father in eternity...

God enjoying God, God stunned by the beauty of God, God searching out God," writes Stuart Greaves (Stuart Greaves, *The Existence and Majesty of God* [Kansas City, MO: Forerunner Books, 2008], 46). Bob Sorge writes, "Oh, the love that draws the Father into the heart of the Son, and the Spirit into the heart of the Father, and the Son into the heart of the Spirit" (Bob Sorge, *Secrets of the Secret Place* [Lee's Summit, MO: Oasis House, 2001], 216).

2. The New International Version says, "The Son is the radiance of God's glory and the exact representation of his being" (Heb. 1:3). He is the effulgence or shining forth of God's glory, being in the likeness of the Father. While He was on earth, Jesus prayed about this glory which He had in eternity: "And now Father, glorify me in your presence with the glory I had with you before the creation of the world" (John 17:5).

3. Professor Wayne Grudem, in his massive work entitled *Systematic Theology*, says, "Theologians speak of…a covenant that is not between God and man, but is among the members of the Trinity." He explains, "This covenant they call 'the covenant of redemption.' It is an agreement among the Father, Son, and Holy Spirit, in which the Son agreed to become a man, be our representative, obey the commands of the covenant of works on our behalf and pay the penalty for sin, which we deserved" (Wayne Grudem, *Systematic Theology* [Leicester, England: Inter-Varsity Press, 1994], 518).

4. The lamb for the burnt offering is a picture of Jesus, the Lamb of God, who would be flayed in pieces by a Roman scourge. God told Moses how to prepare the lamb for the burnt offering: "If the offering is a burnt offering from the flock, from either the sheep or the goats, he is to offer a male without defect. He is to slaughter it at the north side of the altar before the Lord, and Aaron's sons the priests shall sprinkle its blood against the altar on all sides. He is to cut it into pieces and the priest shall arrange them, including the head and the fat, on the burning wood that is on the altar….It is a burnt offering, an offering made by fire, an aroma pleasing to the Lord" (Lev. 1:10–13).

5. See the many Scriptures on the Father's cup in the Bible: Matthew 26:39, 42; Mark 14:36; and Luke 22:42 give Jesus' prayer to the Father about this cup. In the Old Testament, for example, the Psalmist warned, "In the hand of the Lord is a cup full of foaming wine mixed with spices" (Ps. 75:8). The reason spices were mixed into the brew was to increase its intoxicating effect. Ezekiel describes "the cup of horror and desolation" (Ezek. 23:33). God told Jeremiah that this cup in His hand was "filled with the wine of my wrath" (Jer. 25:15). Isaiah described "the cup that made you stagger; from that cup, the goblet of my wrath" (Isa. 51:17, 22). He wrote, "We considered him stricken

by God, smitten by Him and afflicted….The punishment that brought us peace was upon him" (Isa. 53:4–5). We will more fully unpack this subject of the Father's cup in later chapters of this book.

6. Jonathan Edwards, *The History of the Work of Redemption: The Works of Jonathan Edwards*, vol. 1 (Edinburgh: Banner of Truth Trust, 1995), 534.

7. About this eternal covenant of redemption Puritan scholar John Flavel wrote: "When was this compact made between the Father and the Son? I answer, it bears date from eternity. Before this world was, then were his delights in us, while as yet we had no existence, but only in the infinite mind and purpose of God, who had decreed this for us in Christ Jesus, as the apostle speaks, 2 Timothy 1:9" (John Flavel, "A Display of Christ, Part III: The Covenant of Redemption Between the Father and the Redeemer."

8. See chapter 8 for the story of Luther's experience with the cross.

9. Jonathan Edwards, "Christ's Agony," *The Works of Jonathan Edwards*, vol. 2 (Edinburgh: The Banner of Truth Trust, 1995), 867.

10. Ibid.

11. Charles Spurgeon, "How Hearts Are Softened," *Spurgeon's Expository Encyclopedia*, vol. 8 (Grand Rapids, MI: Baker Book House, 1977), 377.

12. See my book *The Unquenchable Flame* (Shippensburg, PA: Destiny Image, 2009), which explores why revivals cease and why the fire burns out from the altar of the church.

13. See Russell Moore's interesting article, "The Blood-Drained Gospel of Rob Bell," March 11, 2011, accessed from the Internet. I'll say more about this article in chapter 18, "A Blood-Drained Gospel," a title inspired by Moore's article.

Chapter 2

THE LAMB *at* CREATION

The Story of Calvary Revealed in Creation

T HE BREATH OF God rushed over Adam. He inhaled deeply and air filled his lungs. His heart began to beat and blood pulsed through arteries and veins. Strength poured into his muscles. Nerves carried impulses to his brain. His eyelids fluttered and vision filled him. He opened his eyes and looked into the face of God the Son.

We know this was the Son because the Scripture says, "All things were made through him, and without him was not anything made that was made" (John 1:3). "All things were created: things in heaven and on earth, visible and invisible whether thrones or powers or rulers or authorities, all things were created by him and for him" (Col. 1:16). So imagine what it was like for Adam when the pre-incarnate Christ "breathed into his nostrils the breath of life" (Gen. 2:7).[1] Now Adam looked into the eyes which shone with eternal love. The Lamb of God smiled down upon him, and glory washed over Adam like an ocean wave, drenching him from head to foot.

The reason we can say this was the Lamb of God is because the Son had already been called "a lamb without blemish or defect...chosen before the creation of the world" (1 Pet. 1:20). Therefore, in that moment of divine glory at the dawn of creation, as the Lamb of God locked eyes with the child of His creation, I'm sure it took Adam's breath away. Adam was undone by a revelation of the Lamb.

ETERNAL LIGHT

Can you imagine the brilliance of the Son shining down on this first created man? Even before Adam was created, Elohim had drawn back the veil from His Son and proclaimed, "Let there be light" (Gen. 1:3). Suddenly the light of the Lamb, which had filled eternity, burst out through the dark and formless universe, flooding time and space.[2]

Out of absolutely nothing (*bārā*), God had created the heavens and the earth,[3] and now the light which filled creation streamed from the face of God's eternal Lamb. Paul later confirmed the source of this light by writing: "For God who said, 'Let light shine out of darkness,' made his light shine in our hearts to give us the light of the knowledge of the glory of God in the face of Christ" (2 Cor. 4:6).[4]

But this preexistent glory of Christ was not just an outer radiance; it was part of His being. He is glory, for "the Son is the radiance of God's glory" (Heb. 1:3).[5] On through the created universe streamed this ineffable glory, rushing from the face of God the Son. Indeed, when the Father unveiled the light of the Lamb at creation, it was as though He was blazing abroad:

> *This is My Son! He is the source of all eternal light. He deserves all the glory, for He is My eternal Lamb!*

THE MASTER CARPENTER

Picture now the Son, compelled by love and commissioned by the Father, coming down to prepare the earth as a platform for the creation and redemption of His bride. The Father was the architect, and the Holy Spirit was the beautifier, but the Son was the master carpenter.[6]

Envision with me now those first few days before Adam was created. Imagine the Son as He scooped out ocean beds, filling them with billowing seas. He sculpted high mountains, capping them with snow which melted into rushing mountain streams. He lavished the earth with fresh vegetation and carpets of grass, dotting it with flowering fruit trees and towering redwoods. He sprinkled the universe with fiery planets and blazing stars, filling the seas with leaping fish, the skies with soaring birds, and the land with crawling insects and creeping animals.[7]

Then came the climax of creation when He reached into the clay of the earth and created the first man. Dipping His hands into dirt, God the Son fashioned the body of a man. What do you think filled the Son's thoughts as He rounded the shoulders and connected them to the back?

Did He think of the day He would be enfleshed in human skin? Did He think about His own shoulders and back which would be ripped to shreds by a Roman scourge?

As He carefully fashioned each hand and foot, did He think of the spikes that would penetrate His own hands and feet? As He smoothed out Adam's side, did He think of His own side, cleft open by a soldier's spear? Whatever were His thoughts, love drove Him to complete this crowning work of creation.

Bob Sorge beautifully writes this about the creation of Adam's emotions: "I can imagine the Son saying to the Father, 'Abba, I want Us to create man with the ability to love as deeply as We love. Because when I take on human flesh, I don't want to be diminished in My ability to love You.'" Sorge continues, "I suppose the Father answering, 'Son, I feel exactly the same way about this. Therefore, let's infuse into Adam's being the ability to experience a full and complete range of emotions, from severe sorrow to extravagant joy and love. In terms of his emotional chemistry, We'll make him exactly in Our image.'"[8]

At last the creation of a man was complete, and as Adam opened his eyes, he looked into the face of God. Because sin had not yet entered his heart, Adam walked in the unclouded glory of Christ. Think of it! Moses would be hidden in the cleft of a rock, only seeing the back of God's trailing glory; Aaron would be sprinkled with blood and covered with the smoke of incense; even the glory was covered with a cloud and veiled in the holy of holies; but Adam walked in cloudless glory. Naked and unashamed, he was clothed with the glory of the Lamb.[9]

When Adam gazed into the beauty and brightness of His face, I'm sure all he could do was fall to his knees and worship. What else can one do when gazing on the glory of Christ? There in the garden, with the love of the Lamb pouring over him like waves lapping over the shore, all he could do was breathe a sigh and adore. "Worship is the heart saying, 'Oh my God,'" says Allen Hood. "It is the heart being rent and undone on a thousand levels, saying, 'I love you,' while trembling at the same time. God has always wanted it this way. He set it up this way in the garden and He hasn't changed."[10]

A BRIDE FROM HIS SIDE

The work of creation, however, was still incomplete. Because there was "no suitable helper" for Adam (Gen. 2:20), God caused a deep sleep to come upon him.[11] Now the Master Carpenter began to carefully slice open Adam's side to take out a rib.[12] "Then the LORD God made a woman from the rib" (Gen. 2:22). Interestingly, the word *rib* comes from the Hebrew *tsêlâ'* which means "a side of a person."

Again, what do you think were the Son's thoughts as He painstakingly pierced open Adam's side to remove a bride? Surely He looked ahead to the day He would hang bleeding like a Lamb on a cross. Then, in the deep sleep of death, His own side would be pierced open and God would take from His side a bride.[13] You see, the church would take her first breath at Pentecost, but she was born at Calvary.

The Bible says that God "closed up the place with flesh" (Gen. 2:21), but it doesn't say there was no scar. When Adam's bride opened her eyes, she looked into the face of her husband. But then, I wonder if her eyes would have slipped down, her gaze arrested by the wound in his side. I can almost see her reaching out and running her fingers over the tender wound in his side, her heart filling with love. This lovely wound spoke volumes. It told her of the sacrifice Adam had made for her.

I believe in that holy moment at the dawn of creation, she fell deeply in love with her Adam, knowing she was now, just as Adam said, "bone of my bones and flesh of my flesh" (Gen. 2:23). Her love was unquenchable when she realized the magnitude of his sacrifice for her.

In a far higher way, when at last the bride of Christ begins to gaze with all her heart upon her wounded Bridegroom Lamb, like Adam's bride, something will happen in her heart. When she looks deeply at His wounds and understands the wrath He endured for her, unquenchable love will fill her. She will love Him as the Father loves Him, just like Jesus prayed "that the love you have for me may be in them" (John 17:26). Then her heart will be undone by a revelation of the Lamb and she will want to live for the reward of His suffering.

Tragically, however, one day the serpent deceived the woman.[14] He whispered to her, "You will be like God" (Gen. 3:5).[15] She fell for the deception, and she and Adam sinned against the Lord. "Then the eyes of both of them were opened and they realized they were naked so they sewed fig leaves together and made coverings for themselves" (Gen. 3:7). And when they "heard the sound of the LORD God as he was walking in the garden in the cool of the day," they hid from Him "among the trees of the garden" and the Lord called out, "where are you?" (Gen. 3:10).

THE STORY OF CALVARY IN CREATION

Now let's come with awe and reverence as we see how Adam was a type or "pattern of the one to come" (Rom. 5:14). Adam foreshadowed Jesus Christ who took the fall of the human race upon Himself, causing Satan's work to be unraveled and undone. Let's see now how the story of Calvary was weaved into the story of creation. Think about it:

- In the garden, Adam and his wife wanted to be "like God" (Gen. 2:5); at the cross, the Son of God chose to be "like a Lamb."

- In the garden, Adam walked naked and unashamed; at the cross, the Lamb hung naked and bearing our shame.

- In the garden, Adam and his wife were bathed in the glory of the Lamb; on the cross, the Lamb was bathed in His own blood.

- At the garden, after Adam sinned, he would toil by the sweat of his brow; in another garden (Gethsemane), the Lamb would toil in prayer until the sweat of His brow became stained with His own blood.

- After Adam was cast out of the garden, thorns cursed the earth; at the cross, those thorns drove into the brow of the Lamb.

- In the garden, Adam sinned and hid behind a tree; but there on Calvary, the Lamb bore our sin while hanging on a tree.

- In the garden, Adam had walked in heaven on earth in the presence of God; but on the cross, the Lamb bore the punishment of hell so we could have the presence of God.

- After the Fall, a son hid from his Father; at the cross of the Lamb, a Father hid from a Son.

- At the Fall, a Father called to a son, "Where are you?" At the cross of the Lamb, the Son cried, "My God, where are you? Why have you forsaken me?"

- In the garden, Adam drank from the river of God; at the cross, the Lamb of God—who created the rivers and streams—languished for a drink.

- In the garden, a serpent deceived the woman; at the cross of the Lamb, "the Seed of the woman" crushed the serpent's head.[16]

- At the Fall, "cherubim with flaming sword" blocked the way into the presence of God (Gen. 3:24); at the cross, a soldier drove his sword into the side of the Lamb, opening the way back into the presence of God.

- In the garden, Adam awakened from sleep and received his beautiful bride; after the cross, Jesus awakened from the deep sleep of death and now, as the Bridegroom Lamb, He prepares to receive His beautiful bride.

- In the garden, Adam's bride gazed at his wounded side and fell in love with him forever; and when the bride of Christ gazes deeply on the wounded side of her Bridegroom Lamb, she will fall in love with Him forever.

- And finally, after the Fall, God slew animals, probably lambs, and clothed Adam and Eve with the skins;[17] now Jesus has been slain and wants to clothe His bride with the glory of the Lamb.

- But it's not just the church He wants to clothe, it's His beloved Jewish people. You see, at the Fall, Adam clothed himself in "fig leaves" (Gen. 3:7), and fig leaves speak of Israel. God wants to strip the veil that covers the eyes of Jewish people. A heart-piercing revelation of the Lamb will open their eyes and cause them to behold their Messiah who became a Lamb.

Yes, through the entire scene of creation and the Fall, God was announcing the message of His coming Son, not just in words but in types and shadows. Through it all He was loudly proclaiming:

> *This is My Son! He will sacrifice Himself for a bride, and she will love Him as I love Him, for My Son will receive the reward of His suffering as a lamb!*

LAMBSKINS

God began unveiling the mystery of His Son as a Lamb from the first stroke of a stylus on parchment in the opening pages of the Bible. The first five books of the Old Testament, called the Torah in Hebrew or the Pentateuch in Greek, were written, not on papyrus, not on cowhide, not even on sheepskin. The Torah was written on *lambskins*! It was as though once again, from the very beginning of His Word, God was saying, "This is My Son! He is My eternal Lamb!"

When you see how this parchment was made, the point becomes even more clear; for a lamb was slain, skinned, and then the skin was soaked in lime water to remove all the hairs. It was stretched out on a wooden frame; and after it dried, it was cut in pieces. The scribe carefully wrote the Hebrew letters on the parchment; then it was pierced at the ends, nailed to two wooden posts, called "the Tree of Life," and rolled into a scroll.[18]

In the same way, Jesus, the Lamb who was slain, was skinned and cut in pieces by the Roman scourge; then He was nailed up to two posts as He was hung upon the tree. Now the cross of Calvary becomes a tree of life to all who come to Him.

LIFE'S GREATEST PURPOSE

I spent so many years as a Christian, not thinking about His sacrifice. But when I bowed my heart at the foot of the cross and began to look into the Father's cup which Jesus drank for me, I realized: the greatest purpose in life is to live to bring Jesus the reward of His suffering. Nothing so pleases the Father's heart, so beats in sync with His heartbeat for His Son, and so gives you a cause for your life.

The Moravians discovered this grand cause. The cry of the Moravians was, "May the Lamb who was slain receive the reward of His suffering!" They had a one-hundred-year prayer meeting and led one of the greatest missionary movements in history. Many Moravians died as they poured out their lives for the Lamb, but not one of them died in vain. They did not waste their lives. They had found the highest calling in life—to live for His reward.

In John Piper's brilliant little book, *Don't Waste Your Life*, he says, "The people who have made a durable difference in this world are not the people who have mastered many things, but who have been mastered by one great thing."[19] That one "great thing"—the greatest work ever accomplished in the entire universe—is the cross of Jesus Christ, God's eternal Lamb. Thus, says Piper, "a cross-centered, cross-exalting, cross-saturated life is a God glorifying life—the only God glorifying life. All others are wasted."[20]

Indeed, the highest purpose in life—the purpose for which you and I were created—is to live for the glory of God. Piper explains, "Life is wasted when we do not live for the glory of God....Christ is the glory of God. His blood soaked cross is the blazing center of that glory."[21]

That's why God has called each of us to draw aside and behold the Lamb until this one pure motive consumes us. Charles Spurgeon, considered the Prince of Preachers, said, "To meditate much on the Lamb of God is to occupy your minds with the grandest subject of thought in the universe. All others are flat compared with it....There is no subject in the world so vast, so sublime, so pure, so elevating, so divine; give me to behold the Lord Jesus, and my eye seeth every precious thing."[22]

So even now, pause to soak in the presence of the Lord. Look up at His beautiful face and let His goodness infuse you. Let the light of His face immerse you. Let His glory cover you. Let the One who is the "sole expression of the glory of God" clothe you with the glory of the Lamb.

But then, like Adam's bride, let your gaze slip down and focus on His wounds. See the wound in His side, still pulsing with love for His bride. See it streaming with love for you.

As He stands in the center of the throne and opens wide His arms, look at Him closely. Every wound bleeds glory.[23] Floods and floods and floods of His glory pour out from His piercings; for as the Bible says, "His glory covered the heavens....His splendor was like the sunrise; rays flashed from His hand, where His power was hidden" (Hab. 3:4). Let that glory flow down on you. Gaze upon His wounds until your heart is melted and completely undone by revelation of the Lamb!

CHAPTER 2 ENDNOTES

1. *Pre-incarnate* means before Christ came in the flesh (in carnate). This is why His birth is called His incarnation.
2. This divine light in Genesis 1:3 did not come from the brightness of the solar sun, for sun and moon and stars were not created until the fourth day: "God made two great lights—the greater light to govern the day and the lesser light to govern the night...and there was evening, and there was morning—the fourth day" (Gen. 1:16–19).
3. "In the beginning God (Elohim) created the heavens and the earth" (Gen. 1:1).This Hebrew word for "created" is *bārā*, which means "to create out of nothing." Scholars use a Latin term: *ex nihilo*, which means created out of absolutely nothing. Wayne Grudem explains that in physics matter and time and space must occur together. Therefore, before God created a material universe, He created time and space. He shows this by the opening words of Genesis: "In the beginning," for *beginning* is a time word. This first verse of the Bible holds a powerful word to those of us who believe that God created the world. Atheists tend to believe that nothing created the world. But nothing cannot create nothing. If nothing creates nothing, then there is nothing. Only God could create (*bārā)* matter out of absolutely nothing.
4. Stuart Greaves, an excellent Bible teacher at IHOP University, affirms, "God speaks for the first time in Genesis 1, declaring, 'Let there be light.' It is my opinion that the first in-breaking of light is the revelation of His glory in the face of Christ (2 Corinthians 4:6)" (Stuart Greaves, *The Existence and Majesty of God*, 90).

5. "The Son is the radiance of God's glory" (Heb. 1:3), and this word *radiance* in Greek is *apaugasma,* meaning "to emit light, to shine." This word is used only one time in the Bible and it refers to the luminous body of the Son. He is called the effulgence or shining forth of God's glory, being in the likeness of the Father.

6. Henrietta Mears, *What the Bible Is All About* (Ventura, CA: Regal Books, 1983), 34.

7. Grudem writes: "One glance at the sun or the stars convinces us of God's infinite power. And even a brief inspection of any leaf on a tree, or of the wonder of the human hand, or of any one living cell, convinces us of God's great wisdom. Who could make all of this? Who could make it out of nothing? Who could sustain it day after day for endless years? Such infinite power, such intricate skill, is completely beyond our comprehension. When we meditate on it, we give glory to God (Grudem, *Systematic Theology*, 271).

8. Bob Sorge, *The Power of the Blood* (Lee's Summits MO: Oasis House, 2008), 12.

9. Remember, this was the pre-incarnate Christ who had already agreed to become a slain Lamb before the creation of the world. So it is correct to say that Adam walked clothed in the glory of the Lamb.

10. Allen Hood, *The Excellencies of Christ: An Exploration Into The Endless Fascination of the God-Man* (Kansas City, MO: Forerunner Books, n.d.), 3.

11. Matthew Henry writes, "If man is the head, she is the crown, a crown to her husband, the crown of the visible creation" (Matthew Henry, *Matthew Henry's Commentary on the Whole Bible*, vol. 1 [McLean, VA: MacDonald Publishing Company, n.d.], 19).

12. Matthew Henry is the author of the famous quote: "The woman was made of a rib out of the side of Adam; not made out of his head to rule over him, nor out of his feet to be trampled upon by him, but out of his side to be equal with him, under his arm to be protected, and near his heart to be beloved" (*Matthew Henry's Commentary*, 20)

13. Matthew Henry wrote, "In this (as in many other things) Adam was a figure of him that was to come; for out of the side of Christ, the Second Adam, his spouse the church was formed, when he slept the sleep, the deep sleep of death upon the cross, in order to which his side was opened and there came out blood and water, blood to purchase his church and water to purify it to himself" (*Matthew Henry's Commentary*, 20).

14. The woman was not called Eve until after the Fall; see Genesis 3:20.

15. This fallacious concept, "you can be as God," is the bottom line deception of most cults today.

16. God told Satan that the "seed of the woman," who is Christ, "will crush your head, and you will strike his heel" (Gen. 3:15). This is known as the *protoevangelium*, which means the first proclamation of the gospel.

17. Jonathan Edwards said, "It is likely that these skins that Adam and Eve were clothed with were the skins of their sacrifices. God's clothing them with these was a lively figure of their being clothed with the righteousness of Christ," (Jonathan Edwards, *The History of Redemption*, John Erskine, ed. [Evansville, IN: 1959], 34).

18. Messianic Rabbi Eric Carlson, "The Wedding," Sid Roth website: "Jewish Roots."

19. John Piper, *Don't Waste Your Life*, (Wheaton, IL: Crossway Books, 2003), 44.

20. Ibid., 59.

21. Ibid, 32, 59.

22. Charles Spurgeon, "Behold the Lamb," *Spurgeon's Expository Encyclopedia*, vol. 3 (Grand Rapids, MI: Baker Book House, 1977), 110.

23. Like Adam, we too need to let the light of God's glory pour over us. It's like when my first grandbaby, William, was born. Because he was jaundiced, as many babies are a few days after birth, his skin was yellowish-orange. The doctor told us not to worry but simply to place him in front of a window where he could soak up the rays of the sun. This would cleanse his bloodstream and soon his skin would be rosy and normal. Most of us are like my grandbaby. Our bloodstream is impure. We need to sit in the presence of the Lamb and soak in the light of His glory. Bob Sorge suggests that "the sun provides heat, light, energy, and ultraviolet rays—radiation. *When we place ourselves in the sun of His countenance, the radiation of His glory does violence to those cancerous iniquities that we often feel helpless to fully overcome.*" In fact, he even suggests, "*When you're in His presence for extended periods, the molecular composition of your soul gets restructured.* You start to think differently and you don't even know why. The secret is simply this: large chunks of time in God's presence—loving Him and imbibing His word" (Bob Sorge, *Secrets of the Secret Place*, 59).

Chapter 3

A REVELATION *of the* LAMB

Beholding God's Lamb through the Bible

A N OLD MAN trudges silently up a hill, his insides heaving with grief. He loves God with all his heart, but what He has asked him to do is unthinkable: "Take your son, your only son, Isaac, whom you love and go to the region of Moriah. Sacrifice him there as a burnt offering" (Gen. 22:2).

Abraham's heart pounds in his chest like a hundred thundering horses' hooves. This was his beloved Isaac, the son of promise. How could he bear to prepare him as a burnt offering? He knew this meant he must slit open his throat, splash his blood on an altar (Lev. 1:11), skin him and slice him in pieces (1:6), arrange the slivers back in their original shape (1:12), then set him aflame as a burnt offering (1:13).[1]

As Abraham climbs, his face flushes and his eyes glaze with tears. He pauses and looks back. His throat runs dry as he sees the son he adores carrying the wood for the sacrifice over his shoulders.[2] Isaac catches up to Abraham now and breathlessly asks, "Father, the fire and the wood are here, but where is the lamb for the burnt offering?" Abraham's stomach lurches, then sickens. He clears his throat, not realizing he is prophesying of another Lamb. "God himself will provide a lamb," he mutters (Gen. 22:7–8).[3]

Finally they reach the top of Mount Moriah, and Abraham quietly takes the rope and ties his son's hands.[4] He lays him on the altar and then draws back the knife. I can imagine his hand shaking violently as he prepares to slash the blade down across Isaac's throat. Black swirls of confusion clog his brain. He feels like he will faint.

Then something happens. A voice from heaven speaks:[5] "Abraham!

Abraham! Do not lay your hand on the lad or do anything to him, for now I know that you fear and revere God, since you have not held back from Me or begrudged giving Me your son, your only son" (Gen. 22:11–12). Suddenly a ram, caught by his horns in the thicket, bleats and Abraham sacrifices him in place of his son (22:13).

I believe Abraham must have burst into tears of relief when he heard the voice and saw the ram, which of course is a mature male lamb. We know this story graphically portrays God's own Son as the coming Lamb. But most of all, it shows the heart of the Father. If we pray into the story and feel what Abraham would have felt, it shows us the trembling heart of God the Father as He reached out His hand to strike His one and only Son with divine punishment.

This story becomes even more compelling when we realize the meaning of the "whole burnt offering," which was the highest kind of sacrifice. The word *whole* comes from "holo" and *burnt* comes from "caust," which becomes the *holocaust* offering.[6] God had essentially told Abraham to offer his own son Isaac as a holocaust offering! Why? Because this is what God the Father would do with His own Son.

This is why this story gives us such a vivid glimpse into the Father's anguished heart. It shows us God's own Son consumed in fiery judgment as a holocaust on the altar of the cross. It was as though God was roaring down from heaven:

> *Can you understand what it meant to Me to give My Son as a lamb? This was My one and only Son who became a burnt offering—a holocaust offering—on the cross!*

FIRE ON THE BURNT OFFERING

Now all through the Bible God unfolds a progressive revelation of the Lamb. Not only was the Torah written on lambskins, but even Adam's son "Abel brought fat portions from some of the firstborn of his flock. And the Lord looked with favor on Abel and his offering" (Gen. 4:4).[7] Some scholars, including Martin Luther, believed that God showed His approval by sending fire down from heaven on the sacrifice, burning up the lamb, for it spoke of Christ His Son, the Lamb of God.

This is exactly what happened when Aaron laid the whole burnt offering on the altar at the dedication of the Tabernacle of Moses: "Fire came out from the presence of the Lord and consumed the burnt offering and the fat portions on the altar" (Lev. 9:24). The same thing happened when David offered burnt offerings at the place where the Temple of Solomon would be built: "The LORD answered him with fire from heaven on the altar of burnt offering" (1 Chron. 21:26). And when Solomon laid the burnt offering on the altar at the dedication of the temple, "fire came down from heaven and consumed the burnt offering and the sacrifices" (2 Chron. 7:1).

Do you see what this means? Oh, I simply can't get over it! The fire of heaven fell upon the sacrifices because God was revealing the fire that would fall upon His own Son as the holocaust offering. In fact, this even happened with Elijah's burnt offering on Mount Carmel: "At the time of the evening sacrifice,[8] Elijah came near" (1 Kings 18:36, AMP) and prayed. "Then the fire of the Lord fell and burned up the sacrifice, the wood, the stones, and the soil and also licked up the water in the trench" (18:38).

PASSOVER'S ROASTED LAMB

The story of the lamb at Passover is equally revealing. The Lord told Moses, "Each man is to take a lamb for his family" and slaughter it at twilight (Exod. 12:2–5). Then the blood of the lamb must be splashed "on the sides and the tops of the doorframes of the houses" to save the firstborn sons from death (12:7). "Do not break any of the bones" (12:46), the Lord insisted, then lift it up on a pole where it will be "roasted over the fire....Do not eat the meat raw or cooked in water; but roast it over the fire—head, legs, and inner parts....If some is left till morning, you must burn it" (12:8–10).[9]

Once again God was bellowing this truth from above:

This is My Son, My firstborn, who will not be spared from death! He will be lifted up on the pole of a cross where He will be roasted over the flames of My holy wrath against sin!

For the next fifteen hundred years this same Feast of Passover would be celebrated among God's people. Even Jesus, as a boy of twelve, would travel to Jerusalem with His parents to celebrate the feast. In fact, when

His parents "found him in the temple courts, sitting among the teachers, listening to them and asking them questions," what do you think He was discussing with them? The Bible says that they were all "amazed at his understanding and his answers" (Luke 2:46–47).

But remember, it was Passover. Alfred Edersheim suggests that Jesus was plying them with questions about Passover, then giving answers, probably explaining to them how God's Son would become the fulfillment of the Passover lamb.[10]

No wonder such a monumental act of God—the Sacrifice of His eternal Lamb—which was the greatest work ever accomplished in heaven or earth, must have this ordinance, called Passover, by which to remember it. For God said, "You must keep this ordinance at the appointed time year after year" (Exod. 13:10). And even after Jesus transformed Passover into the Lord's Supper, Paul said, "Whenever you eat this bread and drink this cup, you proclaim the Lord's death until he comes" (1 Cor. 11:26). It was as though, once again, the Father was announcing from heaven:

> *This is My Son! He will always be honored for His sacrifice as My Lamb!*

BETHLEHEM'S LAMB

A revelation of the Lamb comes into clearer focus when we consider Jesus' birth. Imagine with me those humble shepherds, watching over their flocks in the hills outside Bethlehem, known as the City of David. I can picture the shepherds, having drifted off to sleep, when suddenly explosions of light flood the skies. The men awake, astonished. Glory enflames the sky and bathes each one of them.

The shepherds leap to their feet, rubbing their eyes and trembling. They look on, terrified, as an angel appears in the midst of the brilliance. "Do not be afraid. I bring you good news of great joy that will be for all people. Today, in the City of David, a Savior is born to you; he is Christ the Lord!" (Luke 2:10–11). The angel continues, "This will be a sign to you: You will find a baby wrapped in cloths and lying in a manger" (2:12).

Surely these raw boned, rugged shepherds must have wondered: *A manger? How strange to put a baby in a manger, which is an animal feeding trough. And why would angels come to us? Who are we? We are the poorest of the poor, the lowliest of the lowly. Why would God choose to announce the birth of the Savior to us?*

We too wonder, for these men are not scholars of the Bible. They are not experts of the Law. They hold no lofty degrees. They are only peasants. They merely care for sheep and tend the birth of lambs. And then we realize: Yes, of course, God would choose shepherds, for shepherds always tend the birth of lambs! This is God's Lamb born into the world, and they are chosen above all people on the face of the earth to be the first to attend the birth of God's Lamb!

Now the pieces of the puzzle come together. Now do we see why God's Son was born in a stable, brought forth among sheep and lambs? The answer is because He is God's Lamb, and a stable is a fitting place for a lamb. And why must His only bed be a manger? Because a manger is an animal feeding trough, the perfect place for God's Lamb.

But why did God choose Bethlehem for the birth of His own Son? The answer brings me to my knees in adoring worship. You see, Bethlehem's lambs were born to be slain. Because Bethlehem was only six miles from Jerusalem, the lambs born in these ancient hills were born for sacrifice in the temple.

Several times a year, the shepherds of Bethlehem gathered all the male lambs, those between eight days and one year old, and took them to the Holy City. In the springtime thousands of these lambs would be slain at Passover. Just as these Bethlehem lambs were born to be slain in Jerusalem, in a far higher way, God's Lamb was born to be slain in Jerusalem. This is why God chose Bethlehem to be the birthplace of His own Lamb.[11]

"Behold the Lamb of God!"

Look now across the sun flecked shores of the River Jordan, where waters run icy cold this time of year. Melting snows from Mount Hermon form the headwaters of the Jordan, flowing down to the Sea of Galilee, then south to Jericho, emptying into the Dead Sea.

A crowd has gathered to be baptized by John the Baptist. See the rugged young prophet look up suddenly from his baptizing. He sees Jesus coming, and it must have looked as though a million suns burst across

John's face. I'm sure his face flushed and his body shook with the power and presence of God.

Thirty years before, while he was still in his mother Elizabeth's womb, her pregnant cousin, Mary, had come into the courtyard to greet her. "When Elizabeth heard Mary's greeting, the baby leaped in her womb, and Elizabeth was filled with the Holy Spirit" (Luke 1:41). Of course this baby Elizabeth carried would be known as John the Baptist, who would prepare the way for the coming of the Lord. That's why, as John looks up and sees Jesus coming toward him, I believe his spirit must have leapt again. He lifts his arm, trembling. Pointing to Jesus he bellows across the chilly waters of the Jordan River, "Behold the Lamb of God, which taketh away the sin of the world!" (John 1:29, KJV).

"This was the greatest sermon ever preached," says Charles Spurgeon,[12] for it points us to Christ.[13] But to Jewish thought it was mind-blowing. Jesus is the fulfillment of the Passover lambs, the fulfillment of lambs for the daily burnt offerings, and the fulfillment of all the other millions of bloody sacrifices in Israel.

Once again, God the Father was loudly declaring through John the Baptist:

> *This is My Son! Behold Him now! He is the fulfillment of all the sacrificial lambs throughout the entire Old Testament!*

Oh, how could we ever overlook a revelation of the Lamb again? God gave His one and only Son to bleed like a lamb on the cross! That's why the cross is the turning point of the whole human race. It is the summit, the sparkling mountain peak, the pinnacle of all history. It is the secret to Israel's past history and future history. It is the key to the heart of God. It displays the greatest demonstration of love ever seen upon this earth: "This is love: not that we loved God, but that he loved us and sent his Son as an atoning sacrifice for our sins" (1 John 4:10).

THE LAMB FOR A YOUNG GENERATION

Now I want to tell you a few stories that demonstrate what happened when a young generation of students and then pastors took hold of a revelation of the Lamb. It all began one night at a renewal meeting at Ché Ahn's

Harvest Rock Church in Pasadena, California, where I was attending Fuller Theological Seminary. At the end of a service, a tremendous burden for a young generation came over me. I bent over weeping in intercession for the pain of a fatherless generation. Because of this deep burden from the Lord, I focused my Ph.D. work on this subject, seeking to discover how to reach a postmodern, often fatherless, generation with the gospel. I concluded that only a heart rending revelation of the Lamb, attended by the breath of God in revival, could heal the wounds and set a generation ablaze with the gospel of Christ.[14]

But that was only theory; so after seminary, I followed this burden of the Lord, uprooting from Texas and moving down to start a camp for young people near the Brownsville Revival in Pensacola.[15] Soon I was teaching at the Brownsville Revival School of Ministry (BRSM). I taught Systematic Theology, Old Testament Survey, New Testament Survey, and several other courses. Always I kept the cross at the center of every course. Charles Spurgeon said that just as all roads lead back to Rome, all sermons should lead back to the cross. He said, "I take my text and make a bee-line to the cross."[16] I think the same should apply to biblical teaching as well.[17] As Spurgeon said, "Calvary preaching, Calvary theology, Calvary books, Calvary sermons! These are the things we want and in proportion as we have Calvary exalted and Christ magnified, the gospel is preached."[18]

I had only been teaching at BRSM for a year, when students in my classes began saying, "Dr. Sandy, I've had such an encounter with the cross that I feel like God has pierced my heart for the Lamb!" Other students described a deep burning or a trembling in their hearts, which seemed to come after we studied the cross and the Father's cup. Years earlier, as I've told you, this is what had happened to me when I read about the cup in Edwards' sermon "Christ's Agony"; but I didn't know God would keep on imparting this love-wound into other hungry hearts.

As the years passed, I watched the Lord continue piercing young hearts. I saw them arise with a passion that was like nothing I had ever seen. One night I heard nineteen-year-old Ryan, a student who lived at our camp, pacing up and down, his face beet-red with passion and his heart bursting with holy emotion. With all the fervency of his heart he cried, "Holy Spirit, for the rest of my life I will preach Jesus Christ and

Him crucified! May my heart be pierced every day by the pierced One! May I always feel your wound in my heart! Keep my feet walking in your bloody footsteps!"

Victor was a passionate young revival student, but one day he locked himself in his room and read the chapters on the Father's cup in my original *Glory of the Lamb* book (chapters 5 through 8 in this book). He told me later, "I wept and wept when I saw the Father's cup! Now I know I'll always preach the cross!"

A year later, when pastors in Reynosa, Mexico, saw a video of twenty-two-year-old Victor preaching the cross and trembling under the power of God, they said, "We've got to get this kid to Mexico. He's anointed!" They invited him to come; and he was given the largest stadium in the city, where he held a revival campaign with thousands attending. At one point, a storm blew in and it started to sprinkle. Victor knew that witches sometimes pray against meetings and stir up rain, so he stomped his feet, commanding the storm to leave, and it did.

Powerfully, with passion exploding from his heart, he preached the Father's cup. He told them how Jesus took their place on the cross. He told the story vividly, terribly, graphically; and hearts were pierced with the barb of the true gospel. He spoke with such fiery, penetrating truth that we could all feel the barb thrusting into our hearts. People wept shamelessly; and when he gave the altar call, hundreds raced forward to receive the Lord.

One lady, whose hands were completely gnarled into fists, told of being a witch, a murderer, and having made a pact with the devil. But when she received prayer, her hands opened up and a tumor in her breast dissolved. A girl in a wheelchair couldn't walk; but after being soaked in prayer, she stood and took huge steps across the platform. The joy on her face was worth the whole crusade. Victor lifted his face toward heaven, with tears streaming down his cheeks, and humbly thanked the Lord; for he knew—the only reason this crippled girl could walk was because of the costly sacrifice of the Lamb. Still today Victor leads crusades in Mexico as multitudes are healed and saved by the power of the cross.

Even after revival receded at Brownsville, those who let the Lamb go deep in their hearts rarely strayed from the Lord. A pastor's wife told me, "My daughter has had many powerful experiences with God, but falling on the floor and laughing for hours (as wonderful as that is) could not keep her from sin. What captured her heart and held her in holiness was when she saw the Lamb!"

This is the vision that will heal a young generation and set them ablaze for God. Because of the dryness they've experienced, this generation is indeed highly combustible. But once the spark of revival that shoots out from the message of the cross touches their dry hearts, like a dry field, they will burst into flames. The flames will quickly spread because God is blowing His winds across the field of this generation.

When we took a team of young revivalists to Africa, the pastors responded so dramatically that we established a Kenya Ablaze for the Lamb Ministry School. I watched these strong intelligent pastors weeping before God, repenting for neglecting the cross and for preaching other subjects. When the pastors left the school, they were carrying a theology of the cross that burned with the fire of revival and miracles. Now almost daily I receive texts and emails about revivals breaking out in African villages. These are the hidden places where Western evangelists and television cameras won't be found, but God sees what's happening and He breathes His wind upon the fire.

Pastor John Denge, whose radio ministry reaches his whole nation, cried: "This is the message that must be preached, and I will preach it through all of Kenya!" Pastor Allen called and said, "Oh, Dr. Sandy, the fire of the cross is burning with hundreds being saved and healed in the villages wherever we bring this message!" Pastor Edmond said, "My wife and I shared about the cup yesterday and many hearts were pierced as they wept bitterly for the Lamb that was slain. One old evangelist said to me, 'This message is not joyful to this generation of saints, but it is the true revival!'"

Pastor Henry told me, "Preachers in Africa want to get rich from their people so they preach a message of prosperity. You know how it goes—plant your seed into my ministry and God will bless you!" Then he said, with firm resolve, "That's manipulation and it's wrong! The message that will change lives and change this land is the message of the cross! This has fire and it will spread revival through Kenya and all of Africa!"

But this is not only a message for the young. I have seen older adults, especially those who are still humble enough to know they need more of the cross, come hungrily to the foot of the cross and drink deeply from the river that flows from the side of the Lamb.

Mark and Cathy were in their fifties and sixties when they left everything to come to our internship. People questioned, "Why are you leaving your own successful healing ministry to go be with a bunch of young adults?" But Mark had read my *Unquenchable Flame* book, and he knew he had to get this message. And when they left here, they were carrying the fire of the cross, which revolutionized their healing ministry. Mark says, "It has changed everything for us. We see more fire, more healings and miracles; and my wife, Cathy, who never wanted to preach, has become a fiery preaching woman!"

These men and women were undone by beholding the Lamb. I'm sure this is what God wants to do for you as well. So even now, why not lay aside this book and lift the eyes of your heart to behold the Lamb upon the throne. As someone has said, "Since my eyes have looked on Jesus, I've lost sight of all beside; so enchained my spirit's vision, gazing on the Crucified."[19]

This is not a call to the outer court, but a call to the holy of holies of heaven where the Lamb of God is enthroned.[20] See the One who pulls back His robe and shows you the wounds carved into His flesh. Look up at Him until you can almost reach up and run your fingers over His wounds. Let your heart soften until you begin to be undone by a revelation of the Lamb.

CHAPTER 3 ENDNOTES

1. In Leviticus, when a lamb was prepared for the daily burnt offering, the priest took a young lamb from the flock. It must be "a male without defect" (Lev. 1:10) just as Jesus was a male without defect. After the lamb was slaughtered, "the priest would sprinkle its blood against the altar on all sides" (1:11), for Jesus' blood would sprinkle down across the wood of the cross. Then the priest would flay the lamb in pieces: "He is to cut it into pieces, and the priest shall arrange them, including the head and the fat, on the burning wood that is on the altar" (1:12), for Jesus' own body would be flayed to pieces by the Roman scourge and then cast down on the altar like a Lamb. "It is a burnt offering, an offering made by fire, an aroma pleasing to the Lord" (1:13). Indeed, when the fire of God's wrath burned down upon Jesus on the cross, though it broke the Father's heart, like the

daily burnt offering, He became "an offering made by fire, an aroma pleasing to the Lord."

2. Even as Isaac carried the wood up Mount Moriah, Jesus would carry His own crossbeam up the hill of Mount Moriah where He would be offered as a burnt offering. But the heart-gripping part of this story is what Abraham experienced. He knew that a burnt offering is the highest level of sacrifice, and it must be prepared in a special manner.

3. Adam Clark writes, "Abraham spoke prophetically and referred to that Lamb of God which He had provided for Himself. Who, in the fullness of time would take away the sin of the world, and of Whom Isaac was a most expressive type" (Adam Clark, *The Holy Bible with a Commentary*; quoted in footnote to Genesis 22:8 in the Amplified Bible).

4. According to the ancient historian Josephus, Isaac was about twenty-five years old at that time.

5. The Bible says this voice came from "the Angel of the LORD." Adam Clark points out that the Angel of the LORD is a visible representation of God the Son on earth in the Old Testament. This is known as a Theophany, or a Christophany.

6. *NIV Study Bible*, notes on Leviticus 1:3 (Grand Rapids, MI: Zondervan Publishers, 2011).

7. Even Noah, when he first stepped out on the new creation after the flood, offered burnt offerings—or holocaust offerings—to the Lord (Gen. 8:20).

8. The evening sacrifice was offered daily at 3:00 p.m. It was always a lamb for the burnt offering. In the morning a perfect lamb was also cut in pieces and offered at 9:00 a.m. I believe Elijah knew the power of the burnt offering, and this is why he waited until the "time of the evening sacrifice" (1 Kings 18:36).

9. Jewish historian Alfred Edersheim explains that the Paschal (Passover) lambs in the Temple in Jesus' day would have their throats slit, the blood was caught in golden and silver bowls, and then it was poured out in streams in front of the great altar of burnt offering. Then the lambs would be skinned and pomegranate poles would be pierced through the lamb from "vent to vent" (Alfred Edersheim, *The Temple: Its Ministries and Services as they were at the Time of Jesus Christ* [Grand Rapids, MI: Kregel Publications, 1997], 149–150).

10. Commenting on this meeting of the boy Jesus with the scholars in the temple at Passover, Alfred Edersheim writes, "Judging by what we know of such discussions, we infer that they may have been connected with the Paschal solemnities." Edersheim wonders if the Child Jesus might have raised questions "as to the deeper meaning of the Paschal solemnities, as it was to be unfolded when Himself was offered up,

'the Lamb of God which taketh away the sin of the world'" (Alfred Edersheim, *The Life and Times of Jesus the Messiah* [Grand Rapids, MI: Wm. B. Eerdmans Publishing Co., 1976], 248.

11. These thoughts come from my book Bethlehem's Lamb. Read this story, filled with all the raw emotions and genuine feelings of Mary and Joseph, in this biblical narrative (Sandy Davis Kirk, *Bethlehem's Lamb* [Lake Mary, FL: Creation House Books, 2011]). You can order it from our website www.gloryofthelamb.com or any book store.

12. See Charles Spurgeon's sermon "Behold the Lamb," *Spurgeon's Expository Encyclopedia*, 103–104.

13. This also reveals the secret of true biblical preaching. "Behold the Lamb of God!" the Baptizer cried from the midst of a rushing river. And yet, isn't this the calling of every preacher? Spurgeon said, "It is the preacher's principal business, I think I might say his only business, to cry 'Behold the Lamb of God!'...I can scarce conceive a doom too terrible for the man who dazzled his hearers with oratorical fireworks, when he ought to have lifted up the cross." However, we can only preach what we see. "They preach Christ best who see Him best," said Spurgeon. John the Baptist "fixed his own eyes on Jesus, with fixed wondering, admiring, adoring gaze. John had no eye for anyone but 'the Lamb of God, who takes away the sin of the world,' and therefore his words had point and power in them" (Spurgeon, "Behold the Lamb," 103–104).

14. See my books *America Ablaze, The Cry of a Fatherless Generation, Rivers of Glory, The Pain* (Five steps to healing the hurt inside), and *The Pierced Generation*, available from our website www.gloryofthelamb.com.

15. I had visited the Brownsville Revival several times and was deeply touched by the passion of the youth and the emphasis on repentance and holiness. I rarely have a vision but several times I had seen a vision of the map of the United States with fire burning around it and the words "America Ablaze" written across it. I bought Steve Hill's home, the evangelist who ignited the Brownsville Revival, and turned it into a camp which we called "Camp America Ablaze."

16. Lewis Drummond, *Spurgeon, Prince of Preachers* (Grand Rapids, MI: Kregel Publications, 1992), 223.

17. Spurgeon believed, "There is no true, deep, tender, living conversion except through the cross." This is why he spent his ministry calling people to behold "Christ and him crucified" (Charles Spurgeon, "The Marvelous Magnet," *The Power of the Cross of Christ*, Lance C. Wubbels, comp. [Lynnwood, WA: Emerald Books, 1995], 21).

18. Charles H. Spurgeon, *22,000 Quotations from the Writings of Charles H. Spurgeon*, Tom Carter, comp. (Grand Rapids, MI: Baker Book House, 1988), 46.

19. Spurgeon said, "When a man takes Christ Jesus crucified to be his mind's main thought he has all things in one; doctrine, experience, and practice combined....The crucified Savior is as needful for our meditation as the air is for our breathing" (Charles Spurgeon, "Behold the Lamb," 111).

20. Occasionally someone will raise the argument: "This call to the Lamb is an outer court message because the altar of burnt offering where the lambs were slain was in the outer court of the tabernacle." Respectfully I would argue that we are called to the Lamb upon the throne, which John saw in his vision of heaven: "Then I saw a Lamb, looking as if it had been slain, standing in the center of the throne" (Rev. 5:6). Thus this message, using tabernacle terminology, is a holy of holies message.

Chapter 4

THE STORY *of* HIS GLORY

God's Glory Enfleshed in Human Skin

L IKE A ROARING thunderstorm, the glory of the Lord rushes over the mountaintop. Moses hears God coming. Trembling in the crevice of a rock, he peeks out, and his heart almost stops. Though protected by craggy walls of the rock, the back of God's glory sweeps by, seeping into the crack and soaking Moses' skin with such light that he later has to wear a veil to cover the shining.[1] He has indeed seen glimpses of the Shekinah before, but this is different. Though only the backside of God's trailing splendor passes by, God was unveiling a revelation of the glory of the Lamb.

God had said, "There is a place near me where you may stand on a rock. When my glory passes by I will put you in a cleft in the rock and cover you with my hand until I have passed by" (Exod. 33:21–22). The Bible explains that "the rock was Christ" (1 Cor. 10:4), and the cleft in the side of the rock was a visual foreshadowing of the cleft open side of the Lamb of God. Once again God was declaring:

> *This is My Son! He is My Lamb whose side will be riven open to release My glory to the earth!*

THE GLORY

Let's follow now this "Story of His Glory" through the Bible. The Hebrew word for glory, *kabôd*, means "heavy, weighty, profoundly significant." Because glory has weight, it can be literally experienced with our human senses. Jonathan Edwards described glory as "the refulgence of God," shining down from Him and reflecting back to Him.[2]

Glory is the very essence, the outshining, that flows from the pre-incarnate Son. Because the Son is a Lamb, slain from before the creation of the world, the glory is that which shines from God's eternal Lamb. He is the source, the container, the reservoir of the glory of God. That's why the Bible says, "The city does not need the sun or the moon to shine on it, for the glory of God gives it light, and the Lamb is the lamp" (Rev. 21:23).

"Just as our sun exudes energy and light, God exudes Glory," writes Bob Sorge in *Glory: When Heaven Invades Earth.* "God is such a dynamically blazing inferno that the radiation of His person is called Glory. Glory imbues and sustains all of heaven. It is the air of heaven." His Glory "is the tangible manifestation of the infinite beauty and splendor of His magnificent face."[3]

John Piper in *The Pleasures of God* dreams of the day "my fragile eyes will get the power to take in the glory of the Son shining in his full strength just the way the Father does. The pleasure God has in his Son will become my pleasure, and I will not be consumed, but enthralled forever."[4]

The glory is a summation of all the attributes of God, shining out from the person of Christ. His transcendent attributes—His omnipotence, omniscience, omnipresence, immutability (changelessness), sovereignty, and all of His numberless attributes—stream from the Son of God.[5] His mercy, grace, love, kindness, goodness, and so much more[6] roll like ocean waves from their container in the glorious pre-incarnate Christ.[7] Indeed, all of these perfections together make up the multifaceted glory of the Lamb.

In heaven the seraphim are nearest to the Lamb, and therefore they must cover their eyes from the scintillating brightness of the glory streaming from Him. Stuart Greaves says beautifully, "This wealth of glory is what the seraphim around the Throne call holy or transcendent majesty. God enjoying God, God stunned by the beauty of God, God searching out God, and God desiring that, in the very center of redemption, the Holy Spirit would usher humans into this reality through the cross of Christ Jesus."[8]

THE GLORY IN THE TEMPLE

This same magnificent glory, though veiled in a cloud, actually led the children of Israel from Egypt to the Promised Land. Shimmering over the ark of the covenant, the glory settled in Moses' tabernacle in the wilderness, and later David's tabernacle on Mount Zion, and finally in Solomon's grand temple in Jerusalem. In fact, as the glory flooded the temple, it shone out through the windows which were "narrow within but wide without." The rabbis said this was not to keep the darkness of the world out of the sanctuary, but "to let the light of the Shekinah illumine the world."[9]

Finally, because sin entered Solomon's Temple, God allowed the Babylonian army to sweep in and completely destroy it in 586 B.C. I had always wondered, however, how could these carnal Babylonians destroy the temple without being utterly cremated by the glory of God themselves?

I found the answer buried in the Book of Ezekiel. The Lord showed Ezekiel in a vision that the glory had already lifted from the temple in Jerusalem before the temple was destroyed. It was last seen ascending over "the mountain east of it"(Ezek. 11:23), which is the Mount of Olives.[10] R. Kent Hughes writes, now for almost 600 years, "though the temple was destroyed and rebuilt and rebuilt again, and though godly men and women came and went, the glory was not seen once!"[11]

Please don't miss this crucial point. There was *no glory* left anywhere on earth. So when the second temple was built in 516 B.C., sometimes called Zerubbabel's Temple, the elderly people "who had seen the former temple, wept aloud" (Ezek. 3:12), for they knew something was missing.[12] Matthew Henry explained, "Those that remembered the glory of the first temple which Solomon built...wept with a loud voice."[13]

And though the temple was rebuilt again in Jesus' day, which was called Herod's Temple, there was still *no glory* behind the veil in the holy of holies. The glory would not return to earth until one quiet evening in a little town of Galilee.

THE GLORY OF THE INCARNATION

On the roof of a mud hut in Nazareth the angel Gabriel suddenly appeared and spoke to a young Jewish maiden named Mary. Borrowing from my book, *Bethlehem's Lamb*, I can imagine the scene being something like this:

> "Mary," the angel says, in warm rich tones. Startled, Mary leaps to her feet and wheels around to discover the source of this voice. As she turns, bolts of light strike her eyes. The brightness pulsates with life, radiant and supernal, beyond anything she has ever seen on earth. As her eyes slowly adjust to the light, she can dimly make out the figure of a man enveloped in dazzling, living light.
>
> With wide eyes she gazes at the angel, her face flushed and deeply troubled. What the angel says to her is a mystery too fathomless to fully comprehend: "The Holy Spirit will come upon you, and the power of the Most High will overshadow you. So the holy one to be born will be called the Son of God" (Luke 1:35).[14]

The Greek word for *overshadow* is *episkiazō*, meaning "to envelop in a haze of brilliancy." Amazing! This means that the same glory, which *overshadowed* the mercy seat in the holy of holies, would *overshadow* Mary.

Yes, even as the Shekinah glory overshadowed Moses' tabernacle in the wilderness, later David's tent on Mount Zion, and Solomon's Temple in Jerusalem, in a far higher way, this is what would happen to her. Remember, for over 500 years the glory of God had been missing from the earth. Then late one night it happened. Returning to *Bethlehem's Lamb*, let's envision the scene.

> After all in the household are asleep, she quietly climbs the ladder up to the roof. Now, here on this same rooftop where she met the angel, she continues to pray: *"Oh, Father, how I long for my Messiah! When will He come? I believed what the angel said, but I still don't..."*

Suddenly, before another word could fall from her lips, she feels a mysterious light settling over her. The light intensifies with heat. It reminds her of the warmth she felt in the presence of the angel, but much more intense, so full of glory and fire. Her heart pounds wildly. Her whole body trembles.

Without any warning, a thick heavy glory descends upon her. She knows in an instant—this is the power of God flooding over her. She catches her breath, inhaling deeply of this heavy, weighty presence. Tears swim in her eyes as glory drenches every part of her being. *Oh, my God*, she thinks, *this must be what the angel meant!* Gabriel had said, "The power of the Most High will overshadow you."[15]

Yes, here in this lowly, sometimes despised town of Nazareth,[16] the glory has once again come down into the world. Not in the solemn splendor of the temple in Jerusalem, not amidst the glow of the golden candelabra or the smoky fragrance of the holy of holies—but God has come down on a poor man's rooftop in Galilee. Like the cloud of brilliance which overshadowed the tabernacle, now the glory has overshadowed a virgin, settling in the holy of holies of her womb.

Mary closes her eyes and surrenders completely to this ineffable glory. She feels engulfed, utterly suffused by the presence of God. It is fearful yet exquisitely wonderful at the same time. Tears rush down her face as wave after wave of God's shining essence wash over her, drenching her like warm ocean billows. So close is God's overshadowing presence it is like a divine infusion as He implants a part of Himself. It is something holy. Something beautiful. The very Seed of God imparted into her womb.

Moments pass, she doesn't know how long. But finally her heart overflows to God. Breathlessly she cries, *Oh, Father, can this be happening to me? Have you chosen me to carry your own Son? Have you truly implanted your Seed within my womb? Your beloved Son? My Messiah? Almighty God enfleshed in a baby's skin?*

Yet, somehow she knows—this Holy One inside her did not

begin at conception, as other babies do. He has always been. He is the everlasting, uncreated Son of God. He has existed forever as God's eternal Lamb.[17] Now for this short span of time, He has come to earth, through the womb of a virgin, to transform human hearts and bring us back to God.

Then late one night, as glory guilds the skies over Bethlehem, He is born. Can you imagine the beauty of that scene as Joseph guides the infant out into the world and suddenly a baby's cry splits the midnight air?

> "He's beautiful, Mary!" Joseph cries, as his trembling hands hold up this tiny, squirming, red-faced baby.[18] Mary smiles weakly as she looks at His wet wrinkled little body. Then He cries again, a loud, piercing, powerful wail. Mary gasps. The baby's cry impales her heart, and she realizes, *This is the first time the voice of God has been heard on earth in over five hundred years!* She closes her eyes, exhausted and happy, thinking of the wonder of God in human flesh.
>
> Yes, now at last the voice of God has rung through Israel again. Indeed, He whose voice tumbled galaxies into space now cries in His mother's arms. He whose glory filled the universe now fills a baby's flesh. He who gazed into the eyes of His Father God now gazes into the eyes of a teenage Jewish girl.[19]

Oh, it's the wonder of the ages! The glory of the Incarnation, which means "in flesh." God Himself—a human being![20] He who made man is made a man. Spurgeon marveled: "The infinite God who filled all things, who was and is, and is to come, the Almighty, the Omniscient, and the Omnipresent, actually condescended to veil Himself in the garments of our inferior clay. He made all things, and yet he deigned to take the flesh of a creature. The infinite was linked with the infant, and the Eternal was blended with mortality."[21]

Theologians today call this the *hypostatic union,* the union of God and Man, the merging of the divine with the human.[22] "For in Christ all the fullness of the Deity lives in bodily form" (Col. 2:9). As Allen Hood writes, "Jesus is the 'theanthropos,' the 'God-Man.' Jesus' person is undivided. He is fully God and fully Man in one undivided Person."[23]

And yet He, "being in very nature God, did not consider equality with God something to be grasped, but made himself nothing" (Phil. 2:6–7). This self-emptying of the Son of God is called the *kenosis,* meaning that He gave up the independent exercise of His transcendent attributes and was completely *dependent* on the Father and the Holy Spirit.

And what an incredible self-emptying this was! Samuel Rutherford said "he would like to pile up ten thousand million heavens upon the top of the third heaven to which Paul was caught up, and put Christ in that high place; and then he would not be as high as he deserved to be put; and truly, no honors seem sufficient for him who stripped himself of all he had that he might become the Saviour of sinners."[24]

A beautiful scene in this Story of His Glory took place when Mary and Joseph brought baby Jesus into Herod's Temple: "When the time of their purification according to the Law of Moses had been completed, Joseph and Mary took him to Jerusalem to present him to the Lord" (Luke 2:22). According to the ritual, Mary must hand the priest two pigeons, the offering of the poor.[25] The priest would then cut the birds' throats and sprinkle their blood upon her, declaring her clean from the contamination of childbirth. She must then hand him five silver shekels to "redeem the firstborn."[26]

Can you imagine the irony of this scene? Here stands Mary—sprinkled with the blood which speaks of the cleansing blood of the One she holds in her arms. Now she hands the priest five shekels of silver as the Redeemer Himself is redeemed!

Standing nearby, respectfully waiting for the ceremony to end, an old prophet named Simeon shuffles up to Mary. When he reaches for her baby, she flinches back. But when she sees his sparkling eyes and the glory blushing on his face, she knows the Spirit of God is upon him.

Lifting up Jesus, Simeon cries, "He is a light for revelation to the Gentiles and a glory for your people Israel!" (Luke 2:32). Yes, now at last the glory has returned to Israel, veiled not in a cloud, not behind a curtain in the temple, but in the flesh of a tiny baby. Then the old man turns and looks deep into Mary's eyes. Solemnly he says, "And a sword shall pierce your own soul too" (Luke 2:35). Strangely, Mary can feel these words driving sharp and deep, like the quick thrust of a blade, into her sensitive soul.

FLASHES OF HIS GLORY

Now, as Jesus grows and then steps out in His ministry, every place He walks seems to be aglow with God's holy light. Flashes of His glory break out through His teachings, through His miracles,[27] and even through His tears.

Though He is fully God, Jesus knows the feeling of human tears welling up in His eyes and dripping down His face. His tears are like liquid mercy, distilled in drops of moisture. They contain the passion and pathos of God, dissolved in fluid, spilling from His eyes. His tears show the glory of His love, running down His face.

The Bible says, "When he saw the crowds, he had compassion on them, because they were harassed and helpless, like sheep without a shepherd" (Matt. 9:36).[28] The Greek for compassion is *splanchnizomai*, meaning "bowels that yearn with compassion." Though He came from heaven where no pain exists, He came to us in human flesh so He could know the sensation of hunger gnawing, tears falling, thirst burning, muscles aching, blood shedding, pain wrenching, heart rupturing. Indeed, His compassion revealed the glory and love of the Lamb.

Yet never did His glory shine so brightly from Jesus' face as the night He led Peter, James, and John up a high mountain to pray. Let's dare to imagine what that night was like.

Patches of snow dot the mountainside, reflecting the light of the moon. Finally Jesus stops, lifts His head in prayer and begins to shine. The disciples look on awestruck. In the darkness Jesus glows as bright as the morning sun: "His face shone like the sun and his clothes became as white as the light" (Matt. 17:2). The three men can feel the light flooding out from Jesus. Their hearts drum wildly in their chests and their faces warm with the heat of the glory. So thick is God's presence they can hardly breathe. It seems like heaven on earth.

It is as though the glory, which once hovered behind the veil and rested over the mercy seat, can no longer be contained by the veil of Jesus' flesh. Now the glory within Him exudes out of every pore of His human skin. Spurgeon said, "As the light streams through the lantern, so the glory of the Godhead streamed through the flesh of Jesus."[29] Hughes said, "For a brief moment the veil of humanity was lifted, and his true essence was allowed to shine through. The glory that was always in the depths of his being rose to the surface"[30] and flooded over the mountainside.

That was undoubtedly a transforming vision for the young disciple John who was with Him on the mount. He had heard Jesus teach, watched Him walk on water, seen Him heal blind eyes and raise the dead. But as John beheld His glory, like a fountain of light, rushing out from the reservoir of His flesh on the mount, he knew that Jesus Christ was God. Thus he wrote, "We have seen his glory, the glory of the One and Only, who came from the Father, full of grace and truth" (John 1:14).

And while Matthew emphasized Jesus as King, Mark accentuated Him as Servant, Luke highlighted His human and compassionate side, John displayed Jesus in His glory and divinity. In fact, one day Jesus stood and proclaimed, "I am the light of the world. Whoever follows me will never walk in darkness, but will have the light of life" (John 8:12). With that thundering assertion, Jesus proclaimed Himself as the source of God's glory on earth. He was saying, "I am the glory!"

Hughes writes, "Christ was saying in effect, 'The pillar of fire that came between you and the Egyptians, the cloud that guided you by day in the wilderness and illumined the night and enveloped the tabernacle, the glorious cloud that filled Solomon's Temple, was me!'"[31]

BEHOLDING HIS FACE

Moses' face glowed so brightly after gazing on the trailing glory of God that people "were afraid to come near him" (Exod. 34:30). Paul was blind for three days after beholding His glory, describing Him as dwelling in "unapproachable light, whom no one has seen or can see" (1 Tim. 6:16). And the seraphim, those nearest the Lamb, blaze with such brilliance they are literally called "the burning ones" (Isa. 6:3). But the reason Moses' face shone, Paul was blind, and the seraphim burn is because they had all been gazing on the glory of the Lamb.

And so, may we come, trembling like Moses with holy desperation, longing for the glory of His face. Even now, see yourself hidden in the cleft of the Rock of Christ, and ask Him to grip your soul with His glory. Close your physical eyes, stretch the eyes of your heart, and reach your gaze into heaven. Behold the Lamb of God and look deeply into His shining face. See the love in His eyes. Feel the warmth of His smile.

Drink deeply of His mercy, His grace, His love, and His holiness. Saturate yourself in this fountain of light, as the Psalmist wrote, "You cause me to drink of the stream of Your pleasures. For with You is the fountain of life; in your light we see light" (Ps. 36:8–9, AMP).

Oh, this is His glory! The glory of Christ. Nothing strikes our hearts with such awe as a long steady gaze at the matchless, limitless, timeless glory of the Lamb! This is the beginning of the love wound which will scar your heart forever.

This is what will call forth the highest passion and purpose for living. As Piper says, "Life is wasted when we do not live for the glory of God. His blood soaked cross is the blazing center of that glory."[32] Indeed, this glorious vision of the crucified and risen Lamb will burn within you a desire to bring Jesus, the Lamb who was slain, the reward of His suffering for you. As you behold His beauty, your heart will be undone by a revelation of the Lamb!

CHAPTER 4 ENDNOTES

1. The reason Michelangelo sculpted Moses with horns protruding from his head is because the Bible of his day, which was the Latin Vulgate, mistranslated the word "beams" to "horns."
2. Jonathan Edwards, "God's Chief End in Creation," *The Works of Jonathan Edwards*, vol. 1 (Edinburgh: Banner of Truth Trust, 1995), 119.
3. Bob Sorge, *Glory: When Heaven Invades Earth* (Greenwood, MO: Oasis House, 2000), 10.
4. John Piper, *The Pleasures of God* (Colorado Springs, CO: Multnomah Books, 1991), 28. Piper further says, "The glory of God is the beautiful brightness of God" (John Piper, *God is the Gospel* [Wheaton, IL: Crossway Books, 2005], 74).
5. Scholars call these His "incommunicable attributes" because humans do not possess these Godlike, divine qualities.
6. The "communicable attributes" are those which we humans can actually partake of and be changed.
7. The term *pre-incarnate* refers to the Son before He came in human flesh.
8. Stuart Greaves, *The Existence and Majesty of God*, 46.
9. The Shekinah means "the dwelling presence of God," and is a term used by Hebrews to describe the glory of God (Num. [Rabbah] 15.2,

cited in D. Moody, "Shekinah," *The Interpreter's Dictionary of the Bible* [Nashville, TN: Abingdon Press, 1962], 318).

10. R. Kent Hughes describes the wings of the cherubim "drumming the air like colossal hummingbirds, and above them floated the dazzling glory of God." He continues, "The glory was moving slowly away to the east and upward from the city where it lingered above the Mount of Olives—and then it was gone" (Ezek. 11:23) (R. Kent Hughes, *Luke: That You May Know the Truth*, vol. 1 [Wheaton, IL: Crossway Books, 1998], 348).

11. Ibid., 348.

12. Concerning the cause of their weeping, Jamieson, Fausset, and Brown write, "The chief cause of grief was that the second temple would be destitute of those things which formed the great distinguishing glory of the first; viz., the ark, the Shekinah, the Urrim and Thummim, etc. Not that this second temple was not a very grand and beautiful structure. But no matter how great its material splendor was, it was inferior in this respect to that of Solomon" (Robert Jamieson, A. R. Fausset, and David Brown, *Jamieson, Fausset, & Brown's Commentary on the Whole Bible* [Grand Rapids, MI: Zondervan Publishing House, 1961], 339.

13. Matthew Henry, *Matthew Henry's Commentary: Joshua to Esther*, vol. 2 (McLean, VA: MacDonald Publishing Company, n.d.), 1038.

14. This scene is adapted from my book *Bethlehem's Lamb*, 6–7.

15. The Greek of "overshadow" is ⊠*piskiazō*, meaning "to envelop in a haze of brilliancy." This is also the same word used on the Mount of Transfiguration when "a bright cloud enveloped [⊠*piskiazō*] them" (Matt. 17:5). Again ⊠*piskiazō* is used of Peter's shadow which healed the sick: "People brought the sick into the streets and laid them on beds and mats so that at least Peter's shadow might fall on (⊠piskiazō) some of them as he passed by" (Acts 5:15). R. Kent Hughes asks, "What is described here? Certainly not a sexual union (mating) with divinity, as some have argued. Nothing so crude is suggested here. All leading scholars agree that there are no sexual overtones whatsoever....While it was not a sexual experience, it was surely a conscious experience—something Mary could feel. How could anyone have the Holy Spirit come upon him or her and be overshadowed as in the temple or on the Mount of Transfiguration and not know it?" (Hughes, *Luke*, 34–35).

16. The fact that Nazareth was chosen over Jerusalem, the heart of God's work through the centuries, was shocking. "Nazareth was a 'non place.' It was not even mentioned in the Old Testament or in Josephus' writings or in the rabbinical writings....Nazareth, a shoddy, corrupt halfway stop between the port cities of Tyre and Sidon, was overrun

by Gentiles and Roman soldiers....God bypassed Judea, Jerusalem, and the temple and came to a despised country, a despised town, and a humble woman," writes R. Kent Hughes (Hughes, *Luke*, 29, 32).

17. God's Son did not begin at conception, like other babies. Nor did He commence His life in Bethlehem. He has existed forever in the Triune Godhead, for something happened in the Godhead that still staggers human senses. The Son agreed to come to earth and lay down His life as a Lamb, for He "was chosen before the creation of the world" (1 Pet. 1:19–20). He is indeed God's eternal Lamb, "slain from the creation of the world" (Rev. 13:8).

18. Hughes beautifully describes: "On a cold winter's night, the trembling hands of a carpenter, wet with the blood of birth, held his steaming son in the starlight" (R. Kent Hughes, *Luke*, 348).

19. This scene is adapted from my book *Bethlehem's Lamb*, 48.

20. Oh, the wonder of the Incarnation, which means "in flesh." To think—He who sprinkled the universe with galaxies, stars and planets, making them out of absolutely nothing, was born in human flesh. He, who cradled His head upon His Father's breast, now cradled His head in an animal feeding trough. Spurgeon said, "He might have been born in marble halls, and wrapped in imperial purple, but He scorns these things, and in the manger among the oxen we see a glory which is independent of the trifles of luxury and parade. The glory of God in the person of Jesus asks no aid from the splendor of courts and palaces" (C. H. Spurgeon, "The Glory of God in the Face of Jesus Christ," *Twelve Striking Sermons* [London: Marshall, Morgan & Scott, LTD, 1953], 141–142).

21. Charles Spurgeon, "The Great Mystery of Godliness," *Spurgeon's Expository Sermons,* vol. 3 (Grand Rapids, MI: Baker Book House, 1977), 10.

22. Wayne Grudem, *Systematic Theology*, 558.

23. Allen Hood, *The Excellencies of Christ*, 26.

24. Cited by Charles Spurgeon, "Christ's Crowning Glory," *Spurgeon's Expository Sermons,* vol. 13 (Grand Rapids, MI: Baker Book House, 1977), 380.

25. Alfred Edersheim explains that "The more wealthy brought a lamb for a burnt offering, the poor might substitute a turtledove, or a young pigeon....The substitution of the latter for a young lamb was expressly designated 'the poor's offering'" (Alfred Edersheim, *The Life and Times of Jesus Christ the Messiah*, 195, 196).

26. Edersheim wrote, "And now the priest once more approached her, and, sprinkling her with the sacrificial blood, declared her cleansed.' Her 'firstborn' was next redeemed at the hand of the priest, with five

shekels of silver" (Alfred Edersheim, *The Temple* [Grand Rapids, MI: Kregel Publications, 1973], 222.

27. That's why, in His first miracle at Cana, when He turned water into wine, John wrote, "He thus revealed His glory" (John 2:11). And at the raising of Lazarus from the dead, Jesus said to Martha, "Did I not tell you that if you believed, you would see the glory of God?" (11:40).

28. See also Matthew 14:14 and 20:34.

29. Charles Spurgeon, "The Great Mystery of Godliness," 10.

30. R. Kent Hughes, *Luke*, 350.

31. Ibid., 354.

32. John Piper, *Don't Waste Your Life*, 32, 59.

SECTION TWO

THE AGONY *of the* LAMB

Chapter 5

BLOOD *in the* GARDEN

The Terrifying Contents of the Father's Cup

O N TIPTOE WITH awe, let's follow the Lamb as He leads the disciples out of the city gate and over the Brook Kidron. Because it's Passover, the waters run dark red with the blood of slain lambs, funneled down from the Temple Mount. What an amazing scene this presents as the Lamb of God, whose own blood will run like the crimsoned waters of the Kidron, crosses over the bloody stream.

Come watch Him now as He climbs the Mount of Olives and enters the Garden of Gethsemane, meaning garden of "crushed olives." Here in this garden the air hangs still, cool and crisp on this late night in spring. A full Passover moon casts silvery glints on the olive leaves. Picture yourself asleep on the moist ground of the garden.

Listen now. Can you hear it? It's a deep moaning sound, like an animal howling. A loud masculine sob: *Father!*

It's Jesus, praying "with loud crying and tears" (Heb. 5:7).[1] He seems overcome with torment. To His three disciples He says with deep emotion, "My soul is overwhelmed with sorrow to the point of death. Stay here and keep watch with me" (Matt. 26:38).[2]

Crawl up closer and look. The sight will knock the wind from your lungs. In the bright light of the full moon, you'll see His body bathed in sweat. No! It's not just sweat, it's blood! Without whip, or thorn, or nail to rip through His human flesh, see blood press out through His skin like oil pressed out of an olive. No wonder this is called the "garden of crushed olives."

Here lies the One who contains the glory of eternity, rolling in the dirt, soaked in His own blood: "His sweat was as it were great drops of blood falling to the ground" (Luke 22:44, KJV). This is the first issue of Lamb's blood, offered up like a high priest in the holy of holies of prayer.

But notice that the blood fell in huge drops; as Spurgeon said, "He not only sweat blood, but it was in great drops of blood coagulated and formed in large masses."[3] Edwards explained, "The distress and anguish of his mind was so unspeakably extreme as to force his blood through the pores of his skin....so plentifully as to fall in great clots or drops" which "congealed or stiffened"[4] as it hit the cool night air.[5]

And though some try to dismiss this as merely heavy drops of sweat, sweat never congeals to form clots. Only blood thickens when air hits it. This could be nothing else but rich, red human blood, issuing from the veins of the Lamb. In fact, the Greek word for "drops of blood" (Luke 22:44) is *thrombos*, meaning, according to W. E. Vine, "large, thick drops of clotted blood."[6]

But why? What caused the Savior to sweat great drops of blood? Was it terror of the Roman scourge, embedded with bits of bone and metal that would rip His human flesh to shreds? Was it fear of thorns gouging His brow or spikes impaling His hands? Did He shrink from the shame and humiliation of His enemies, gawking like hungry hawks at His naked, bleeding body?

Was it dread of bearing the filth of humanity's sin which the Father would plunge upon Him? Did He cower from the torment of Satan's demons flinging themselves against Him, feeding greedily on the sin? Did He recoil from the rupture of His heart or flinch from the sword piercing His side, emptying out every drop of His blood? Did the chilling thought of death overwhelm Him? Did the morbid thought of the cold slab of a tomb cause Him to shrink back in fear? Many martyrs have courageously hung from crosses or laid their necks on chopping blocks for their faith in Christ. Was Jesus more cowardly than His own followers?

Did He cringe from the grief of losing His Father's presence? To be sure, the abandonment of His Father was terrifying beyond measure. Through all eternity He had dwelt in "the bosom of the Father" (John 1:18, KJV) in face-to-face communion in the Triune Godhead, but was the thought of this separation what caused blood to rush from His pores and fall in clots to the ground?

I'm asking *you*, why did Jesus' own blood burst out of His pores as He prayed in the garden? Do you know why? What could cause such extreme anguish in the heart of our Lord? The answer is found in His prayer. Peer again through the olive leaves in the garden and listen: "Father," He roars, "If you are willing, take this cup from me" (Luke 22:42).

Jesus fervently prays about this cup in Matthew, Mark, and Luke, known as the Synoptic Gospels (Matt. 26:39, 42; Mark 14:36; Luke 22:42).[7] In John's Gospel, Jesus shows us the profound significance of this cup when He says to Peter, "Put your sword away! Shall I not drink the cup the Father has given me?" (John 18:11). What then is this cup?

We've looked at it briefly, but now let's dare to gaze into its terrifying contents. I tremble inside whenever I look into the Father's cup. I can feel the heat rising in my heart and burning on my face. It never fails. Ever since I first read Jonathan Edwards' sermon over twenty-five years ago and then released it briefly in that Methodist class, I still feel the burning. I think you'll feel it too.

A REVELATION OF THE CUP

As our Savior knelt to the ground, bleeding and sweating, Old Testament verses must have reeled through His mind; for as John Stott says, "This Old Testament imagery will have been well known to Jesus."[8] For example the Psalmist warned, "In the hand of the Lord is a cup full of foaming wine mixed with spices" (Ps. 75:8). Ezekiel describes it as "the cup of horror and desolation" (Ezek. 23:33).

God told Jeremiah that this *cup* in His hand was "filled with the wine of my wrath" (Jer. 25:15). Isaiah described "the cup that made you stagger; from that cup, the goblet of my wrath" (Isa. 51:17, 22). He wrote, "We considered him stricken by God, smitten by Him and afflicted....The punishment that brought us peace was upon him" (53:4–5).

Jeremiah said that when the nations drink from this cup of wrath, "they will stagger and go mad" (Jer. 25:16). I believe this speaks of the cry of dereliction, which Jesus screamed out in near madness, "My God, my God, why have you forsaken me?" (Matt. 27:46). No wonder a view of this cup was killing Him as He said, "My soul is overwhelmed with sorrow to the point of death" (Matt. 26:38).

Though some people interpret the cup to refer simply to Jesus' suffering in general, a careful study of Scripture proves this incorrect. The passages above show otherwise; as Cranfield says, "In the Old Testament the metaphorical use of 'cup' refers predominantly to God's punishment of human sin." He adds, "'*His* cup' is the cup of God's wrath against sin."[9] The apostle John heard an angel from heaven give a clear description of the contents of this cup, it is "the wine of God's fury which has been poured full strength into the cup of his wrath" (Rev. 14:10).

Imagine the scene now, as Jesus, His hair dripping with blood and sweat and His robe splattered with clotted blood, returns to His disciples and finds them asleep. "Are you still sleeping and resting? Enough!" He cries (Mark 14:41). It must have crushed young John when he later realized he had slept through such a desperate time in the Lord's life.

In our day, however, there is something far worse than falling asleep like John. He fell asleep *before* Jesus drank the cup on the cross. Today Jesus has already engulfed it, and many of us still sleep! Philip Ryken writes, "Like the disciples, we are often asleep in the Garden, dozing through the Christian life, ambivalent about our sin. But were we to watch and pray, to kneel beside our Savior in the grass, to hear his cries of anguish, and to see the bloody sweat upon his brow, then we would see the fearfulness of God's wrath. And then we would know the sinfulness of our sin."[10]

Before I read Jonathan Edwards' sermon, I was sound asleep to the cup. I had never looked into its fiery ingredients. As I said, maybe once a year I would think about the nails and whip and blood, but I never let the Father's cup grip me. I never looked until my heart was undone by a revelation of the Lamb.

Yet this is the zenith, the crux, the high point of the cross. The cross is the central message of the entire Bible; as Leon Morris says, "The cross is at the heart of all New Testament teaching."[11] James Denney wrote, "Scripture converges on the doctrine of the Atonement,"[12] but the cup is the pinnacle of the Atonement. As Jonathan Edwards said, His "principal errand" for coming to earth was "to drink that cup."[13]

Oh, why have we so neglected this monumental subject? The cup is the climax of Jesus' work on the cross. He proves this when Peter tries to interfere, and He commands, "Put your sword away! Shall I not drink the cup the Father has given me?" (John 18:11).

Can you imagine what would have happened if Jesus had not engulfed the dregs of that cup of eternal wrath? We would have plummeted into hell! We would have received the punishment that we deserve for sin! We would have had to "drink of the wine of God's fury, which has been poured full strength into the cup of his wrath." We would "be tormented with burning sulfur in the presence of the holy angels and the Lamb" (Rev. 14:10).

HIS BAPTISM OF FIRE

On that day long ago when I first began to study about the cup of God's holy wrath, I experienced fire like I've never known. That's when I began to understand the fiery contents of the cup which Jesus saw in the garden.

When He looked into the Father's cup, He saw the flames leaping. He saw the fire from heaven blazing down upon the burnt offering on the altar, and He saw Himself as the burnt offering. He saw Himself as the Passover lamb, roasting over the flames. He saw the "bush burning with fire," which, said Jonathan Edwards, "represented the sufferings of Christ in the fire of God's wrath."[14] He saw Himself thrust into Nebuchadnezzar's fiery furnace; as Edwards wrote:

> He was brought to the mouth of the furnace that He might look into it, and stand and view its raging flames and see the glowing of its heat....When He had a full sight of the wrath of God which He must suffer, the sight was overwhelming to Him. It made His soul exceeding sorrowful even unto death. Christ was going to be cast into a dreadful furnace of wrath, and it was not proper that He should plunge Himself into it blindfolded, by not knowing how dreadful the furnace was. Therefore, that He might know what was in this cup....God brought the cup that He was to drink and set it down before Him that He might have a full view of it, and see what it was before He took it and drank it.[15]

This is what Jesus meant when He said, "I have a baptism to undergo, and how distressed I am until it is completed!" (Luke 12:50). This was a *baptism of fire* which He would experience in this furnace on the cross. What was this furnace? It was the eternal wrath and judgment of

Almighty God, into which the Son would be thrust while hanging from two strips of wood and bleeding from every wound.

A preacher stunned the students in a Baptist seminary when he invited them to look into the garden and see Jesus wrestling over this cup. He said, "The Savior staggers—he does not sin—but he staggers as he contemplates the weight of this horrific prospect. In the garden he is not contemplating the physical pain of the crucifixion; he is contemplating the fierceness of God's wrath poured out upon him for our sin."[16]

Not only did God fill this cup with His "furious and righteous wrath,"[17] but He took His eternal wrath, *condensed* it, and poured it into that cup. He *distilled* His judgment against sin, which is the very lake of fire, and emptied it into that cup. He placed hell's blazing fury into this cup and asked His Son to drink it.

In fact, Edwards said that Jesus would endure "the very pains of hell"; not *after* the cross but *on* the cross. The contents of this cup were "fully equivalent to the misery of the damned for it was the wrath of the same God."[18] Stott said, "We may even say that our sins sent Christ to hell," not in a battle down in hell after His body went into the grave, but on the cross "before His body died."[19]

Arthur W. Pink said, "Not all the thunderbolts of divine judgment.... not all the weeping and gnashing of teeth of the damned in the lake of fire" ever gave such a demonstration "of His infinite hatred of sin as did the wrath of God which flamed against His own Son on the cross."[20]

If you doubt that hell was in this cup, look again at this powerful verse explaining what is in the cup, which all who reject Christ will drink: "He, too, will drink of the wine of God's fury, which has been poured full strength into the cup of his wrath. He will be tormented with burning sulfur in the presence of the holy angels and the Lamb. And the smoke of their torment rises forever and ever" (Rev. 14:10).

Now do you see why blood burst out of His skin in clots and streamed down on the ground? It was from a violent inner struggle as He grappled with the horrors of drinking the Father's cup. Edwards said, He was "covered with clotted blood" which "had been forced through His pores through the violence of His agony."[21]

In the midst of it all, surely the Father must have whispered to His Son,

Oh, Son, My Beloved, don't You remember the eternal covenant of redemption We agreed upon before creation? I showed You My cup and asked You to become a lamb, consumed in the fire of My wrath. Son, do You remember? You agreed to become the Lamb, slain before the creation of the world!

Look at Jesus there in the garden. Tears gush from His eyes, love weeps in His heart, and blood squeezes from His pores. But now see that climactic moment when Jesus falls again to His knees and cries, "My Father, if it is not possible for this cup to be taken from me unless I drink it, may your will be done" (Matt. 26:42).

Jesus must have then slumped to the ground, limp and weak, coated in His own blood. He was exhausted from wrestling in prayer with God, but ready to drink the Father's cup.

WHY DID HE DO IT?

Oh, how could He do it? Why would He surrender to drinking this cup? Do you know why? Of course He wanted to be obedient to His Father, and He knew He must fulfill the eternal covenant of redemption. But there was another reason; one so gripping it will melt you in tender devotion.

He could have said, "No," and watched the whole human race plummet into hell. But He looked into that furnace of wrath and saw something compelling. It was something beautiful. He would rather go through the flames of hell than let this treasure slip away.

You see, He looked into the furnace of hell and He saw *you*!

He saw you enduring the punishment you deserve for sin. It's not that God is cruel and vindictive, looking for people to punish. But God is holy, and He wants you near Him. Unholiness cannot come into the presence of a holy God. So He threw Himself in front of the Father's eternal wrath—to save you! This story helps illustrate what He did:

A train roared around the side of the mountain, sounding its warning whistle. It came earlier than usual that day, catching the mother of five children off guard. When she heard the whistle, she quickly searched the house and yard to be sure the children were safe. She found four of them playing outside, but where was the youngest?

She raced through the yard and looked over the embankment. There he was, her two-year-old, sitting on the tracks, oblivious to the impending danger. She tore down the hillside, flailing her arms and calling out to her child, but he didn't notice. He looked up just in time to see the terror on his mother's face. Then he saw the oncoming train, and he froze in fear.

The conductor didn't see the child, and the train was only yards away, rumbling down upon the baby. The mother saw that her child couldn't move out of the way in time, so she drew in her breath, gave a piercing cry, and lunged forward, pushing her baby out of the way. But she couldn't escape the train. The train barreled across her body, crushing her and killing her instantly. The child escaped unharmed, saved by his courageous mother.[22]

That's what Jesus did for you and me! He saw us playing on the train tracks of sin, oblivious to the danger. But He could not bear to live in heaven without you, so He left the glory of eternity, and raced down the embankment of time and space into this earth. Then He threw Himself upon the cross, pushing us out of the way, and taking the full crushing impact of God's punishment against sin.

Theologians call this "propitiation," which means "a sacrifice to avert wrath."[23] That's what the Bible means when it says, "He Himself is the propitiation for our sins" (1 John 2:2, NAS; see also Rom. 3:25; Heb. 2:17; 1 John 4:10).[24]

It tells of a Savior who came all the way from heaven to rescue us from hell by taking it upon Himself.[25] As John Piper writes: God sent His Son to be the "wrath absorbing" propitiation for us. As our Substitute, Jesus "does not just cancel the wrath, he absorbs it and divests it from us to himself."[26]

Now do you see why blood squeezed out from Jesus' pores when He prayed in the garden? He dreaded the cup, but something far deeper than fear motivated Him. Love compelled Him to come. Edwards said, "Those great drops of blood that fell down to the ground were a manifestation of an ocean of love in Christ's heart."[27]

Yes, though agony and grief submerged His soul, His love overcame His anguish. For never has there been such a monumental display of love as the cross of Jesus Christ. That's why only at the feet of the Lamb can we really begin to "grasp how wide and long and high and deep is the love of Christ" (Eph. 3:18).

STUDENTS TRANSFORMED BY A VIEW OF THE CUP

All through the years, as I've taught this message of the cross, it has always been the Father's cup that captures and transforms hearts. Old and young alike have been undone by this heart-ripping view. Students kept telling me of a love wound which God was carving into their hearts. The more we looked into the contents of the Father's cup, the more their hearts were gripped. Soon the Lord began sending them out to preach the message of the cross and the cup with amazing power. One of the most tremendous preachers was Mary.

Mary came here from the UK as a lost and rebellious eighteen-year-old, simply wanting a holiday in America. But her wise parents, pastors in England, agreed to pay for the trip if she would stay in Christian places. They heard about us and booked her for a few weeks at our camp. I picked her up at the airport while she was still hung over from a week of partying.

But after being here for two days, she went to church and heard Evangelist Steve Hill pouring out the passion of his heart for souls, every word dipped in his own tears. She was overcome with conviction, and soon she was weeping her way to the Savior. She set aside all her plans to attend Nottingham University in England and came to the Brownsville Revival School of Ministry (BRSM) where she was one of my students.

One Saturday night Mary accompanied me to a meeting with the evangelism students where I had been invited to preach about the Lamb. During the message, I felt the Holy Spirit on me so strongly that I could barely talk, especially as I told about the Father's cup, which Jesus wept over in the Garden of Gethsemane and fully engulfed on the cross.

After the message, I invited students to come forward so that I could pray for them to receive a revelation of the Lamb. I cannot impart this revelation to anyone, but I can pray and ask the Holy Spirit to do so. I started to pray, and then I saw Mary. No one had touched her, but she was on the floor weeping her heart out. By now she had been saved for two months, but she later told me, "I fell in love with Jesus when I saw Him as the Lamb."

A year later I accompanied her to England where we preached in her father's church and she spoke in the public schools. Mary courageously gave her testimony in her own former school, where students, especially teachers, were shocked at the transformation. In one public school the students gathered around her in tears, wanting to know how they too could find God.

Back in America one night at a mission for former drug users and alcoholics, I gave a message on the cup and Mary came and gave the altar call. With passion blazing in her voice and tears running down her face, she cried, "If Jesus drank the cup for you, then what else can you do but come and give Him everything?"

Men and women raced to the altar. I saw big strong men, gripping their hearts and falling on their faces. It was as though God Himself was reaching in and piercing some of their hearts. The sword was the cross and its blade was the message of the cup. It was just like Charles Spurgeon had said; hearts were being pierced as they gazed upon the cup Jesus drank for them.

And now, eight years later, Mary has grown into a powerful preacher of the gospel. I've heard her preach in England, Canada, Bulgaria, Romania, Mexico, Taiwan, and Peru, and each time the power of God roars from her burning heart. When she preaches, the passion trembling inside her burns out of her mouth and into the hearts of those listening. She has now finished her Master's degree at Fuller Theological Seminary, and she and her husband Kevin now lead our Unquenchable Flame Internships and will be directing our new school.

Oh, this is the message we must bring back to the center of Christianity! Before our very eyes we see a young, abused, hopeless, sometimes suicidal, and often fatherless generation rejecting Christ and sliding into hell because they haven't found something to capture their hearts. They must have something that stirs their passion and gives them a purpose to live. A deep revelation of the Lamb will grip them and cause their hearts to burn with undying passion to bring Him His reward.

But we've been so preoccupied with material blessings and a humanistic gospel we've almost lost a whole generation of young people. Do you know why? Because they haven't been given a clear enough reason to give up sin and follow the Lamb. It's like Mary's mother told me years ago, "My daughter never had a reason to quit sinning until she saw the Lamb!"

That's why I am convinced—we must have a theological revolution in the church. It's not about building big ministries. It's not about achieving great fame. It's not about making a name for one's self. It's about lifting up *Christ and Him crucified* until Jesus receives the glory He deserves for giving Himself as the Lamb.

So even now, won't you get on your face before God and look into the face of Jesus? See Him there in the garden, blood oozing from His brow, mixing with tears spilling from His eyes. See Him looking into the Father's cup of eternal wrath. But see something else. See yourself in that cup. See your sin immersing you and see eternal wrath and judgment consuming you.

But then watch Jesus. Hear Him cry, "No Father, let Me drink that cup instead!" Meditate deeply on what He did for you until something in your heart begins to bleed. Let the blade of the sword cut deep until a revolution takes place within you.

Oh, please—this doesn't come from reading the pages of a book. It comes from your own trembling encounter with God. Let Him show you what your sin did to Jesus. See the horrors of hell which He took upon Himself for you. Let the cup go deep, deep, deep inside you, until the very motives of your heart are exposed.

You see, most of us have been serving God for all the wrong reasons. All the wrong motives. But when we truly see the depth of our Savior's sacrifice, we can only live for one burning cause. Living to bring Jesus, the Lamb who was slain, the reward of His suffering, becomes the driving purpose of our lives. It becomes our compelling motive behind all that we do for the Lord. This is what pierces our hearts, for nothing so slays our selfish ambitions, revolutionizes our theology, and fills us with pure burning passion as gazing deeply on the glory of the Lamb until our hearts are undone!

CHAPTER 5 ENDNOTES

1. Spurgeon said Jesus was "encompassed, encircled, overwhelmed with grief...He was entirely immersed with woe" (C. H. Spurgeon, *Spurgeon's Sermons on the Death and Resurrection of Jesus* [Peabody, MA: Hendrickson Publishers, Inc., 2005], 122). Thomas Goodwin said, "He was plunged head and ears in sorrow and had no breathing-hole" (Thomas Goodwin cited in C. H. Spurgeon, *Spurgeon's Sermons on the Death and Resurrection of Jesus*, 122.

2. Leon Morris writes, "There, as Jesus prayed, His soul was in veritable torment. 'He...began to be greatly amazed, and sore troubled' (Mark 14:33). This is very forceful language. Of the word translated 'sore troubled,' J. B. Lightfoot says, it 'describes the confused, restless, half-distracted state, which is produced by physical derangement, or by mental distress, as grief, shame, disappointment,' and H. B. Swete refers to it as conveying 'the distress which follows a great shock.' The language is vivid, almost shocking. Clearly, the evangelists were describing no ordinary perturbation. Jesus was in agony as He faced death" (Leon Morris, *The Cross in the New Testament* [Exeter, England: The Paternoster Press, Ltd, 1965], 46–47).

3. C. H. Spurgeon, *Spurgeon's Sermons on the Death and Resurrection of Jesus*, 128.

4. Jonathan Edwards, "Christ's Agony," 868.

5. The Bible says that because the night "was cold," over in the courtyard of the high priest "the servants and officials stood around a fire they had made to keep warm" (John 18:18).

6. W. E. Vine, *Vine's Expository Dictionary of Old and New Testament Words* (Nashville, TN: Thomas Nelson Publishers, 1996), 185.

7. The word *synoptic* is important to understand so you will know what commentators mean in some of the more scholarly written works. "Synoptic" is from a Latin word, meaning "seeing alike," (Syn: alike, optic: seeing). The Gospels of Matthew, Mark, and Luke see Jesus from a similar perspective and were written earlier than the Gospel of John. It is believed that John's Gospel was written after his revelation on the Island of Patmos so he had a far broader and even more spiritual perspective than the Synoptic Gospels. He had beheld the Lamb in eternity, and this is reflected in his Gospel.

8. "This Old Testament imagery will have been well known to Jesus," writes John R. W. Stott, *The Cross of Christ* [Downers Grove, IL: InterVarsity Press, 1986], 77).

9. C.E.B. Cranfield, cited in Leon Morris, *The Cross in the New Testament*, 47. G. E. Ladd says, "The awfulness of the cup of God's wrath against sin is so bitter that he cannot but cry out for deliverance—'If it

is possible'" (Mark 15:34) (G. E. Ladd, cited in Leon Morris, *A The-ology of the New Testament* [Grand Rapids, MI: Baker Book House, 1975], 191).

10. Philip Graham Ryken, "Take from My Hand This Cup," *Commentary on Jeremiah and Lamentations* (Googlebooks.com., 1973), 372–373.

11. Leon Morris, *The Cross in the New Testament*, 375.

12. Carl F. H. Henry quoting James Denney in the forward of his book, *The Death of Christ* (New Haven, CT: Keats Publishing, Inc., 1981), n.p.

13. Jonathan Edwards, "Christ's Agony," 869.

14. Jonathan Edwards, *The History of the Work of Redemption*, 546.

15. Jonathan Edwards, "Christ's Agony," 867.

16. The preacher is only identified as "C.J.," who preached a sermon on "The Cup" at Southeastern Baptist Theological Seminary (Tony Reinken, February, 2008).

17. Ibid.

18. Jonathan Edwards, "Christ's Agony," 868, 871.

19. John Stott, *The Cross of Christ*, 79.

20. A. W. Pink, *Seven Sayings of Jesus on the Cross* (Grand Rapids, MI: Baker Book House, 1958), 72.

21. Jonathan Edwards, "Christ's Agony," 869.

22. I heard this story told by an elderly preacher about a woman in his church.

23. Leon Morris, *The Atonement* (Downers Grove, IL: InterVarsity Press, 1983), 169. Professor Wayne Grudem explains that "propitiation" actu-ally means "a sacrifice to avert wrath and turn it into favor." Please remember this—if God has given you favor, it is all because of the wrath Jesus took on Himself and turned into favor! (Wayne Grudem, *Systematic Theology*, 580).

24. Sadly, many of the modern versions of the Bible no longer use the word *propitiation* but they use words like *atonement* or *expiation*. This weakens the meaning of the original Greek word "hilasmos" or "hilastērion." The King James Version and the New American Standard Bible still correctly use *propitiation*.

25. Leon Morris said, "Propitiation points us to the removal of divine wrath, and Christ has done this by bearing the wrath for us" (Leon Morris, *The Cross in the New Testament*, 405).

26. John Piper, *The Passion of Jesus Christ* (Wheaton, IL: Crossway Books, 2004), 20.

27. Jonathan Edwards, "Christ's Agony," 867.

Chapter 6

ENGULFING *the* FATHER'S CUP

When Jesus Became Our Substitute Lamb

COME NOW TO follow the Lamb up a tear-stained hill outside Jerusalem. Draw near this burning bush until you can almost feel the heat of the flames warming your face. Like Moses you may almost need to slip the shoes from your feet, for you stand on holy ground.

As you stand on the crest of the hill looking up, feel the tension crackling in the air. Hear the thunder rumbling in the distance. See the black clouds rolling toward Mount Calvary. Hear the moans and cries, but then tune your ears above the din of the crowd. Hear beyond the weeping women, scoffing priests, cursing Romans, shrieking thieves, and groaning earth.

This is the pivotal event of all human history. This is the hub around which all heaven revolves. It is the central view of adoring angels. The hinge of eternity. The bedrock foundation of our Christian faith. It is the focus of the Father's heart. No other event in universal history ever displayed the glory of God's love so magnificently as the day the Lamb gave His life on a cross.

Look with all your heart at Jesus. Focus your gaze on the face of the One, flung up on two strips of wood. See the blood seeping from puncture wounds in His brow, dripping down His face into His eyes and nose and beard. See the cold sweat lathering His body, the tears and spittle coating His cheeks.

Jesus is a visage of bruised and macerated flesh. The Roman flagellum, with its sharp protrusions of bone and metal, has ripped out great hunks of human tissue. He looks like He's been through a meat grinder. John

Piper says, "No manner of execution that has ever been devised was more cruel and agonizing than to be nailed to a cross and hung up to die like a piece of meat. It was horrible. You would not have been able to watch it—not without screaming and pulling at your hair and tearing your clothes. You probably would have vomited."[1]

THE DARKNESS OF SIN

Watch now as the sky turns ominously dark. The sun hides its face. All nature seems to react to this hideous scene. A shuddering awe falls upon the mass of people at Calvary. How amazing—at Jesus' birth it was midnight and the sky glowed bright with the glory of God; now at His death it is midday and the sky is dark as night.

Matthew Henry tells about a Christian martyr who was fastened to a stake and set aflame. As the flames leapt around him, he prayed, "Son of God, shine upon me." Instantly the sun in the sky burst from behind a dark cloud and shone so brightly he had to turn his head away. He was comforted by God in his dying hour; but not so the Son of God.[2] In His dying hours, the last three hours on the cross, the sky turned black and the Father hid His face from His Beloved.[3]

Now Jesus' body thrashes wildly beneath this gruesome weight of darkness. God has rolled all the sin of the ages down on the innocent Lamb, just as He had planned in the Godhead in the great covenant of redemption before the creation of the world. "God made him who had no sin to be sin for us" (2 Cor. 5:21). "He was pierced for our transgressions; he was crushed for our iniquities" (Isa. 53:5). Indeed, He is "the Lamb of God who takes away the sin of the world" (John 1:29).

Please pause here and let this go in deep. This is your sin He bears. He is about to be punished in your place. Oh, when I think of my sin upon Jesus, I shudder with sorrow. Dear God, I hate the sin that riveted my Savior to the cross! My sin drove thorns into His brow. My sin hammered spikes into His hands and feet. My sin caused Him to engulf the Father's cup. Spurgeon writes:

> Let us abhor the sin that brought such agony upon our beloved Lord. What an accursed thing is sin that crucified the Lord Jesus! Do you laugh at it?...Sin murdered Christ; will you be a friend

to it? Sin pierced the heart of the Incarnate God; can you love it? Oh, that there was an abyss as deep as Christ's misery, that I might at once hurl that dagger of sin into its depths, whence it might never be brought to light again.[4]

If only we could grasp the wretchedness of sin. Sin pollutes the soul. Sin opens us to demonic attack. Sin dulls our senses, causing hopelessness and depression. Sin corrodes our hearts, making us hard and numb inside. Sin destroys homes, and families, and relationships. Most of all, God is holy; and sin separates us from the holy presence of God: "Your iniquities have separated you from your God; your sins have hidden his face from you" (Isa. 59:2). That's why sin is so awful.

But most of all, sin is repulsive because of what it did to Jesus. If you ever doubt the dreadfulness of sin, if you ever find yourself winking or smiling as people recount their stories of sin, stop and think what this sin did to the Son of God. This will show you how hideous sin is.

Today people don't want to face the issue of sin. Refusing to call sin "sin," they wonder—where is God's presence? Why don't I feel Him anymore? Does God even love me? Sin blocks our awareness of God's presence. This is why we must bring our sin to the cross and crucify it. "Contemplations of the Saviour are the death of sin, but no other weapon will destroy it," said Spurgeon.[5]

An obscure story in the Bible illustrates this point. The Israelites were being bitten by poisonous snakes, so the Lord told Moses to make a brass serpent and lift it up on a pole. Then He called all who were sick from snakebite to come look up at the one upon the pole. He told them they would live if they looked "attentively, expectantly, with a steady and absorbing gaze" (Num. 21:9).

This is our answer to the sin problem; for even as the serpent carried venomous poison, the Son of God on the cross carried the venom of our sin. "Are you tormented with the power of sin?" asked Spurgeon. "Beloved, if you long to conquer sin within you, behold the Lamb of God!"[6]

So pause for a moment and think about your own sin crushing down on Jesus. Look long and deep at Him, writhing under this heavy load of sin. No matter what you've done—whether it be pride and gossip, or gluttony and bitterness, or murder and hatred, addictions or the filthiest sexual sin—all of this infuses Jesus. He who is holy, innocent, and full of love becomes permeated with your sin. Now, like the Israelites in the wilderness, look at Jesus "attentively, expectantly, with a steady and absorbing gaze." Look until you are grief-stricken over your sin. Look until a spirit of repentance falls upon you and you are melted with godly grief.

Now repent with "godly sorrow" over it. Repent hard and deep, asking God to give you a gift of repentance. He will. Repentance is one of the most powerful gifts He has given us. It cleanses the soul and gives us the power to turn completely from our sin. Even if you slip and fall again, run over and over to Calvary until at last your sin is starved and defeated in the finished work of the cross. Indeed, there is cleansing, healing, and forgiveness in a long steady look at the Lamb.

THE CUP POURS DOWN

Look up again at Jesus, writhing under this heavy load of sin. Spikes tug against the holes in His hands as He tosses under this crushing weight. Ropes burn His arms, holding Him to the wood, preventing the nails from ripping through the flesh of His hands.[7] Raw wounds on His back scrape against the rough-hewn wood.

But suddenly His body stops thrashing. His whole body stiffens. The color in His face drains. His eyebrows rise in shock, and His eyes fly open wide. What is happening to Jesus?

A look of terror covers His face. His eyes tell the story. They are swollen and red, bulging with tears, filled with untold horror. We saw that same look of fear in His eyes before, in the moonlight of Gethsemane, when Jesus was crying out to His Father about the cup.

Jesus looks up and sees it coming. There it is—God's cup of wrath, trembling in the Father's hand. The cup tips. Jesus shuts His eyes tightly and braces Himself against this oncoming flood.

God's eternal judgment against sin mounts like a massive tsunami wave. It swells and crests. Then it breaks and bursts down over Jesus. Wave after wave after wave of God's furious wrath slams down upon the Son of God.[8]

Watch now as this furnace of wrath opens over Jesus, and God casts

Him, like a Passover lamb, into the roaring flames. See His body hanging rigidly as the fire of heaven rushes down on the burnt offering. Watch the bush burn with fiery judgment as eternal wrath tumbles down upon the Son. See the lake of fire empty out upon Him as hell crashes and burns against the Lamb. Look on as the Father baptizes His Son in wrath. It is just as the Scripture says, "All your waves and breakers have passed over me" (Ps. 42:7). "He was smitten and afflicted by God; the punishment that brought us peace was upon him" (Isa. 53:5).

Close your eyes and think about it. Picture your innocent Jesus, burning like a Lamb, in the flames of God's wrath. This is what will pierce your soul. This is what will revolutionize your theology. Oh, why have we so neglected this high point of the cross? This is what Jesus came to earth to do. Above all, He came to drink His Father's cup. So let the sword go deep. Let it pierce the veil that covers your heart. Let it transform your thinking.

Now over and over and over and over again, the waves of God's wrath explode upon the innocent Lamb, crushing, rushing, roaring, spilling, billowing hot boiling judgment down from above.

Jesus holds His breath, almost unable to breathe under the weight of such devastating punishment. His eyes roll upward. His brows knit with anguish. His fingers seem to grasp for God. His eyes speak of a mystery too deep for words. He searches the heavens as if to silently scream, *Where is God? Where are You, Father? Why do You abandon me now, Holy Spirit, when I need You most?* But still He opens wide and drinks in every broiling drop of the Father's cup of wrath.

My heart stands still when I gaze up at Jesus drinking His Father's cup. It hurts to look, but I must look until I can see. This is what's been missing from our theology. This is the part of the cross we've overlooked. If we are going to bring the gospel back to the center of the church, we must understand this great mystery. We must bring back this fundamental truth. It's the apex, the summit, the most vital part of the gospel and most of us have overlooked it.

This is essentially what the "Prince of Preachers" Charles Spurgeon spent his whole life defending. In his latter years the fight almost overwhelmed him because so much liberalism, called "higher criticism," was slipping into the church in England.

But our day is no different. Rarely do you hear a sermon, read a book, or view a video or a television program which is saturated in the pure gospel of Christ. Even in our Charismatic/Pentecostal stream, it's as though we must move on beyond the cross into "deeper things." There is nothing deeper than the cross! Nothing is higher and more revolutionizing than a profound understanding of the Father's cup of wrath which Jesus engulfed for us.

If we miss this, we miss it all. Then we wonder why revivals cease, teenagers backslide, and pornography grips so many Christians. We've forgotten that Jesus became our substitute on the cross. Spurgeon said, "If you put away the doctrine of the substitutionary sacrifice of Christ, you have disemboweled the gospel, and torn from it its very heart."[9]

I've taught hundreds of students through the years, and when they hear about the cup, they almost always say, "Why didn't anyone ever tell me?" The reason we haven't told them is because our theology has become so weak and wishy-washy. We've forgotten to tell them the most essential part of biblical theology, and it has left them with a tremendous void in their hearts.

The young generation is weary of the hype and glitz they see in some churches and on television. They need something real, something into which they can sink their spiritual teeth. Most of their lives have been shaken from the divorces of their parents, and they need a solid rock foundation. They long for something they could die for so they can truly live. Something that stirs their passion and gives them a reason to serve Jesus with all their hearts. But when they hear about the Father's cup, they are truly undone! They are gripped with a passion that compels them to live for Jesus Christ.

That which stirs them most deeply is hearing that Jesus took their hell. They know they deserve hell. Many of them have trashed their lives on drugs and sex and porn. They know how wicked they are. But when they discover that Jesus took their hell, they are undone! Now they are gladly willing to give their whole lives to bring Jesus, the Lamb who was slain, the reward of His suffering.

CALVARY'S HELL

You might be thinking, *Please don't mention hell again. It makes me too uncomfortable!* But how uncomfortable did the Father's cup make Jesus? If we can't mention this volatile but vital subject, we can't tell others what Jesus actually did for them. We can't show them a Savior who took their punishment of hell upon Himself and already paid their price. Oh, what a great gospel we have to share with the world if we will boldly tell about the Father's cup which Jesus engulfed for them!

Spurgeon said, "There was the cup, hell was in it, the Savior drank it—not a sip and then a pause...but He drained it until there is not a dregs left for any of his people."[10] Do you realize what this means? Hell is an "eternal fire prepared for the devil and his angels" (Matt. 25:41), but now Jesus is taking that hell upon Himself. He is swallowing down "the wine of God's fury which has been poured full strength into the cup of his wrath" (Rev. 14:10).

Jesus described hell as a place of outer "darkness where there will be weeping and gnashing of teeth" (Matt. 8:12).[11] "Into that outer darkness the Son of God plunged for us," writes John Stott.[12] Billy Graham explains, "Jesus' suffering was not simply that of a man dying a cruel and painful death—terrible as that was. His greatest suffering was the spiritual agony He endured as He took upon Himself the death and hell you and I deserve. Yet by allowing His Son to suffer the pangs of death and hell, God demonstrated how much He loves us."

Do you see? This is all for *you and me!* He is taking the punishment we deserve for sin. Spurgeon said, "O Christian, pause here and reflect! Christ was punished in this way for you! O see that countenance so wrung with horror, those horrors gather there for you!"[13] How then can we neglect so great an act of our Savior? How can we continue to preach and teach every other subject, when most Christians don't even know about the Father's cup?

What's even more amazing—this is not simply the wrath of one person's hell. This is the accumulated hell for all humanity. God has saved all the punishment which Old Testament sinners deserved as well, and poured it on His Son: "In His forbearance he had left the sins committed beforehand unpunished—he did it to demonstrate his justice at the present time" (Rom. 3:26). Yes, from Adam to the last person conceived on earth, from Adolf Hitler to Osama Bin Laden, to you and me—Jesus is taking our punishment for sin.[14] He is "stricken by God, smitten by him, and afflicted." He is "pierced for our transgressions, crushed for our iniquities; the punishment that brought us peace was upon Him" (Isa. 53:4–5).

What a travesty it is when someone chooses hell instead of choosing Jesus, for God sends no one to hell. Hell was prepared for the devil and his angels, but now because of sin, those who reject God's gracious gift of His Son send themselves to hell. But, for all who put their faith in Christ, Jesus has already emptied their cup of punishment and hell. This is the grace and mercy of our God. It is the mystery unveiled in the covenant of redemption before the world's creation. It is the foundation of our Christian faith, the heart and soul of the gospel, the theological basis for all that we believe. That's why we must allow this cup to revolutionize our theology.

SPREADING THE MESSAGE OF THE CUP

I took a team of young revivalists from our school to the UK to spread this message. God opened doors in churches and even public schools all over England. One day we were at a public school in London, facing three to four hundred students. Now remember, this is England, where many students tell us they've never heard anyone even talk about God, and certainly not in the public schools. The schoolmaster told us with a frown, "You cannot preach! You cannot pray! You cannot read the Bible! You cannot testify!" I thought, *What are we going to do?*

Then one of our students, John, who always listens to the Lord for guidance, smiled and said sweetly, "Can I tell a story?"

She thought for a moment, and said, "Yes." So John began telling this story, which he's heard me tell a hundred times.

> A young mother awakened one night to the cries of her baby. Sitting up in bed, the smell of smoke filled her senses. She shook her husband awake and raced upstairs to the baby, but a wall of flames drove her back. "Honey, we've got to get out!" her husband cried. "But the baby!" she wailed. He picked her up and carried

her outside where neighbors had now gathered and firefighters were hooking up their hoses. Soon they were spraying the blaze, and preparing to enter the house. But the mother kept hearing the cries of her baby from the upstairs window. Her husband held her back, knowing there was nothing they could do.

Finally, she broke from his grip and tore into the house. Covering her face with her hands, she charged up through the wall of flames into her baby's room. Gathering her from her crib, she placed the little one inside her robe and pressed back through the flames. She could feel her hair burning and the skin of her face melting. When she reached the door she was delirious with pain. She struggled to open the door and fell to the ground outside, a crumpled heap of charred human flesh.

A medical helicopter rushed the mother and her baby to a burn center, where the baby soon recovered with very few burns. But the mother was burned almost beyond recognition. For the rest of her life she was horribly disfigured, but to this little mother, the sacrifice was worth it, for she had saved her baby.

Years later, the baby girl matured into a beautiful teenager. When her friends came to her home, occasionally someone would rudely ask, "Why is your mother so ugly?" Always the girl would beam with a smile as bright as the sun, "Oh, my mother is the most beautiful woman in the world! Because she went through the fire for me, I'm alive today!"

As John ended this story to the English students sitting before him, most of whom were now weeping, he said boldly:

> That's what Jesus Christ did for you! Like the mother who heard the cries of her baby, He heard your cries. He came all the way from heaven to go through the fire of God's wrath against sin. And just to prove how much He loves you, He holds out His hands to show you the scars of His sacrifice. Now, like the teenage girl whose mother was forever scarred by the fire, if you will receive Christ as your Savior, you too can cry, "Jesus is the

most beautiful Man in the world! Because He went through the fire for me, I'm alive today!"

My throat tightened as I heard John's final words, knowing the schoolmaster would be furious. Here he was—actually explaining the fires of hell through a metaphorical story—in an English school where they don't believe in God or sin and certainly not hell. But I looked over at the schoolmaster, and she was wiping away tears. It was amazing; and that day we were allowed to meet with interested students in a classroom. We led them in prayers to repent of their sins and receive Jesus Christ as their Savior. It was an incredible victory, but it happened because a young man boldly told them what Jesus Christ did for them when He drank the Father's cup and went through the fire for them.

So now when people ask you, "How could a good God send sinners to hell?" Tell them the whole story. Tell them about a God who took hell in their place so they could have His heaven. Help them understand His wrath, so they can understand the depths of His love. But don't hesitate to tell them—if they refuse to accept the Savior who took their punishment on Himself, then they will have to bear their own punishment.

"MY RIVER STILL RUSHES"

One day I stood weeping in our prayer garden, covered over with a canopy of oak leaves and branches. Through the years, here in this prayer garden, revival students had preached the Lamb, enacted dramas of the cross, and prayed in fire tunnels.

As I already told you, I had bought Evangelist Steve Hill's property in Alabama, just outside Pensacola, turned it into a camp, and the place had exploded with the presence of God. Then for five years I had been teaching at BRSM and praying for people at the Brownsville Revival; but now revival was lifting, and it broke my heart. As I cried to the Lord, I whimpered, *"Father, what should I do? Do you want me to close everything down and go back to Texas?"*

As clear as if it were an audible voice from heaven, the Lord spoke warmly into my spirit, *"My River still rushes."* That's all He said but those four words spoke volumes. They told me that God is still moving, even if revival seems to have lifted from Brownsville. Even more, they told me—this message must go on.

So rather than packing up in defeat, as soon as BRSM closed, we built a chapel at our camp and started Glory of the Lamb Internships so that we could continue pouring the message of the Lamb into hungry hearts. Because we've seen God raise up so many students who now carry the fire of the cross and the power of revival, we've changed the name of our internships to "Revivalists of the Cross" and "Unquenchable Flame" Internships. One of our main purposes is to raise up men and women who pray and preach with fire; for indeed, the message must go on.

One night I heard four of our interns from England praying in a corner of our chapel. I could see the passion bursting from their hearts. We could all feel the fire of God's presence pouring out through the chapel as they prayed. I slipped up close to listen.

Sophie cried, *Oh, Jesus, You drank the cup of wrath on the cross for me! You were punished for me! You cried that cry for me!* Michelle wailed, *Father, this is Your Son! Your Son!* Mandy wept, *Oh, Father, how can we bring Him His reward in England? People have forgotten the cross of Your Son in America—in the church—but how can we make Christ crucified known again?*

As they prayed with all the passion of their hearts, their faces reddened, tears streamed down their cheeks, and their bodies rocked back and forth. I was melted by their prayers, for I knew they had touched the Father's heart for His Son. They were crying out to bring Jesus the reward of His suffering as a Lamb.

This is indeed what the Father waits to see. He searches the earth to find those who will burn for His Son's sacrifice. He longs to find a generation who will unveil the depths of the cross, who will reveal the agony of the cup Jesus drank, who will cherish every drop of His sacred blood, who will walk in the finished work of the cross, who will pray their hearts out to see Jesus receive His glory, and who will live their whole lives to bring Him His reward.

One day I saw Stephanie sobbing before God on the floor of our chapel. I had been teaching on the Father's cup in our summer internship, and I could see something precious was happening between her and the Lord. She had been one of my students at BRSM, and now served on staff at our internships. She had always had a tender heart toward the Lamb, but today she was experiencing an encounter with God on the cross.

She later told me that suddenly she was able to see Jesus immersed in the Father's fiery wrath. Repentance came over her like a flood, and she has not been the same since. She said, "Dr. Sandy, we have to take this gospel to the nations. It's not just a message. The cup is it! It's the pinnacle!"

Oh, I tell you, I just can't get over it, and I pray I never will. I never knew He went to such an extravagant extent on the cross. All I ever heard was "Jesus died for you," but that doesn't tell the whole story. Jesus became our Substitute. He took the judgment we deserve so we could be forgiven. He engulfed every burning drop of hell so we could have His heaven.

So I want to ask you to pause right now, close your eyes and see Him, hanging in shreds on the cross. Watch again as the Father tilts His cup over Jesus, preparing to punish Him for you.

See wave after wave of violent wrath tumble down on the innocent Lamb. See every drop of the hell you deserve immerse the One you love. Over and over and over again, the judgment of God smashes the Son of God. Please don't lose sight of the fact—this is all for you! Look until the cup is more than mere head knowledge. Until the cross is more than an historical event. Gaze at your bleeding Savior until you can feel it. Until you experience the power of the cross. Until your heart dissolves into tears. Cry out to Him, *Oh, Lord, plunge the sword of the cross into my soul! Pierce me, Jesus! Break me! Wreck me! Ravish me for the Lamb!*

Then fall on your face and worship. Pour out upon Him all the gratitude of your heart. Pray something like this:

> *Oh, Jesus, thank You, thank You, thank You! For the rest of my days I will never stop thanking You for drinking the Father's cup for me. Because You did this for me, I will live my whole life for this one great cause—to bring You, the Lamb who was slain, the reward of Your suffering for me. For You have melted my heart until it is utterly undone!*

CHAPTER 6 ENDNOTES

1. John Piper, *Don't Waste Your Life*, 50.
2. Matthew Henry, *Matthew Henry's Commentary on the Whole Bible*, vol. IV, 564.
3. 'The darkness of Calvary did not, like an ordinary night, reveal the stars, but it darkened every lamp of heaven. His strong crying and tears denoted the deep sorrow of his soul. Well may I tell you that this unutterable darkness, this hiding of the divine face, expresses more of the woes of Jesus than words can ever tell' (Charles Spurgeon, "The Three Hours' Darkness," *The Power of the Cross of Christ*, 98).
4. Charles Spurgeon, "Lama Sabachthani?" *The Power of the Cross of Christ*, 117.
5. Charles H. Spurgeon, "Behold the Lamb," 113.
6. Ibid.
7. I completely disagree with the commentators who tell us that Jesus was not nailed through His hands but through His wrists. While it's true that in order to prevent the spikes from tearing through the hands, some were spiked through the wrists under Roman crucifixion. However, when ropes are tied to the arms, the spikes will not tear through the hands. I believe Jesus was nailed through His healing hands, the very hands—not wrists—that were laid on the sick, on little children, and on the suffering masses.
8. John Piper writes, "In that moment when the Son was taking upon himself everything God hates in us, and God was forsaking him to death, even then the Father knew that the measure of His Son's suffering was the depth of his Son's love for the Father's glory" (John Piper, *The Pleasures of God*, 176.
9. Charles Spurgeon, *2200 Quotations from the Writings of Charles H. Spurgeon*, 200,
10. Charles Spurgeon, "It Is Finished!" *The Power of the Cross of Christ*, 141.
11. When Jesus cried, "My God, why have you forsaken me?" Spurgeon said, "This was a cry of spiritual agony as God heaped the judgment of hell upon His Son" (Henry Drummond, *Spurgeon, Prince of Preachers*, 25).
12. John Stott, *The Cross of Christ*, 79.
13. Charles Spurgeon, "Cries from the Cross," *Spurgeon's Sermons on the Cross* (Grand Rapids, MI: Kregel Publications, 1933), 158.
14. By no means does this mean that all people are saved. Jesus died for everyone, but only those who repent of their sin and receive Him as Savior and Lord are saved. The view that all people are saved is called "Universalism," which is a heresy.

Chapter 7

ABBA'S PAIN

The Father's Looks Down on Calvary

THE WRATH OF God smashes down upon the innocent Lamb of God, as He hangs suspended between heaven and earth, bleeding from every wound. Jesus drinks and drinks and drinks of this tremulous cup in His own Father's hand.

Pause for a moment now and lift your gaze higher. With the eyes of your heart, look into heaven and consider how the Father feels as He punishes His blameless Son. I am sure He aches with unthinkable sorrow. His heart shakes violently as the cup of wrath trembles in His hand. I can almost hear Him sobbing as He looks down on His Beloved. Though some accuse Him of being cold and heartless, punishing His Son with merciless anger, in reality, I'm sure that Abba Father bears the deepest pain of all. I hear Him crying:

> *This is My Son! Do you understand what His sacrifice does to Me? Can you see that this cup of wrath breaks My heart, too? Can you feel what I feel for My Son?*

THE FATHER'S HEART

This is the One He held in face-to-face communion through all eternity. No one loves Jesus as deeply as the Father loves Him. And no one feels anguish over this cup of wrath as Abba feels it.[1] John Piper writes, "In the very moment when God's curse rested most heavily on Jesus because of sin, the Father's love for his Son reached explosive proportions."[2]

Now we understand a little better why God dropped a curtain of darkness over those last three hours at Calvary. It almost seemed He was veiling from open view this most colossal event in all human history.[3] It was a mystery too sacred to reveal before the mocking eyes of priests and the calloused hearts of Roman soldiers.[4]

Not only was the mystery of the cup veiled to taunting eyes, but the unspeakable anguish of the Father's heart was hidden as well. The divine agony in the heart of God is an immeasurable mystery. "In giving his Son he was giving himself," writes John Stott. "Through the person of his Son he himself bore the penalty which he himself inflicted....There is neither harsh injustice nor unprincipled love nor Christological heresy in that; there is only unfathomable mercy....Divine love triumphed over divine wrath by divine self-sacrifice."[5]

How could we ever take this sacrifice of the Father for granted? How could we ever think He was being calloused or heartless in this act of divine judgment? The pain it caused Him when He punished His Son in our place was unthinkable. It was the ultimate expression of love.

Oh, how it grieved the Father God to have to feed the darling of His heart into His undying flames of wrath. It's like the time, during the Holocaust, when a Jewish boy had to feed his own father into the flames of a crematorium. How much more it would grieve a father to feed his own son to the fire. What infinite grief it causes the Heavenly Father as He casts His own beloved Son into the crematorium of Calvary.

The following story helps us relate to the feelings of the Father:

> Late one night a pastor received an emergency phone call asking him to come to the home of a family in his church. When he got there, the scene was unimaginable.
>
> The father, a dedicated family man and church member, had been cleaning his shotgun with his ten-year-old son by his side. The boy stood for a moment and walked in front of the barrel of the gun. Just then an explosion jolted the father. He looked up suddenly to see a look of shock on his son's face. The boy grabbed for his chest and fell over, blood gushing from his aorta leading from his heart.
>
> The horrified father jumped up and reached for his son, as he was in the throes of dying. "I'm sorry! I'm sorry! I love you! I love you!" he screamed, holding his son near. "It's okay, Dad,"

his son whispered. Then his eyes fixed, his body went limp in his father's arms, and he died.

As the pastor entered the room, he found the man sitting in stunned shock. The boy's body had been removed, but blood still splattered the room.

For a long time the pastor held this anguished father as together they cried. Finally, the man looked up and wailed, "Pastor, I killed my own son!"

Just then the Lord spoke to the pastor and said, "Tell him I killed My Son too. You did it by accident, but I had to kill My own Son on purpose. Tell him I understand His hurt and grief, but My pain was even deeper!"

The pastor knelt beside the broken man and began to pray for him. In his prayer he spoke those words, "Father, this dear brother's son died by accident, but You killed your Son on purpose so that his boy could live forever."

That night a devastated father received some comfort as he meditated on the Father's pain at the cross of His own Son. And though this is a heart wrenching story, it helps illustrate how the Father felt at Calvary.

Indeed, we need to understand Abba's pain as He looked down on His own precious Son, bleeding like an innocent Lamb. Though His heart was bursting with love, He turned His face away and pummeled Him with punishment. The agony this brought the Father is unthinkable. Sorrow engulfed His tender heart. He felt each stroke of pain and judgment Himself.

It's like the beautiful painting of the crucifixion which hangs in an Italian church. At first glance, one hardly notices, but as you look more closely, writes George Buttrick, "there's a vast and shadowy Figure behind the figure of Jesus. The nail that pierces the hand of Jesus goes through to the hand of God. The spear thrust into the side of Jesus goes through into God's."[6] For in the sacrifice of His Son, God gave His very best and suffered with Him.

A heresy has recently arisen saying that if Jesus suffered punishment on the cross, then the Father is the "ultimate child abuser." Think about this. To accuse the Father of the crime of child abuse when He suffered so much pain in giving this supreme sacrifice—this is sheer blasphemy! Especially when He did it all for us! Now to twist His sacrifice for us by turning it against Him and calling it "child abuse" is the height of sacrilege! It is a desecration of the Father's love!

Justice Satisfied

Now let me bring up a thorny issue. Evangelical scholars talk about "appeasing God's wrath," "divine justice satisfied," and the "satisfaction of the demands of God's wrath." I don't disagree with that theology, but I disagree with the language. This gives the impression of a cold and heartless God, vengefully punishing His Son with no feelings at all, simply satisfying His demand for righteousness.

But we miss the mark by a long shot if we don't realize how it hurt the Father to pour His wrath upon the Son of His heart. We misrepresent Abba if we don't tell our students about the divine pathos—the emotions and feelings of God. Let me tell you how I learned about this theological issue, which I think reveals part of the reason why we have so little teaching or preaching on the cup of wrath today.

I was sitting in a systematic theology class in seminary one day, when the professor said, "It wouldn't have mattered if Jesus had died of a heart attack. How He died was unimportant. That He rose from the dead is what matters."

I jumped out of my seat in front of 300 students and cried, "Oh, no Sir! That's not right!" I began explaining about the cup of wrath which the Bible says filled Jesus' prayers in the garden of Gethsemane. I told about the terrors of drinking that cup on the cross, backing it up with quotes from Jonathan Edwards.

He calmly dismissed my words with, "I believe God is a loving God and He would not punish His Son."

"But Sir, God punished His Son because of His great love!" I countered.

"You're talking about the 'satisfaction of divine justice theory' and I don't accept that forensic language."

"What do you mean?" I asked.

"Anselm, Calvin, and Luther all had legal backgrounds and they used this forensic, or legal language to describe the crucifixion." When he said this, lights went on in my head.

"Then, Sir, let's change the language but not the truth!" I then began explaining how Jesus never called it "satisfaction of divine justice." He called it drinking the Father's cup. He used family terms, simple and warm, calling Him Abba and Father, not divine justice! We had many more such talks, and he ended up giving me a high A in the course and writing me a long letter, thanking me for my theology.

This was one of my fondest memories from seminary, for it challenged me to see what we are up against in the theological world. One of the primary reasons the Father's cup has been dismissed by liberal theologians is because the wrong language has been used—forensic, legal, law-based language—and the words must be changed to use the language of our Lord. That's what I'm trying to do in this book.

As Christian leaders—those who believe in the new birth, in being washed in the blood of Christ, and in the inerrancy of the Word of God—we must do all we can to bring solid, biblical, cross-centered theology back to the church. This is what has been missing, not just in liberal churches but many Evangelical churches as well, especially Charismatic and Pentecostal churches.

Do you see how an understanding of the Father's cup can produce a theological revolution and bring the church back on course? I believe the Father burns to see His Son glorified as the Lamb. How could the Father sacrifice so deeply, only to hear us mention this supreme sacrifice once a year at Easter? Our silence is deafening, and I am sure it hurts the Father's heart.

By failing to tell others about the Father's cup of wrath which Jesus endured for us, we have trifled His sacrifice. We have sugarcoated the message and presented a blood-drained gospel. Most of all, we've presented a wrath-drained gospel, which is not biblical, and it leaves people blinded to His full atoning work. By slighting the full weight of the Father's cup of eternal judgment, we have grieved His heart.[7]

Now the Father's heart is raw and sensitive to every reminder of His Son's sacrifice. Bob Sorge writes in *The Power of the Blood*, "I am persuaded that there is nothing God feels more strongly about than the cross of His Son....Never has anything torn and lacerated the infinite depths of God's heart as deeply and severely as the crucifixion of His beloved Son. And He will never forget it....When you come to the cross, you are getting God at His deepest passions."[8]

How much longer can the Father endure watching His church neglect His sacrifice? How much longer will He put up with our self-centered, humanistic, materialistic gospel? When His Son paid such an immeasurable price, when Abba Himself gave until His own heart was gutted, how much longer will He wait? The late David Wilkerson said, "The one thing God will never endure is the casting aside of the preaching of the cross."[9]

I believe the Father is shaking the whole earth, and He will continue to shake until a theological revolution takes place in the church. Until we come back to the cross of Calvary.[10] Until the Lamb is the center of the church as He is in heaven. Until Jesus—His one and only beloved Son—receives the glory and honor He deserves for drinking the Father's cup. Until our lives are riveted to the cross and the cross is riveted into us.

When we begin to understand this mystery, it's like climbing a high mountain and looking down to survey the scene below. The whole Bible makes sense and comes alive when we stand on this pinnacle of truth. Understanding the Father's cup changes everything. Once we realize the magnitude of His sacrifice, what else can we do but live for the greatest purpose on earth? What else can we do but live our whole lives to bring Him the reward of His suffering?

This is the Father's deepest desire. Nothing means more to Him than to see His Son honored on earth as He is in heaven. There He stands as a slain Lamb. Think about it. If John "saw a Lamb, looking as if it had been slain" (Rev. 5:6); and if angels continually cry out, "Worthy is the Lamb who was slain" (Rev. 5: 12), then, as Mary Wells points out, "The Father also sees Him like a slain Lamb, and it breaks His heart!"[11]

Yes, every glimpse of His beloved Son, looking like a wounded Lamb, ravishes His tender heart. His heart burns for Him to be honored for His costly sacrifice. Nothing is more important than this—to live to bring Jesus, the Lamb who was slain, the reward of His suffering for you.

GRIPPED BY THE FATHER'S CUP

With all my heart I believe we have wounded the heart of God by overlooking the depths of His Son's sacrifice.[12] And yet, most of us have never even looked into His cup. If you are like me, you've rarely if ever heard a sermon on the cup or read a book which reveals its ingredients.

It's like the time Mary and I were ministering in Asia, when Dr. Earnest Chan, the leader of the entire Asian Network of conferences, said, "I have been in ministry for forty years, but I have never even heard about the cup!" This highly educated man with a Ph.D. from Fuller Theological Seminary was willing to humbly admit his need, urging everyone in the conferences in Taiwan and Hong Kong to let this message of the Lamb transform their lives.

One of the most striking experiences for me was in China where I taught the Glory of the Lamb course in the Agape School of Ministry in downtown Hong Kong. At first the students seemed somewhat reserved, but when I began describing the Father's cup, something started happening all over the room.

These beautiful Asian students loved the Lord dearly and had committed themselves to Christian ministry. But never had they looked into the Father's cup. When they gazed with all their hearts into the wrath Jesus engulfed for them, all through the room students began to grip their hearts and cry out. Then several of them screamed, fell out of their chairs, and hit the floor. It was because they were realizing for the first time in their lives what their Savior did for them and they were undone.

I saw something even more amazing in Africa. I told you in an earlier chapter about founding a Kenya Ablaze School of the Lamb, for pastors and leaders in Kisumu, Kenya. Let me tell you more about the fire of God that fell upon these precious pastors.

It was the first week of the first school in Kenya. Most of the pastors were skeptical about receiving anything from a white *"mazunga"* team, much less a white woman. But when they saw the eternal covenant of redemption and then when we looked into the Father's cup of wrath, these young pastors came undone. Most of them had been preaching a prosperity message because they saw nothing special in the message of the cross; and as some told me, "It wouldn't make us rich!"

On the third night, I invited those who wanted to resolve to follow the Lamb and preach the cross of Christ to come up to the altar. I always ask our team to wait to lay hands on people until we invite the Holy

Spirit to come down. This way we are able to let Him lead and we aren't trying to make something happen.

We waited, and then suddenly—without any warning, the lightning of God struck a young pastor named Allan. Though dressed in his best clothes, he cried out and hit the dirty floor, shaking violently and praying loudly in Swahili, "*Moto! Moto!*" which means "Fire! Fire!"

The Lord was indeed "confirming his word with signs following" (Mark 16:20). The sign was the fire. This is the fire of the Holy Spirit which God sends down on the message of the cross and especially the Father's cup. Like touching a match to dry tinder, the fire of God spread through the whole room. Pastors gathered around Allan, and the fire consuming him swept out like a contagious flame, igniting them with the same holy fire.

Pastor Allan told me later, "I didn't even know I was on the floor in my clean clothes, but suddenly I saw a very bright light, like lightning in a thunderstorm." From that time on, Allan, has been like a man aflame. He has faithfully gone to the villages, preaching the gospel with indescribable passion and power. People scream and run to the altar, and many are physically healed when he lays hands on them.

The next night I saw the same fire fall on Pastor Newton. Again we had invited people forward and waited on God. Newton opened his mouth and gasped. Suddenly, he fell to the concrete with no one touching him. He trembled and shouted and prophesied until everyone in the room was burning with the same spreading fire.

A few days later, I heard him preaching in the slums in Kisumu. In all my life, I have never heard such powerful preaching. He was like a man set ablaze. It reminded me of what John Wesley said, "When you set yourself on fire, people come to watch you burn!" He was like a burning man as he vividly and dramatically preached the cross and the Father's cup of wrath, and people were irresistibly drawn to Jesus.

One day Sophie, Pastor Newton, and Pastor Allan were preaching in a village when it started to rain. In spite of the rain, they continued to preach and the fire of God fell. People ran to the altar as the power of God began striking them down, and they fell to the muddy ground. So aflame were their hearts they didn't even care that they were lying in muddy water. Many of them cried out, "I feel fire!" "I'm on fire!" and many of them were healed.

Oh, I tell you, this is what I live for! To see men and women experiencing the pure fire of God when they preach the message of the Father's cup to their own people, I know this touches the Father's heart. We aren't trying to build something for ourselves. To the contrary, we are simply giving the message away to the nationals, the indigenous pastors, and they are spreading the news. All I can do is weep when I hear these stories, for I know that God's Son is receiving what He deserves on earth. And most of all, I know that Abba's heart is pleased.

Can you see how this can eventually erupt into a theological revolution in the church? When people of every tribe and tongue and nation receive the full understanding of the Father's cup, they will at last know what Jesus did for them. Christianity will no longer be just another religion, for it is the only religion of hope. It tells of a God who took their punishment of hell so they could have His heaven. This is an irresistible gospel.

ABBA'S HEARTBEAT

Almost every single day, early in the morning, I walk out to our chapel, dip communion bread into juice, and hold the blood-soaked bread before the Lord. I thank the Father for the pain He was willing to suffer. Then I step back, lift my hand toward heaven, and cry out with all the passion of my heart. Would you join me in this earnest prayer?

> *Father, this is Your Son! Oh, when will You vindicate Him on earth? When will You allow Him to receive the reward of His suffering? When will You remove the veil over the eyes of the church and show her what our Savior has really done? Oh, when, Father? My heart weeps with Your heartbeat. I can feel Your heart pounding hard with love for Your Son! Please, Father, open our eyes and let us fall in love with Your Son as Your eternal Lamb!*

This story helps us relate to how the Father must feel as He sees His Son's blood being trampled today.

One day a father was working in his office when he received a phone call from the police. "I'm sorry, Sir," the police officer on the other end of the line said, "Your son has been killed in a head-on collision. He was pronounced dead at the scene."

Shock swept over the father as he leapt from his desk, threw on his jacket, and rushed to his car. Tears blinded his eyes as he raced toward the scene of the accident. He finally reached the location and swerved to the side of the road. The wrecked cars had been towed away and his son's body had already been taken to the morgue. He looked out across the road where he saw blood still splashed across the highway—his son's blood! Cars now traveled carelessly across the blood-stained road, oblivious to what had happened. Delirious with grief, the man ripped off his jacket and charged out in front of the traffic. Waving his jacket in front of the cars, he screamed, "Stop! Can't you see? You're traveling over the blood of my son!"

That's how the Father in heaven feels! He looks down upon this earth where His own Son's blood dripped into the ground, and I believe He roars:

Can't you see? You're traveling over the blood of My Son!

The Bible warns, "If we deliberately go on sinning after receiving the knowledge of the truth" we have "trampled the Son of God under foot" and "treated as an unholy thing the blood of the covenant" (Heb. 10:26, 29). But this is what we've done in the church. We've emptied the blood from the gospel and presented a sterilized, seeker-friendly version. We've presented a blood-drained gospel. We've grieved Abba's heart.

When I finish crying out for God's Son to be glorified on earth as He is in heaven, sometimes I step back and listen. Often I can hear Him speaking—not in audible words—but with a deep resonating voice in my spirit. I hear His voice thundering over the courts of heaven breaking over the threshold pouring, roaring, spilling, and filling my heart. The voice of eternity cries:

This is My Son! Hear Him! Behold Him! Live to bring Him what He deserves! Give your whole life to bring Jesus, the Lamb who was slain, the reward of His suffering for you!

When I hear this heartbeat of Abba, I want to fall on my face and worship, for my heart has been undone by a revelation of the Lamb!

CHAPTER 7 ENDNOTES

1. Abba is the intimate name for the Father which Jesus sometimes called Him.
2. John Piper, *Pleasures of God*, 176.
3. Pastor Wil Pounds writes, "No wonder God pulls the curtain across His holy of holies so no profane eyes could see the terrible spiritual suffering the Lamb of God was enduring as punishment for our sins. God permitted no one to look on the physical convulsions of the vicarious suffering of God's Servant. This is how far He traveled from heaven's glory to save your soul. It was a place of outer darkness, or god-forsakenness and God caused a thick darkness to fall upon the land." (Wil Pounds, "My God, My God, Why Have You Forsaken Me?" 2007, www.abideinchrist.com [accessed September 3, 2011]).
4. Jesus said, "Do not give dogs what is sacred; do not throw your pearls to pigs" (Matt. 7:6). It would be like casting the most exquisite Pearl of Heaven before the trampling feet of this mocking multitude.
5. John Stott, *The Cross of Christ*, 159.
6. George A. Buttrick, *Jesus Came Preaching*, 207; cited in John Stott, *The Cross of Christ*, 158.
7. Furthermore, we've tolerated unholiness, not realizing that when we do, this drives nails again through His wounds, for we are "crucifying the Son of God all over again and subjecting him to public disgrace" (Heb. 6:6). Yes, "If we deliberately keep on sinning after we have received the knowledge of the truth" we have "trampled the Son of God underfoot" and "treated as an unholy thing the blood of the covenant" (Heb. 10:26, 29).
8. Bob Sorge, *The Power of the Blood*, 1.
9. David Wilkerson, "They Have Done Away with the Cross!" *Times Square Church Pulpit Series* (New York City: Feb. 23, 1996), 2.
10. Spurgeon said, "The minister who has failed to cry, 'Behold the Lamb of God,' may expect at the last to be cut up in pieces and to have his portion with the tormentors" (Charles Spurgeon, "Behold the Lamb," 103).

11. Mary Clay Wells, which she preached in a sermon here at our internship in Alabama.
12. Piper says, "Though he knew the wrath of his Father was being poured out on him, he also knew that he was bearing it for the Father's glory, and that his Father loved him for it's 'for this reason the Father loves me,' Jesus said, 'because I lay down my life, that I may pick it up again' (John 10:17)" (John Piper, *Fifty Reasons Why Christ Came to Die* [Grand Rapids, MI: Crossway Books, 2006]).

Chapter 8

"ELI, LAMA SABACHTHANI?"

A Window into the Father's Cup

J ESUS FINALLY DRAINS the last bitter drops of eternal wrath. As the ninth hour nears, He pushes down on the spike in His feet, lifting His chest to take in a chestful of air. The pressure of His weight on the spike tears open the wound in His feet. Blood spurts from beneath the cold iron, spilling down His feet and toes, dripping down the wood and soaking into the ground.

Jesus turns His gaze upward. Tears quiver in His eyes. He throws back His head. His mouth flies open wide as though He's about to speak. He spoke three times in the first three hours, once to forgive, next to save a dying thief, and third to place His mother into John's care. Mary had other sons, but Jesus chose the tenderhearted John to care for her, which he did to the end of her life.

Now with this third word from the cross, a long period of silence follows. The pain has been too deep for words. The horror of the Father's cup has crushed His breath away. But He can no longer hold His silence. Now He is about to release what scholars call "the cry of dereliction."

This is the most heart-stunning sentence in the entire Bible. This is the cry that shook the earth at Calvary. It shook Martin Luther's heart and led to a reformation of the church. And it shook my heart as well, causing a theological revolution in my life. To look into this cry flings back the shutters, lifts the shade, and throws open the window, allowing the sunlight of revelation to penetrate the mystery of the cross.

THE CRY OF DERELICTION

For a moment, time stands still at Calvary. The crowd hushes. Tension charges the atmosphere. Hearts thunder in every breast as Jesus opens His mouth to shout. With a deep, guttural, animal-like roar, He shrieks: *Eli, Eli, lama sabachthani?* which is Hebrew for "My God, my God, why have you forsaken me?"

The crowd stands appalled, paralyzed by this staggering outburst. Birds' songs freeze midair. The wind ceases to blow. The sun still hides its face. Dark clouds, heavy with moisture, hang low as though ready to drop a load of tears.

Jesus' plaintive cry resounds across the hillside. He doesn't whimper like a lamb; He roars like a wounded lion, just as the Scripture says, "My God, my God, why have you forsaken me? Why are you so far from saving me, so far from the words of my groaning?" (Ps. 22:1).

Puritan scholar John Flavel explains that the Hebrew here for *groaning* "comes from a root that signifies to howl or roar as a lion; and rather signifies the noise made by a wild beast than the voice of a man." Said Flavel, "It is as though Christ had said, 'O My God, no words can express My anguish: I will not speak but roar, howl out my complaint; pour it out in volleys of groans.'"[1]

When I try to wrap my thoughts around this hideous cry, I realize I can never fully comprehend it. As Spurgeon said, "It is measureless, unfathomable, inconceivable. This anguish of the Savior on your behalf and mine is no more to be measured and weighed than the sin which needed it, or the love which endured it. We will adore where we cannot comprehend."[2]

This cry of dereliction is an audible revelation of the depth of His suffering. It unveils the Father's cup, for it reveals "the crisis of His sufferings."[3] It shows the terrible cost of our sin. It unveils the horror of the wrath of God. Spurgeon writes, "To be deserted of his God was the climax of Christ's grief, the quintessence of his sorrow."[4] F. W. Krummacher in *The Suffering Savior* writes that such "distress overpowered Him," such "horror and death-like terror appalled Him," and such "infernal temptations roared around Him" that it wrung this ghastly cry from His lips.[5]

Though Jesus spoke seven times from Calvary, this fourth cry so astonished Matthew and Mark that these were the only words from the cross either of them recorded. All other cries paled in comparison, and they wrote only of this one heart-rending utterance from the lips of the Lord.[6]

This cry ushers us beyond the veil into the deepest heart of the Triune Godhead. When we look into this desperate cry, we are touching the most sensitive nerve in God's heart. It reveals the bursting heart of the Son, the grieving heart of the Father, and the aching heart of the Holy Spirit. Only when we know the depths of their immeasurable sacrifice, can we know the infinite heights of God's love.

Jesus never cried, "Why must I be scourged to a bloody pulp?" "Why must I have thorns crushed like ice picks into my brow?" "Why must I have spikes gouged through the tender nerves in my hands and feet?" No, He remains silent during all of these: "He was led like a lamb to the slaughter, and as a sheep before her shearers is silent, so he did not open his mouth" (Isa. 53:7).

But now, He's been gulping down the fiery wrath of the Father's cup and He erupts with all the emotion and terror of His soul: *My God, My God, why have You forsaken Me?* But notice that He doesn't cry, "Why have You poured Your wrath on Me?" "Why have You punished Me?" "Why have You tumbled Your judgment upon Me?" "Why have You plunged Me into the utter depths of hell?" No, none of these are His complaint. His cry is "Why have You forsaken—abandoned—deserted Me?" "Why have you left Me all alone in the midst of such unutterable suffering?" "Father, I could bear this horrible wrath if I had Your sustaining presence, but why have even You forsaken Me when I need You most?"

Drinking the Father's cup caused unthinkable horror and pain, but to bear it all alone, with no comforting presence of His Father, was more than He could endure.[7] Spurgeon writes, "Our Lord's heart and all His nature were, morally and spiritually, so delicately formed, so sensitive, so tender that to be without God was to Him a grief that could not be weighed."[8]

As this cry rips from the lips of the Son, it blazes up through the atmosphere, into the realms of heaven. Like an arrow dipped in the poison of sorrow and pain, it soars through the outer court, into the inner court, right into the throne room of God. It finds its target in the heart of the Father.

How do you think the Father felt when this cry of His Son penetrated His heart? Oh, I don't know how He could bear it, but I'm sure He must have doubled over with divine grief. I can almost see Him breaking open and sobbing in fathomless sorrow. This is why God shows us Abraham's sacrifice in Genesis 22, for this story gives us a brief glimpse into His heart.

Can you imagine what it would have been like for a father to tie up his son, lay him on an altar, then lift a knife above him? His hand must have trembled and tears gushed down his cheeks as he prepared to plunge the knife into the heart of his son. He knew that He must then cut him into pieces, like a lamb for the burnt offering, and then light the fire that would consume his body. At that moment, Abraham must have felt like the knife was plunging into his own heart.

But that's how the Father in heaven felt! When the cry of dereliction shot into His own heart, I'm sure the very gates of heaven must have trembled. Angels must have bowed and wept with the Father God. Seraphim must have shut their eyes more tightly and barely whimpered, "Holy." Indeed, I'm sure all heaven must have hushed, silenced by the outburst of pain and emotion from the Father.[9]

Oh, this is why I still pray almost daily, *Father, this is Your Son! Your Son!* I roar it up to Him because I can feel just a small bit of what He feels. I pray, *Please vindicate the One You love! Please honor Him on earth as He is honored in heaven.* I cry to Him with all my might because I feel what He feels for His Beloved.

But it's not only the Father who weeps; it's the Holy Spirit as well. In Hebrew Jesus cried, "Eli, Eli," but Mark translates His cry into Aramaic, which is "Eloi, Eloi" (Mark 15:34). This is a plural name for God, so Jesus is crying out to the Holy Spirit too. He who is so loving, gentle, and sensitive must surely be shattered by this cry of the Son. He too must grieve like never before in all eternal history. The apostle Paul warns us not to "grieve the Holy Spirit" (Eph. 4:30), for, like a dove, He is easily wounded. But now the Holy Spirit is sorrowing over the One He dearly loves. Oh, can you imagine the divine pathos of the Father and the Holy Spirit in the Godhead as they hear this piteous wail of the Son?

But this horrific cry breaks the Son's heart as well, for all this time Jesus' heart has been swelling and filling with grief. The wrath of God has smashed and beaten against Him, until His heart is ready to burst. Now with this cry wrenched from His lips and shot up in His Father's face, His own heart begins to tear and bleed.

Even now the veil in the temple trembles, ready to rip in two. Already the earth rumbles, for the cracking rocks, the quaking earth, and the darkening sun are nature's proclamations that a rupture is taking place in the heart of God.[10]

How could we ever take this sacrifice of the Father for granted? How could we ever accuse Him of being cruel and vindictive toward those who suffer? This is God's answer to human suffering—the cross of His own Son! God's own Son entered our world of human sin and suffering and took it on Himself. But the pain it caused the Father when He punished His Son in our place was inestimable.

This cry of dereliction is the heart cry of the ages. Martin Luther said that all theology should be developed "within earshot of the dying cry of Jesus."[11] In fact, this is indeed the cry that jolted Luther and opened his eyes to the truths that led to the Protestant Reformation. Let's look more carefully now at his story, most of which is told by Mark D. Tranvik, Luther's translator.

LUTHER'S ANFECHTUNG

A thunderstorm blew fiercely down on the village of Erfurt, Germany, as the young law student walked from his home to the university. Suddenly, a bolt of lightning struck the ground near him. He cried out for mercy to Saint Ann, promising he would become a monk if he could be spared from death.

It was July 2, 1505, and two weeks later Martin Luther left his law studies to keep his promise to God. He entered an Augustinian monastery to live as a monk. Here in the monastery, Luther struggled night and day to find God. Through fastings and prayer and self-flagellations, he sought to find salvation, but all to no avail.

Haunted by doubt and failure, he was sure God hated him. He often experienced bouts where he believed God was punishing him with wrath and judgment. At other times he found himself wrestling with the devil, who tormented him with thoughts of failure, depression, and doubt.

Germans have a word, which we don't have in English: *Anfechtung*, which means "a profound sense of being lost, alienated, and out of control." It is far more than a case of "the blues" or simply depression. It involves an unbearable mental and spiritual torment.[12] This sense of *Anfechtung* plagued young Luther as he wrestled with God in the monastery.

He went on to study at Wittenberg University where he completed a master's degree in theology and finally a doctorate, becoming a professor of theology at the university. But studying the Bible, which he did earnestly, only aggravated his misery. As he read, he saw what a wretched sinner he was. He wrestled with Paul's writings, but only found solace in the Psalms where he could identify with David's emotional highs and lows. If only he could somehow achieve enough good works, perhaps he could earn his salvation and be free from this plaguing *Anfechtung*.

To feel Luther's quandary, think for a moment about your own worst sin. Do you remember the torment of guilt and shame and despair you felt? Can you imagine the shame of a pedophile or the guilt of a guard in a concentration camp where millions of Jewish people were gassed? The guilt would be more than the human conscience could endure. That's how Luther felt. Though he lived a moral life, guilt had mounted over him like an ominous black cloud. He admitted, "I did not love, yes, I hated God who punishes sinners, and secretly, if not blasphemously, certainly murmuring greatly, I was angry with God."[13]

One day, while reflecting on Psalm 22, the crucifixion Psalm, Luther was struck by the first verse, "My God, my God, why have you forsaken me?" (22:1). He grappled with the words for hours. Why would God's Son have to experience the *Anfechtung* that plagued him in the monastery?

Charles Spurgeon told how "hour after hour that mighty man of God sat still, and he was so absorbed in his meditation that those who waited on him almost thought he was a corpse. He moved neither hand nor foot and neither ate nor drank, but sat with his eyes wide open, like one in a trance, thinking over these wondrous words: 'My God, my God, why hast thou forsaken me?' And after many long hours in which he seemed to be utterly lost to everything that went on around him, he rose from his chair, and someone heard him say, 'God forsaking God! No man can understand that!'"[14] *Why would Christ be abandoned by God?* he wondered. Christ loved God perfectly, purely, whole-heartedly, yet He was absolutely forsaken by God. It didn't make sense.

Out of this intense time of wrestling with God over the meaning of this dying cry of Jesus from the cross, fresh light began to break over his soul. Like the lightning that struck in the midst of the thunderstorm and changed the course of his life, this verse had a lightning like effect on his theological thinking. It dawned on Luther that Jesus screamed this cry because He was bearing the sin of the human race. He who knew no sin had voluntarily taken the sin and punishment of the entire world on Himself.

Now Luther began to realize: *If Christ took the sins of all humanity on Himself, then He took my own sin as well. This means that I need no longer carry the guilt of sin and therefore I need not be punished for my sin.* As he continued to study Paul's writings, he came to a "fresh and bracing interpretation of the Christian faith." He concluded that "grace alone and faith alone are possible because of what Christ alone did on the cross."[15]

In spite of all Luther's self-efforts, "the cross, with a force like lightning, became the pathway to life," wrote historian Mark A. Noll in *Turning Points.* For Luther, God reveals the mystery of Himself at the cross, where "the loftiest heights came down to the deepest depths," where "the hands of men pierced the hands that made humankind. There could be no greater mystery."[16] From that point on Luther was undone by this revelation of God through the cross of His dying Son.

Luther's revelation of the cross permeated all of his thinking.[17] It was the key that opened the Bible to him and revealed the mystery of justification by faith alone.[18] It led to the posting of the "95 Theses" on the door of the church in Wittenberg, which exposed the deception of indulgences, sold ostensibly to free people's loved ones from purgatory. The money was used to pad the pockets of priests as well as to build the magnificent Saint Peter's Basilica in Rome.

We gasp in shock that such materialism and sheer manipulation could enter the church of that day; and yet, in our day subtle forms of materialism and manipulation have slipped into the church and cracked our foundation as well. It took the Reformation to shake the foundations of the church in Luther's day, and it will take another reformation to shake the foundations in the church today.[19] Our theology needs to be undone and refounded on the cross of the risen Lamb! We need theology ablaze!

Carving a Love Wound

Luther's eyes began to open when he meditated on this cry of dereliction, "My God, my God, why have you forsaken me?" Indeed, once we have looked upon the Lamb consumed in God's fiery cup of wrath—something within us awakens. It's as though God performs an operation on the eyes of our heart. The veil which once blinded our spiritual sight is removed and we can really see.

Spurgeon said, "The hardness of the heart dies when we see Jesus die in woe so great....The cross is God's hammer of love, wherewith he smites the hearts of men with irresistible blows....When the Holy Spirit puts the cross in the heart, the heart is dissolved in tenderness....We see the Lord pierced, and the piercing of our own hearts begins."[20] As Charles Wesley wrote, "Oh, Jesus, let Thy dying cry pierce to the bottom of my heart."

Through the years I have seen this heart-piercing love-wound carved in many students, both young and old. When they see the extraordinary love of God displayed in the Father's cup, and then when they hear this cry roaring from the lips of our Lord, they are utterly undone.

So many times I've seen students weeping on the floor of our chapel, as the Holy Spirit draws His sword through their hearts. I believe this is what Simeon meant when he said to Mary, "And a sword will pierce even your own soul—to the end that the thoughts from many hearts may be revealed" (Luke 2:35, NAS). A sword pierced Mary's soul when she looked up at her Son on the cross; but Mary is a type of the church, birthing Jesus to this earth. She's a picture of what God wants to do in His bride as He pierces our hearts with an unquenchable love for His Son. In the last chapter I told you about students in a ministry school in Hong Kong who began crying out and falling to the floor when they heard about the cup. I had simply been describing the Father's wrath and the cry of dereliction as graphically as I could. But when they saw what Jesus really did for them, they broke open like an alabaster box, spilling out the liquid contents of their tears.

Later they began testifying to the class, telling us what had happened. Some said they saw an angel with a huge sword or a spear in his hand piercing their hearts with the blade. One lady said, "When my sister began telling about this piercing angel, I was silently mocking her in my heart. Then suddenly, I looked up and saw the angel for myself! As soon as I saw him, he drove his sword into my heart. I screamed and fell to the floor, weeping."

Personally, I never saw the angel. I only know that the Holy Spirit wrecks hungry hearts when they look into the cup. They are undone by a revelation of the Lamb. You see, the Word of God is the "sword of the spirit" (Eph. 6:17), but the blade of this sword is the message of the cross, which has cutting power. Like the thousands who were "cut to the heart" at Pentecost when Peter preached the gospel (Acts 2:37), the cross has the power to sever the veils that cover our hearts.[21]

I think of all the places we've ministered the cross, I've never seen such deep repentance as in Germany.[22] In a conference with at least fifteen nations represented, the place exploded on the first night. I had been telling about the Father's cup when people began crying out and running forward, throwing themselves prostrate on the floor. And after such deep repentance, the Lord pierced their hearts and the fire of God began to fall and flow among the people.

I saw this wounding of hearts in many pastors in our Kenya Ablaze for the Lamb School. God began supernaturally piercing the hearts of these young pastors. But one young man, Pastor Zacheaus, felt a bit left out. Nothing was happening to him. He saw people groaning over the cross, gripping their chests, and falling before the Lord. *Why can't I feel anything?* he wondered. He was desperately hungry for more of God, and he wouldn't give up like so many do when they see God touching others. He was willing to contend with Him like Jacob,[23] until He blessed him with this divine heart touch. He wasn't striving for an experience; He was contending for more of God. He knew the Bible says, "You will seek me and find me when you seek for me with all your heart" (Jer. 29:13).

So he cried out with all his might, "Please, Lord, let me encounter You!" Later he told me, "Suddenly I felt a Person standing in front of me. It was Jesus. He reached in and squeezed my heart until I lost my breath." That's when Zacheaus cried out and hit the floor. Jesus Himself was gripping this pastor's heart. The passion I've seen in him and in the pastors who had this same encounter with God has been indescribable.

Oh, please know—I am not talking about a painful or sorrowful wound. This is a glorious wound. It causes one to fall more deeply in love with Jesus. It fills the heart with a trembling fire, an aching love, a burning passion for the Lamb. Please understand, it's so difficult to describe the indescribable. But let me try because I want your own heart to be undone.

Again, it's like Isaiah; when he saw the Lord, he cried, "Woe is me! I am undone" for my "eyes have seen the King, the Lord of hosts" (Isa. 6:5). It's seeing Him that causes this heart-rending experience. Just like Joel said, "Rend your hearts and not your garments" (Joel 2:13). This heart-rending encounter with the cross brings us to our knees in repentance and on our faces in worship.

But as I keep saying—this is not a new revelation. It is as old as the Bible. It is a revelation—an uncovering—of the Word of God. It is an unveiling of a truth that's been overlooked for a long, long time. It brings Scripture alive. It discloses the Lamb in the Bible as never before. It displays truth about Jesus. Remember, we are not talking about a mystical, flakey, speculative subject. We're talking about the cross of Jesus Christ! The bedrock of our Christian faith! Indeed, our passion burns deep and peripheral subjects fade in the light of a revelation of the Lamb.

I believe this incision of the heart is what Paul meant when he said, "Circumcision is circumcision of the heart, by the Spirit" (Rom. 2:29). "Revival springs from a heart that has had a deep, deep incision of the knife of God, which is the cross of Christ, to the point of 'circumcision of the heart' (Rom. 2:29)," wrote Peter Madden, in *The Secret of Smith Wigglesworth's Power*.[24]

Circumcision is the cutting away of a veneer or covering. The Western church has had a veneer over the eyes of our hearts because we've wandered so far from the pure gospel. The cross is the blade that cuts away the scales covering our spiritual eyes. It is the scalpel used for divine surgery so that we are able to see more of Christ. The instrument that wounds is the instrument that heals.

When our hearts are "crucified with Christ" (Gal. 2:20), resurrection glory pours in and through our very lives. It's like the tearing of the veil in the temple, which was torn in two by the power of the cross. We, who are "a temple of God" (1 Cor. 3:16), need to have the veil that covers our hearts torn in two by the power of the cross.

This precious heart-wound can only come from gazing at Jesus as the Lamb of God. So even now, close your eyes and meditate on that cry of dereliction that fell from the lips of our Lord. He shrieked this horrific heart cry because of the agony of drinking our cup of wrath and hell. Let that soak into your heart. Let it go in deep. Let the words, "My God, My God, why have You forsaken Me?" which were roared like a wounded lion from the lips of our Lord, pierce to the depths of your soul.

Now picture that heart-rending cry piercing up into the Father's heart. See the arrow strike its mark. Look until you can almost see the Father grab His chest and bend over weeping as the cry strikes its target like a penetrating arrow. Gaze at Him until you can almost feel His pain—shattering, heart-wrenching, soul-tearing pain. Oh, nothing can so affect your sensitive spirit as feeling the Father's heart for His Son! Let the Father's love for His Son fill your whole being. Let it melt you within until your heart and your theology are utterly ruined, captured, wrecked, dissolved—undone by a revelation of the Lamb!

CHAPTER 8 ENDNOTES

1. John Flavel, *The Works of John Flavel*, vol.1 (London, UK: Banner of Truth Trust, 1969).
2. Charles Spurgeon, "Lama Sabachthani," 103.
3. *New American Standard Bible,* study note on Psalm 22:1, 730.
4. Charles Haddon Spurgeon, *The Gospel of Matthew*, Larry Richards, ed. (Grand Rapids, MI: Baker Book House Company, 1987), 406.
5. F. W. Krummacher, *The Suffering Savior* (Grand Rapids, MI: Kregel Publications, 1947), 383.
6. Leon Morris writes, "These are the only words that Matthew and Mark recorded....This gives the words special meaning" (Leon Morris, *The Cross of Jesus* [Grand Rapids, MI: William B. Eerdmans Publishing Company, 1988], 71).
7. It could be said that the central question of the Christian faith is wrapped up in this anguished cry of Jesus: "My God, why have you forsaken me?" The answer is simple if you understand the Father's cup. The answer is—He was forsaken and punished because He carried our sin and stood in our place as the One who took our punishment.

8. Charles Spurgeon, "Lama Sabachthani," 109.
9. John Stott writes, "It was 'God himself' giving himself for us. Karl Barth did not shrink from using those words. 'God's own heart suffered on the cross,' he added. 'No one else but God's own Son, and hence the eternal God himself….' (Karl Barth, *Church Dogmatics*, II. 1, 446 ff)." Stott continues, "Similarly, Bishop Stephen Neill wrote, 'If the crucifixion of Jesus…is in some way, as Christians have believed, the dying of God himself, then…we can understand what God is like' (S. C. Neill, *Christian Faith Today*, 159). And hymns of popular devotion have echoed it, like this phrase from Charles Wesley's 'And Can it Be': 'Amazing love! How can it be that Thou my God, should'st die for me?'" (Stott, *The Cross of Christ*, 153).
10. The entire Godhead feels this wound. In a sense, the Father, Son, and Holy Spirit are experiencing a divine piercing. That's why God said, "They will look on me the one they have pierced and mourn for him" (Zech. 12:10).
11. Jürgen Moltmann, *The Crucified God: The Cross of Christ as the Foundation and Criticism of Christian Theology* (Minneapolis, MN: Fortress Press, 1993), 201.
12. Martin Luther, *The Freedom of a Christian*, Mark D. Tranvik, The Translator's Introduction, "Martin Luther's Road to Freedom" (Minneapolis, MN: Fortress Press, 2008), 12.
13. Martin Luther, "Preface to Latin Writings," 1535, *WA* 54: 185–86; *LW* 34:336–37; cited in Martin Luther, *The Freedom of the Christian*, Mark D. Tranvik, The Translator's Introduction, "Martin Luther's Road to Freedom," 13.
14. Charles H. Spurgeon, *2200 Quotations from the Writings of Charles H. Spurgeon*, 272.
15. Martin Luther, *The Freedom of a Christian*, 17.
16. Mark A. Noll, *Turning Points: Decisive Moments in the History of Christianity* (Grand Rapids, MI: Baker Book House Co, 1997), 169–170.
17. Jürgen Moltmann, in his masterpiece *The Crucified God*, explains that Luther's theology of the Cross is "the key signature for all Christian theology." He says, that according to Luther, all theology should be developed "within earshot of the dying cry of Jesus" (Jürgen Moltmann, *The Crucified God*, 72, 201).
18. Luther realized, writes Noll, that "the cross was where God had most completely revealed himself." He saw that if one wants to find God, one must "look to Calvary where God has made himself known" (Mark A. Noll, *Turning Points*, 167, 169).

19. A reformation must have a cause. It must be driven by a forgotten but compelling biblical truth. Justification by faith alone, undergirded by Luther's foundational theology of the cross, was the energizing truth behind this world-changing Protestant Reformation. Indeed, it took a revelation of the cross to ignite a fire in young Luther's heart, and it will take a revelation of the cross to rekindle the flame and ignite a reformation today.

20. Spurgeon, "How Hearts Are Softened," 377–378, 380.

21. Leon Morris said, "The cross is at the heart of all New Testament teaching" (Leon Morris, *The Cross in the New Testament*, 375); John R. W. Stott wrote, "The centrality of the cross originated in the mind of Jesus himself" (John R. W. Stott, *The Cross of Christ*, 25). Stott further said, "The three major letter-writers of the New Testament—Paul, Peter, and John—are unanimous in witness to its centrality, as are also the letter to the Hebrews and the Revelation." In fact, explains Stott, Paul defined "his gospel as 'the message of the cross,' his ministry as 'we preach Christ crucified,' baptism as initiation 'into his death' and the Lord's Supper as proclamation of the Lord's death" (John R. W. Stott, *The Cross of Christ*, 35).

22. This was an Unquenchable Flame Conference held in Germany in 2011 and sponsored by Pastor Greg Violi and his church. I know that the main reason the people repented so deeply is because Pastor Violi had been teaching "The Lamb's Heart," and he had taught his people the power of true repentance. I strongly recommend his teaching on a Lamblike nature for Christians. See Pastor Greg's website: www.gregvioli.startlogic.com .

23. The piercing of the heart comes when we agonize over the cross of Jesus, letting it go in deep. Only God can wound our hearts, but we have to be proactive about engaging the Lamb of God until our hearts are *undone*. Sometimes I've seen people actually get angry, saying we shouldn't have to "strive" to get our hearts pierced or undone. Remember, however, that Jesus said, "Strive to enter in at the strait gate" (Luke 13:24, kjv). He used a Greek word, *agōnizomai*, which means "to strenuously endeavor to accomplish," to "struggle with concentration and intensity." Also Paul wrote, "I strived [*agōnizomai*] to preach the gospel" (Rom. 15:20, kjv). (I am using King James Version here because it uses the word "strive.") Paul urged that the Philippians be "of one mind, striving [*agōnizomai*] together for the faith of the gospel" (Phil. 1:27, kjv). You might argue that Paul also said to Timothy, "the servant of the Lord should not strive," (2 Tim. 2:24), but the Greek word here for strive is not the same. It is *machomai*, which

means to war, quarrel, or dispute. The point is, sometimes we give up too quickly.

24. Peter Madden, *The Secret of Smith Wigglesworth's Power* (New Kensington, PA: Whittaker House, 2000), 64.

Chapter 9

FORSAKEN

God's Answer to the Theodicy Question: Why Human Suffering?

T HE CRY OF Jesus still thunders soundlessly over the hillside at Calvary. The crowd stands petrified. Not a muscle moves. Not a breath or a shuffle. Even the moans of the women, the mocking of the priests, and the groans of the two thieves cease.

No one comprehends the meaning of this shriek of abandonment, "My God, why have You forsaken Me?" It shocks the human senses. God forsaken by God. In this one cry lies the answer to the question of the ages, called the theodicy question, which is, "Why does God allow human suffering?" Pause with me now to probe this question until we find the answer to a problem which baffles believers and unbelievers alike and plagues humanity all over the world.

THE THEODICY QUESTION

Today millions of orphans, destitute and desperately hungry, wander the streets of Africa, India, and countries all over the world. Two-thirds of the world's population live in abject poverty, with millions of children bound in the sex trade.

You too have probably experienced your own kind of suffering, sometimes soaking your pillow with tears, crying out in the darkness, *"My God, why?"*

At no other time in human history does this question loom more bewildering than during the Holocaust, when six million innocent Jewish people were annihilated.[1] Elie Wiesel, who was a boy during the Holocaust, tells how he used to run to the synagogue on Sabbath evenings to worship the God of Abraham and pray for the coming Messiah.

But then came the Holocaust, and his faith dissolved in the black coils of smoke rising up from the crematory where his mother and sister were cremated. In his Nobel Peace Prize winning book, *Night*, he recalls sleeping nearly naked in thirty below zero weather. He describes babies thrown into the air and used as targets for machine guns. He remembers a young man who had to feed his own father to the crematory oven.[2]

In the prison camp, young Wiesel's stomach wretched as he watched thousands of Jewish prisoners fall prostrate before God on Rosh Hashanah, crying, "Blessed be the name of the eternal!" Bitterly he wept to God, "These men here, whom You have betrayed, whom You have allowed to be tortured, butchered, gassed, burned, what do they do? They pray before You! They praise Your name!"[3] He remembered a Rabbi, a little bent man whose lips trembled constantly as he recited whole pages of the Talmud by memory. One day the old man told Wiesel hopelessly, "It's the end. God is no longer with us."[4]

Perhaps the most faith crushing experience of all for young Wiesel, that which consumed his faith forever, was the day thousands of prisoners gathered to watch the hanging of two men and a boy. As the noose tightened around the three necks, all eyes riveted on the child, whose pallid face was like that of an angel. Chairs were kicked from beneath them and the two men died quickly, but the boy writhed in the throes of death for more than thirty minutes. As the prisoners were forced to march in front of the victims, weeping as they walked, young Wiesel heard a voice behind him say, "Where is God? Where *is* He?" Wiesel said, "I heard a voice within me say, 'Where is He? Here He is—He is hanging here on this gallows.'"[5]

Seventy years after the Holocaust, the suffering continues in a different form today, as millions of innocent children are held captive, trafficked in child prostitution. Patricia McCormick, in her book *Sold*, tells the story of thirteen-year-old Lakshmi from Nepal, sold into sex slavery by her parents for a few hundred dollars. After being promised a better life, the predators transported her to the red-light district of Calcutta where she was locked in a room, drugged, and beaten into mindless submission. For over a year she became the sex toy of thousands of men, unspeakable abuses forced upon her.[6] But this is what happens to millions of trafficked children, who live in brothels until they are used up, riddled with disease, and kicked out on the streets to die like dogs.[7] How can this be? If God is a merciful God, why does He allow so much human suffering? Especially among innocent children?

When the Twin Towers fell on September 11, 2001, and 3,000 Americans lost their lives, believers and unbelievers alike asked, "If God is good, how could He allow this to happen to us?"

People have grappled with the theodicy question for centuries, many even losing their faith over it.[8] Why is there so much suffering in this world? Why earthquakes killing thousands, famines starving tens of thousands, tsunamis drowning hundreds of thousands, AIDS destroying millions? Why is there so much cancer, and death of loved ones, and divorce, and addictions, and wars, and poverty, and starvation, and child prostitution, and suffering little children?

If God is all powerful, why doesn't He step in and heal the suffering masses? Is He angry with us? Is He helpless? Did He just set the world in motion and let it go like the Deists believe? And what about the Holocaust with the gassing and cremation of millions of innocent Jews? Why the genocides in Bosnia and Darfur and Cambodia? If God is a God of mercy and love, why does He do nothing? Is He powerless? If the Bible is true, why does God allow a good man like Job to suffer? Why does God seem to punish some and allow others to live in evil? Why, why, why?

MY PERSONAL STRUGGLE WITH SUFFERING

I too wrestled with this thorny question: "Why?" I want to be very vulnerable with you right now. In all my books and teachings for the last thirty years, I have never been as open about my personal life as I'm going to be now. I know my story doesn't hold a candle to the suffering of Holocaust victims and child prostitutes, but it's my story and I want to be real about my own struggle with the theodicy question.

Almost forty years ago, as a young mother of a three-year-old and twin baby girls, I often wept alone in prayer. My husband went out drinking almost every night, usually coming in drunk and often violently abusing me. I felt like my heart had been peeled raw, tossed to the side of the road and trampled. *"Why, God? Why must I suffer like this? Why don't You intervene?"* I cried in the midnight hours.

Always my husband would use as his excuse, "It's your......religion!" It's true I had been filled with the Holy Spirit, but I could never regret such a heavenly blessing. The Holy Spirit made me softer and more loving and more devoted as a wife and mother.

But still I wrestled in prayer with God. I fasted and prayed and pleaded, like the woman with the unjust judge. I confessed positively, recited all the formulas, and submitted earnestly; but nothing changed. *"God, why don't You intervene?"* I pleaded. My story has a beautiful ending, but at that point I couldn't understand why God wouldn't help me. I wrestled with the question that so many today struggle to understand. But still the drunkenness and abuse continued until finally I had to take my three young children and flee to a place of safety. Soon my marriage to the only man I had ever loved ended. I could not imagine why God would allow me to suffer so deeply when I was so dedicated to Him.

I didn't realize it, but a slow, subtle bitterness toward the Lord was setting into my heart. It all seemed so wrong. If God is sovereign and omnipotent, then He certainly possesses the power to save me from my suffering. But He does nothing! Why?

SEARCHING FOR ANSWERS

As I searched for answers, I came across this story one day. I told it in my *Unquenchable Flame* book, but I tell it again because I think it begins to explain God's answer to suffering. It was told by a Messianic Jewish pastor to a Messianic congregation.

> One day, while looking for work, a Jewish boy entered a Messianic church building, not realizing it was a place where Jewish Christians worshiped. Inside, the pastor was lighting candles for Passover. The young man asked if he had any jobs open, and as the boy talked, the old pastor discerned pain and bitterness in the boy. He asked him to sit down and tell him about his life. "What is really bothering you, Son?" he asked.
>
> The young man hesitated, then sat down and opened his heart. "Well, you see, Sir, my dad was a young doctor in Poland, but he suffered in the concentration camp at Auschwitz. He survived,

and when the war was over, he married my mother, whom he had met in the camp."

The young man cleared his throat and shifted uncomfortably. Brushing away a tear, he continued. "After the war they came to America and tried to start over. But my dad could never get a good job and he was always told he was a Christ-killer. He couldn't take it anymore and last year he shot himself in the head." The boy covered his face in his hands and began to weep. The pastor reached out an arm, and the young man fell against the old man's chest, sobbing.

Finally, he looked up at the pastor and cried, "How could God let us suffer so much? If we are God's chosen people, why has He hurt us so badly?"

Moments passed as the wise old pastor waited. When the boy's tears finally subsided, he said, "Son, I want you to go over to that picture of Yeshua hanging on a cross. I want you to look at it and tell Him everything that is in your heart. Don't be afraid to tell Him about your hurt and anger."

The boy walked over to the picture and looked up. He saw the crimson marks streaked across the Savior's body. He saw the tears etching down His cheeks. He saw the love gleaming in His eyes. The artist had been saved from a life of sin and pain. He had painted his whole heart into that picture. He had painted mercy into every drop of blood, forgiveness into every stroke and gash across His chest. Love burned in every tear. Grace and forgiveness shone in every brushstroke.

The boy began to bark out his complaints to Christ. "How could you let babies die in the Holocaust? How could you cause bodies to burn? How could you stand by and let children cry? How could you let my dad kill himself?" he railed. "How could..." Then he paused and read the little verse of Scripture engraved at the bottom of the picture. "For God so loved the world that He gave His only begotten Son so that whosoever believeth in him should not perish but have everlasting life" (John 3:16, KJV).

Suddenly, it rushed over him, *God didn't do this to me. He gave His one and only Son!* As he looked upon the wounded

One in the picture, he saw the love of God blazing out from the canvas. He slipped to his knees, weeping.

The old man telling the story said, "In that moment, the Scripture was being fulfilled: 'They shall look upon me the one they have pierced and mourn' (Zech. 12:10, kjv)." He concluded, "That day an angry teenage Jew gave his life to Yeshua." Then with his face glowing, he exclaimed, "I know. I was that young man!"

I was like that young Jewish boy. I too had blamed God for my hurt. But then, as I told you earlier, I began studying Jonathan Edwards' writings, and he opened my eyes to the magnitude of Jesus' suffering as a Lamb.

When I began to look into what God had done to solve the problem of human suffering, revelation began to dawn. My view of God had been too small. But when I began to look into God's plan to offer His Son as a Lamb before the creation of the world, it was like windows of vision flew open and light from heaven shone in, broadening my understanding of God's plan and magnifying my view of Him. I began to see, from God's vantage point, what He has done about human suffering.

I saw a God who was willing to step down from the heights of heaven into our world of suffering and pain. This was when I realized that I had been asking the wrong question. The question is not, *"Why?"* The question is *"What?"*

THE ANSWER

Yes, the question is not *"Why* does God allow suffering?" The question is *"What* has God done about human suffering?" The answer to this question is stunning; but before we can fully discover God's solution, we need to think back into eternity past.

Before God flung planets into space, sparkled the universe with stars, and breathed life into Adam's nostrils, He saw what sin would do to the human race. He saw the genocides of Saddam Hussein in Iran and Kurdistan, the slaughters of Idi Amin in Uganda, the murders of the Ayatollah Khamenei in Iran, the killing fields of Pol Pot in Cambodia.

He saw the maniacal Hitler, possessed by a demonic scheme to bring a "final solution" to the Jewish problem in Germany. He saw the pain of divorce and drugs and alcoholism and rape and murder and war and theft and the litany of sins against humanity that would cause such suffering.

He further saw what the Fall would do to the perfect world He created, causing nature to erupt in disease and death and volcanoes and famines and tsunamis and earthquakes and tornadoes and hurricanes, increasing as the earth ages.

What did God do about this epidemic of sin that would ravage the earth and run rampant through the veins of every human being? The answer is fathomless: He asked His Son to become a Lamb.

God the Son would step down from the glory of eternity and hang between heaven and earth. Here on two stakes of wood He would twist and thrash under the gruesome burden of sin. Like a raft on a storm tossed sea, He would pitch and flail in agony under this horrific weight. And then, while bleeding from every wound, He would become God's holocaust.

This is what forever arrested my heart and caused me to understand God's answer to human suffering. Gazing into the Father's cup infinitely enlarged my view of God. It staggered my senses to think of innocent Jews being gassed to death and thrust into crematoriums, reducing their bodies to ashes. But it stunned me even more to think of our tender Lord Jesus, who was not even dead when cast into this boiling inferno of wrath. He was fully alive as He drank down the last scalding drops of the Father's cup. He felt every pang, every horrifying flame, as He plunged into the crematorium of the punishment of hell.

It's like the story I tell about the little mother who raced up the stairs and plunged herself into the flames to save her baby girl. God's precious, uncreated, eternal Son, who lived with His Father in the bosom of eternity, raced down to Jerusalem, flung Himself upon two strips of wood, and then plunged into the flames of infinite wrath—in *our place*. He became our substitute as "the punishment that brought us peace was upon him" (Isa. 53:5).

No one on earth has ever come close to the intensity of human suffering as He experienced. Again, as Arthur Pink explained, "Not all the thunderbolts of divine judgment which were let loose in the Old Testament times, not all the vials of wrath which shall be poured forth" during the end times, not all the "wailing and gnashing of teeth of the damned in the lake of fire" ever gave or will give such a powerful demonstration of the divine justice and holiness, "of His infinite hatred of sin, as did the wrath of God which flamed against His own Son on the cross."[9]

Oh, I tell you, I cannot get over the extent to which God went to solve the problem of human suffering! This was why God the Son offered Himself as a Lamb before the world's creation. Understanding His master plan "which God devised and decreed before the ages" (1 Cor. 2:7, AMP) unlocks a great mystery. God's answer to human suffering is infinite. It is measureless. It is the cross of His own Son.

Sadly, however, many will reject this answer, "for the story and message of the cross is sheer absurdity and folly to those who are perishing" (1 Cor. 1:18, AMP). It defies human logic, for "God chose the foolish things of the world to shame the wise; God chose the weak things of the world to shame the strong" (1 Cor. 1:27).

In the Holocaust a doctor was given a choice to either stop operating on a Jewish prisoner and let the prisoner die or else he would be shot dead on the spot. In spite of the threat, the doctor finished operating, sutured up the wound, and was shot dead on the spot.[10] That's what Jesus did. In order to extract sin and suture up the wound of a bleeding human race, He was shot dead on the spot. But He rose again to breathe the life of God on suffering human souls.

Again, it's like the three hundred firefighters, when the jet planes slammed into the Twin Towers in Manhattan. They raced to the scene of destruction to rescue dying people. These heroes took no thought for their own lives as they threw themselves in front of harm's way. Charging up the stairs of the crumbling towers, the buildings tumbled down upon them, crushing them in the rubble.

But that's what Jesus did! In a sense, we can see how the tragedies that have befallen humanity descended on Him there on the cross. As the sin of all the ages tumbled down, it was like the crumbling Twin Towers, crushing down upon Him. Though reduced to a bleeding mass of quivering flesh, He endured the hurricane winds of divine judgment storming against His human frame. He took tsunami waves of God's wrath crashing over Him in black swirling terror. He bore the gasses of

Dachau and Auschwitz while consumed in the flaming crematorium of hell on the cross. And like the seismic heaving of an earthquake, His heart heaved and tore until it quaked open. He was indeed God's holocaust Lamb![11]

Was this justice? No, not by human standards, but from God's vantage—yes! This was Supreme justice! It was divine self-sacrifice to answer the impending problem of human suffering. And you can be sure the Son will receive the justice He deserves when He receives His bride, the one who is the reward of all His suffering.

NEVER FORSAKEN

Through the years, whenever I've taught the Glory of the Lamb course, whether it be to the street boys in the garbage dumps of Kenya, or among the gypsies of Bulgaria, or the gifted students in Kings College at Cambridge University, I've tried to release this pain-filled cry of Jesus, *"My God, why have You forsaken Me?"* with all the passion of my heart. This cry from the lips of God the Son actually asks the question that so many have asked through the ages: *"My God, Why?"*

But almost always, in my secret thoughts, this cry takes me back to a young mother, crying out in the darkness, *"Why God? Why have You forsaken me?"* I couldn't understand it then, but when I see what God has done through the years, at last I understand. It took a revelation of the Lamb to open my eyes and make sense of my pain, for this is indeed God's answer to human suffering.

Then one night, a miracle happened. I never dreamed I would see this day. But my former husband, the man I had loved so deeply and with whom I had three children, walked over to where I was sitting and took my hands. We had buried his mother that day, and his heart was especially tender. His health had been failing and he had completely given up his old way of life.

He lifted me to my feet, looked in my eyes and said brokenly, "Sandy, I am *so sorry* for what I put you through." Then his head dropped on my shoulder and he cried like a baby.

I could hardly believe it. At first I was too stunned to respond. Then I too wept and repented to him for the way my deep faith had made him feel rejected. We held each other and sobbed as years of pain and unforgiveness floated away like trash on an outflowing tide, rushing, washing, cleansing, healing.

God in His foresight knew that day would come, and now when I think of that young mother crying out, *"Why, God? Why have You forsaken me?"* sweet joy fills my heart. For through the years, the cross has been my anchor. And God has opened floodgates of glory surrounding the Lamb. He has poured out fires of revival on the message of the cross in so many lives, and the presence of God has been indescribable. I have never been forsaken by God.

That's why this terrifying question, *"My God, why have You forsaken me?"* asked by Christ Himself on the cross, answers a million questions. To all who feel hot tears running down your face and drenching your sheets in the midnight hours; to all who have felt rejected by friends and family; to all who have suffered divorce, sickness, and loss of loved ones; to all who have screamed in the darkness, *"My God, why have You forsaken me?"* this cry of Jesus offers comfort.

It shows us a God who feels our pain. A God who willingly left heaven's comfort to experience human grief, to taste human tears, to bleed human blood, to bear hell for human sin. It shows us that God is not a distant, aloof, dispassionate God. He's a God who knows the gut-wrenching agony of human emotions.[12] He knows the feeling of salty wet drops forming in His eyes and sliding down His cheeks.

Most of all, it shows us the wonder of the ages—when God forsook God! Why was He forsaken? So that even in the midst of suffering, we would never, never, never be forsaken by God.

Why did He do it? How could the Father make such an unspeakable sacrifice? How could the Son endure such unthinkable suffering? There is only one reason. One monumental reason—*love.* "For God so loved the world that He gave His one and only Son" (John 3:16).

That God would love so deeply breaks us in repentance for blaming Him for our suffering. "The thief comes only to steal and kill and destroy; I have come that they may have life, and have it to the full," said Jesus Christ Himself (John 10:10). We have blamed Him for what He didn't do.

Dear God, forgive us for blaming You and for not understanding this immeasurable sacrifice from Your heart!

So now, when people ask—what is God's answer to human suffering? You have a simple but profound answer: the cross of His own Son. This is such a marvelous mystery. It is the mystery of all mysteries. The secret of all secrets. That He would give so deeply, from the bowels of eternity, from the very "bosom of God" (see John 1:18), melts us to our knees. It flattens us to our faces where our hearts are forever undone by God's answer to human suffering—a revelation of the Lamb!

CHAPTER 9 ENDNOTES

1. In a bitter prayer, Zvi Kolitz cried, "I want to say to You that now, more than in any previous period of our eternal path of agony, we, we the tortured, the humiliated, the buried alive, the burned alive, we the insulted, the mocked, the lonely, the forsaken by God and man— we have the right to know what are the limits of your forbearance?" (Yossel Rakover in Zvi Kolitz, 'Yossel Rakover's Appeal to God,' in Albert H. Friedlander, ed., *Out of the Whirlwind: A Reader of the Holocaust Literature* [New York: Shocken, 1976), 390–399); quoted in Michael Brown, *Our Hands Are Stained with Blood* (Shippensburg, PA: Destiny Image, 1992), 159.
2. Elie Wiesel writes of seeing men reduced to wild beasts, fighting, biting, tearing at each other for one crust of bread. He tells of a night in which one hundred people were crammed into a cattle car, traveling from the death camp of Auschwitz to Buchenwald. Suddenly, he heard, "Wailing, groaning, cries of distress hurled into the wind and the snow." Soon hundreds in other cattle cars moaned and wailed in a cry that seemed to come from beyond the grave. He describes, "It was the death rattle of a whole convoy who felt the end was upon them" (Elie Wiesel, *Night* [New York: Random House, Inc., 1960], 95–98).
3. Ibid., 64.
4. Ibid., 73. A Yiddish poet wrote despondently, "Even an outcry is now a lie, even tears are mere literature, even prayers are false (Arthur Hertzberg, *A Jew in America,* 299; quoted in Ronald Takaki, *A Different Mirror* (New York: Bay Back Books, 1994), 375).
5. Elie Wiesel, *Night,* 61–62.
6. Patricia McCormick, *Sold* (New York: Hyperion Paperbacks, 2006).
7. Ibid., 265.

8. This same haunting question plagued New Testament scholar Bart Ehrman. After earning his M.Div. from Wheaton College and a Ph.D. from Princeton Seminary, he began teaching a course on the theodicy question at Rutgers University. In the course, he reasoned, "If God is an all-powerful God, He can do anything He wants. And if He is all loving, He doesn't want people to suffer....If God is a God who intervenes, Why doesn't He?" He also grappled with various books in the Bible such as the Prophets, Job, and Revelation, and he found differing answers in every book, which he called "discrepancies." He said, "After I finished my class at Rutgers, I experienced a lot of suffering myself as did other people." Finally, he said emphatically, "I became an agnostic. I no longer believe in the God of the Bible. I do not believe in a good and all powerful God" (See debate with Bart Ehrman and Denesh De'Sousa on You-tube, "The Theodicy" Debate).

9. Arthur W. Pink, *Seven Sayings of Jesus on the Cross*, 72.

10. Judita M. Hruza, "The Making of a Physician," in Jack Canfield, Mark Victor Hansen, Rabbi Dov Peretz Elkins, *Chicken Soup for the Jewish Soul* (Deerfield Beach, FL: Health Communications, Inc., 2001), 251.

11. This paragraph is taken essentially from my book, *The Unquenchable Flame* (Shippensburg, PA: Destiny Image, 2009), 111.

12. John R. W. Stott says, "In the real world of pain, how could one worship a God who was immune to it?" He tells of entering many Buddhist temples in Asia as he gazes respectfully at the statue of Buddha, "his legs crossed, arms folded, eyes closed, the ghost of a smile playing round his mouth, a remote look on his face, detached from the agonies of the world." But always, adds Stott, "I have turned instead to that lonely, twisted, tortured figure on a cross, nails through hands and feet, back lacerated, limbs wrenched, brow bleeding from thorn-pricks, mouth dry and intolerably thirsty, plunged in God-forsaken darkness. That is the God for me!" (John R. W. Stott, *The Cross of Christ*, 335–336).

SECTION THREE

THE TRIUMPH *of the* LAMB

Chapter 10

"TETELESTAI!"

The Cosmic Power Encounter

JESUS' LIPS ARE cracked and dry. His tongue feels parched from drinking the Father's fiery cup. He hangs His head and groans, "I thirst" (John 19:28, KJV).

A soldier wets a sponge with posca, a cheap vinegar wine, and lifts it up to Jesus. The wine stings the cracked lips of the Savior, but He is oblivious to the physical pain. Now with His tongue moistened, the Master prepares to shout—not a cry of defeat, but a transcendent cry of victory.

Look into His eyes. No longer are they filled with terror. Can you see the glint of triumph? Yes, all this time, unseen by human eyes, a power encounter has been raging. Here on the battlefield of Calvary, an epic conflict between Christ and the kingdom of darkness has been taking place. Let's look now into the mystery revealed in this battle of the ages.

THE COSMIC POWER ENCOUNTER

At the head of the ranks of evil stands Satan himself. He smirks, thinking he's got Jesus just where he wants Him. This is the One who humiliated him long ago, casting him out of heaven to the earth. The Bible says, "You said in your heart, I will ascend to heaven; I will raise my throne above the stars of God....I will make myself like the Most High. But you are brought down to the grave, to the depths of the pit" (Isa. 14:13–14).[1]

As Jesus "was suspended there, bound hand and foot to the wood in apparent weakness," writes F. F. Bruce, all the forces of evil "imagined they had him at their mercy and flung themselves upon him with hostile intent."[2]

125

Ah, such sweet revenge! Now this Son of God is getting what He deserves as He hangs in utter defeat, forsaken even by His Father. What Satan doesn't understand, however, is that his only ground of attack on God's Son is sin. Because the Father has poured our sin on Jesus, Satan and all his minions have a legal right to attack Him. Apparently, they have forgotten the great "*protoevangelium,*" which is the first proclamation of the gospel in the Bible. It was spoken by God to the serpent himself: "And I will put enmity between you and the woman, and between your seed and her seed; he shall bruise [margin: crush] you on the head and you shall bruise him on the heel" (Gen. 3:15, NAS).

In fact, these demons don't seem to comprehend the divine mystery hidden since before the creation of the world. They don't know that the Lamb has agreed to drink His Father's cup of wrath—punishing and annihilating sin in Himself! Yes, as Jesus drinks the last bitter drops of the Father's cup, sin is obliterated in Him. As the Bible says, "He has appeared once for all at the end of the ages to do away with sin by the sacrifice of himself" (Heb. 9:26). Another version says, He has come "to abolish sin by the sacrifice of himself" (Heb. 9:26, TCNT).[3]

Now with the Father's cup consumed, sin is fully punished, and Satan has no more hold on Jesus. Like Haman in the Book of Esther who was hanged on his own gallows (see Esther 7), the very instrument on which Satan meant to kill the Savior has defeated him. "Like a magnet he drew upon himself all the forces and reserves of evil," writes N. Micklem. "He compelled them to a supreme and final test; they must break him, or he will infallibly break them."[4] As Martin Luther put it, Satan has fallen into the trap. The One who looks like "a worm and not a man" (Ps. 22:6), has dangled on the cross, and like a greedy fish, Satan has gobbled the bait. Now he is hooked in the jaw, ensnared by God on the cross.[5]

And though men have marred Jesus' flesh with spittle and thorns, drawn His blood with scourge and spikes, and thousands of principalities and powers have sunk poisonous fangs into His body, they are no match for the Lord of glory.

The battle has been hot and the dust thick, but it is almost over. Satan rears back and hurtles forward, rushing like a battering ram in one final charge against the Lamb.

But what is this? There is no more sin for him to feed on! Jesus has fully consumed the final dregs of the Father's cup and sin has been fully punished in Him. Now Satan slams his head against the heel of Christ's foot, and his neck breaks. He falls, crushed beneath the feet of the Seed of the Woman.

Now all the demons fall, vanquished—stripped, exposed, defeated— around their head-crushed leader. There they lie in a heap beneath the feet of the Lamb. Now Jesus, with His tongue moistened, prepares to give the final shout of victory.

The Master pushes down with all His might on the spike in His feet to raise His chest for air. The wound in His feet tears open and blood trickles down, dripping on the demonic forces beneath Him. The blood of the Lamb splashes over them as they gasp and sputter in utter defeat.

Yes, at long last the victory is won at Calvary, for Christ has come "to destroy the devil's works" (1 John 3:8). He overcame him, not in some mythical battle in hell after the cross—but *on the cross*. It is just as the Bible says, "Having disarmed the powers and authorities, he made a public spectacle of them, triumphing over them by the cross" (Col. 2:15). As Leon Morris writes, "The cross is the place of victory. The crucifixion is the triumph."[6]

Now hear the triumphant sixth word from the Conqueror's lips: "It is finished!" (John 19:30). The Greek is *tetelestai*, in the perfect tense meaning that "it has been and will forever remain finished."[7]

The words of victory blast from the Champion's lips like the sound of rams' horns at a feast. They resound across the hillside, jolting every heart, shaking the very gates of hell. The ring in the Master's voice and the look on His face, like the red flush of victory after a long and decisive battle, tells you that something of infinite significance has taken place.

Yes, an eternal victory has indeed been won, and now the greatest work in all human history has been accomplished. Even as God finished His work of creation on the sixth day, He now finishes His work of redemption with His sixth word from the cross.

Now the types and prophecies as well as the Law are fulfilled. Sin is fully punished, and the Father's cup of eternal wrath is drained. For all who receive Jesus Christ, hell has been emptied for them. Indeed, the new covenant has been cut in the flesh of God's own Son.

Yes, at last, that eternal covenant of redemption, planned before the creation of the world, is fulfilled. As Spurgeon said, "The words, 'It is finished!' consolidated heaven, shook hell, comforted earth, delighted the Father, glorified the Son, brought down the Spirit, and confirmed the everlasting covenant to all the chosen seed."[8]

Furthermore, death is now overcome in Him, for Jesus has come to "destroy him who holds the power of death—that is, the devil" (Heb. 2:14). Disease is conquered, for on the cross He "took up our infirmities…and by his wounds we are healed" (Isa. 53:4, 5; 1 Pet. 2:24). Now the spiritual David has cut off the giant's own head, using Goliath's own sword—the sword of the cross!

So stand back now and look up at your conquering King upon the throne. Now the bleeding Worm has become the blazing Warrior! The suffering One has become the sovereign One! The tortured Lamb has become the triumphant Lamb! The gory Victim has become the glorious Victor!

Yes, the cross of misery has now become a cross of majesty. Indeed, the cross, which was meant to destroy Him, becomes like a magnificent throne. "There is no tribunal so magnificent, no throne so stately, no show of triumph so distinguished, no chariot so elevated" as is the cross "on which Christ has subdued death and the devil and trodden them under his feet," wrote John Calvin.[9]

THE VICTORY OF THE CROSS

No wonder the early church could "trample on snakes and scorpions and…overcome all the power of the enemy" (Luke 10:9). This is why the apostle Paul could take his stand "against the devil's schemes" and "against the rulers, against the authorities, against the powers of this dark world and against the spiritual forces of evil in heavenly realms" (Eph. 6:11–12).

Confidently Paul could say, "No, in all these things we are more than conquerors through him who loved us" (Rom. 8:37). He could proclaim, "Thanks be to God! He gives us the victory through our Lord Jesus Christ" (1 Cor. 15:57), for "They overcame him by the blood of the Lamb" (Rev. 12:11).

Yes, the early church saw something in the cross that many of us have missed today. They understood that because wrath engulfed the Lamb, because sin was abolished in Him, and because Satan's work was undone at Calvary, they had authority over sin, sickness, death, and the devil. Their authority came from the finished work of the cross.[10] Now "he may tempt," said Spurgeon, "but he cannot compel; he may threaten, but he cannot subdue, for the crown is taken from his head." Jesus has "dashed in pieces our enemies and divided the spoil with the strong."[11]

Christ has indeed conquered the weaker one, just as He said, "When a strong man, fully armed, guards his own house, his possessions are safe. But when someone stronger attacks and overpowers him, he takes away the armor in which the man trusted and divides up the spoils" (Luke 11:21–22). Jesus Christ, the Lamb of God, is the stronger Man who overpowered Satan on the cross.

And this is why we can stand our ground at Calvary, taking authority over the evil one. Derek Prince, after decades of a successful deliverance ministry, explained:

> The cross is the sole basis of the total defeat of Satan. Through the cross, Christ administered to Satan a total, permanent, and irrevocable defeat. Satan cannot change that. He realized it too late because when he procured the death of Jesus on the cross, he procured his own defeat. Ever since then he has been doing everything he can to obscure that fact and to keep it from the eyes of the church.[12]

Do you see why we have been blind to the full work of the cross? Satan has blinded our eyes! One way he has done this is through a false teaching which has weakened our understanding of the finished work of the cross.

DID JESUS SUFFER IN HELL?

Regent University's J. Rodman Williams in his massive work, *Renewal Theology*, writes, "The teaching in some circles that the victory occurred after a three-day-and-night struggle with Satan in hell is wholly contrary to Scripture."[13] He quotes one well-known author who gives a description of a battle that took place after the cross before Jesus arose from the dead.[14] This same author said that Christ "suffered hell's agonies for three days and three nights."[15] This fanciful battle in hell flatly contradicts what Paul wrote: "Having disarmed the power and authorities, he made a public spectacle of them, triumphing over them by the cross" (Col. 2:15).

Professor Wayne Grudem wrote an article entitled, "He Did Not Descend into Hell: A Plea for Following Scripture Instead of the Apostles' Creed." Here he explains, "It is surprising that the phrase 'descended into hell' was not found in any of the early versions of the Creed. Before A.D. 60 it was found in the creeds of the Ariens who did not believe in the deity of Christ, asserting that the Son was not eternal but was created by the Father. After that, 'he descended into hell' was generally understood as 'He descended into hades (the grave), not gehenna (the place of punishment).'"[16]

So apparently, Jesus did descend to Hades, which is not the same as Gehenna, the place of eternal punishment.[17] But the purpose was not to suffer in a battle with the devil. It was to take back "the keys of death and hades" (Rev. 1:18) and to proclaim to the captives the victory of the cross (see Pet. 3:18). He did not suffer in hell after the cross. He makes this clear with what He says from Calvary.

To the thief He did not say, "This day you will be with me in hell." He said, "This day you will be with me in paradise" (Luke 23:43). Paul places paradise in the third heaven (2 Cor. 12:4) and John does as well (Rev. 2:7, 22:2, 14).

With His sixth word Jesus didn't say, "It is almost finished!" He said, "It is finished!" (John 19:30), which reveals the triumph over Satan and proclaims the finished work of the cross.

And finally, He didn't cry, "Satan, into your hands I commit my spirit!" No, He cried, "Father, into your hands I commit my spirit" (Luke 23:46), which shows that He released His spirit, not to the devil for three days of suffering, but to God His Father.

Sadly, however, many preachers today embellish the story, graphically describing the torture Jesus endured at the hands of the devil. Of course, according to this myth, He finally won the battle and rose victoriously from the grave. However, this leaves a gaping hole in our understanding of the cross. It implies that the work was done in hell, after the cross, which twists truth and diminishes the message of the cross. But this is exactly what Satan wants! He wants us to underestimate the finished work of the cross because this is the place of his demise.

THE AUTHORITY OF THE CROSS

If we don't understand the power of the finished work of the cross, then we won't use this triumphant weapon against Satan. Derek Prince explained that if you deal with demons on the basis of anything but the cross, you will be defeated because he is much stronger and cleverer than we are. Says Prince, "When you deal with them on the basis of Jesus on the cross, then it really is true that demons believe and tremble. And I've seen demons trembling many times when confronted with the reality of the defeat that Satan suffered on the cross."[18]

Now do you see why Satan has worked overtime to blind our eyes to the power of the cross? This is a truth which, as Prince said, "the enemy would wish that we never discovered, and he'll do everything in his power to prevent us apprehending it, understanding it, or applying it."[19]

Why haven't we understood this? Because the "god of this age has blinded the minds of unbelievers so they cannot see the light of the gospel of the glory of Christ" (2 Cor. 4:4). But it's not only unbelievers' eyes that have been blinded. It's ours as well. I know mine were, until I began to understand the Father's cup.

Because we have not looked with unflinching gaze into the Father's cup, we haven't understood the finished work of the cross. We have failed to see that because the cup of wrath was fully consumed, now sin was fully punished and Satan had no more grounds on which to attack the Lord. Then, when the blood of God dripped down upon this earth, spilling over demons and splashing over Satan, his power was broken. This is why we can boldly proclaim the verse, "They overcame him by the blood of the Lamb!" (Rev. 12:11).

We took our Glory of the Lamb School to a rehab center in Mobile, and hope exploded in the hearts of men and women who had been abused and severely addicted to drugs and alcohol. When they opened wide and let the depths of the Father's cup melt their hearts, their eyes could suddenly see.

To illustrate the victory of Christ over Satan on the cross, I held up a rubber snake, threw it on the floor, and cried, "The Seed of the Woman crushed the serpent's head under His heel. Now He calls you to crush the devil's influence in your life—under your feet!" Then I challenged, "Is there anyone here tonight who would step forward and stomp on the serpent's head?" Earlier that day they had deeply repented for their sin at the foot of the cross, so they were ready to experience the victory.

One young man shot out of his seat and began stomping the snake, shouting, "I crush my addictions to alcohol and crack cocaine!" Instantly others jumped up and, one by one, began pounding on the serpent and breaking their addictions. They knew they were only doing this because Jesus had already conquered Satan on the cross.

Do you see what an immeasurable victory was completed at Calvary? For too long we've let the enemy wreak havoc over our souls, when all along Jesus was calling, "Run to the cross where I already completed the work!"

Oh, I wish you could have seen what happened when I showed Jesus' triumphant victory over Satan to the pastors in the Kenya Ablaze for the Lamb Revival School of Ministry. They did not know that Jesus defeated the devil on the cross. They either thought He won the victory in hell, which diminishes the power of the cross; or they thought Satan will not be overcome until Jesus comes back. In Africa demonic forces run rampant because of all the witchcraft, voodoo, and false religions. The reason missionaries don't see much victory over these forces is because they haven't grasped the power of the cross over Satan.

But when these young pastors saw the Lamb conquering the devil on the cross, not in hell after the cross, they rose up and took authority like nothing I've ever seen. They knew they had the right to "trample on snakes and scorpions and to overcome all the power of the enemy" (Luke 10:19).

So again, as a prophetic act, I threw a fake serpent to the floor and challenged the pastors to step up and trample on the serpent's head. Pastors ran to the front of the church, stomping on the serpent's head and shouting bold proclamations of victory over the devil in Africa.

Suddenly one woman screamed and fell to the floor. She slithered and foamed at the mouth, but in moments she was completely free. Later she explained that she had formerly been a Muslim and this was what bound her, but the demons were no match for the finished work of the cross. A few other visitors fell to the concrete floor, slithering and groaning as pastors cast demons out of them. Soon they fell, weak, limp, and delivered but filled with the joy of God's presence.

Finally, Pastor Newton called for a panga (a large machete like knife), then sliced off the serpent's head and threw it toward the cross. The whole place exploded in victorious dancing as Cathy, one of our team members, sang a song she had written:

> Tetelestai! It is finished! The work is now forever done.
> Tetelestai! It is finished! Christ, the Victory He has won!
>   Amen.
> Disease and sickness now are broken; in His wounds we now
>   are healed.
> In the cross our God has spoken; God's great act of love
>   revealed! Amen.
> The cup is emptied; Jesus drank it; He engulfed our wrath
>   and pain.
> Sin is banished; Hell is vanquished. He has wiped out all
>   our shame. Amen.
> Powers of darkness, they are conquered, by the cross where
>   blood was shed.
> Christ has triumphed over Satan; He has crushed the devil's
>   head! Amen.

As I stood back thinking how the cross had impacted these pastors, I thought back to Pastor Ambrose, an apostle over nineteen churches in Kenya, where we preached a year ago. The night before we came, he was agonizing in prayer about the Muslim spirit that was taking over his village. The Lord spoke to him and said, "If you will preach the power of the blood, the Muslim authorities cannot stop the power of the cross, and a revolutionary move of God will start."

Pastor Ambrose had invited us to preach in his church, but he had no idea we would be preaching the power of the blood, the victory of the cross, and the fire of revival. Several team members preached, and then I called the people to close their eyes and look up at Jesus. I described the Lamb upon the throne, still bearing wounds from His sacrifice. I told them to focus on the blood of Christ which gives them the power to overcome Satan: "They overcame him by the blood of the Lamb" (Rev. 12:11).

The people looked up to Jesus and the whole place erupted as they began proclaiming the power of the blood of the Lamb. The generator ran out of fuel and the mic went dead, but it didn't matter. The Holy Spirit had broken loose in this Kenyan church, and Pastor Ambrose knew this was the answer to his prayer. Indeed this is the power that will overcome the enemy in Africa. It's the powerful blood of the Lamb!

One evening we took our team and a busload of children from the orphanage to a nearby village. Draping several sheets sewn together over the bus, we showed *The Passion of the Christ* movie.

I watched the people's faces as cruel Romans drove spikes through Jesus' hands and feet. The people had never seen such a thing. They had barely even heard of Jesus. Many had been influenced by Islam or witchcraft. But when they saw the God who came to earth in human flesh and laid down His life on a cross, they wept and wept.

When we stopped the movie, Pastor Allan rose to the platform and blazed out a gospel message in Swahili. When he gave the altar call, at least one third of the people rushed to the front, calling out to be saved.

I stood back in wonder as I saw the power of the gospel exploding in a little African village. Rarely will a Western evangelist go into these hidden villages where there are no television cameras. This would never be seen by the world, but the eyes of God saw it. And I'm sure He was pleased, for nothing is so dear to His heart as seeing His Son receive the reward of His suffering.

Do you see what I'm trying to tell you? There is power in the message of the cross. Again and again, the pastors in Kenya told me, "This is the message that will set Africa ablaze with the Lamb!" Like the apostle Paul, they had discovered the power of preaching the cross. Paul said, "The message of the cross...is the power of God" (1 Cor. 1:18). It is God's burning bush. Even as God's fiery wrath descended on the Lamb on the cross, now the fire of revival descends when the cross is lifted high.

Indeed, Jesus overcame Satan in a cosmic power encounter at Calvary. It's a finished work: *Tetelestai*—the work is now and forever finished! Now He gives us the authority to walk in what He purchased on the cross. He did the work. Now we have to apply His finished work by stepping out, telling others what He did, and breaking demonic strongholds as we encounter them.

Just think—a group of almost one hundred African pastors humbled themselves and admitted they needed to learn more about the cross. Believe me, it took humility to receive from a female white *mazungu*! But they allowed this message to be carved into their hearts, and now they are shaking their nation with the finished work of the cross, for their hearts and their theology have been undone and set ablaze by a revelation of the Lamb.

CHAPTER 10 ENDNOTES

1. See also Ezekiel 28:12–19.
2. E. K. Simpson and F. F. Bruce, *Commentary on the Epistles to the Ephesians and Colossians, New International Version Commentary on the New Testament* (Grand Rapids, MI: Wm. B. Eerdmans Publishing Company, 1957), 239.
3. TCNT refers to the *Twentieth Century New Testament* (Chicago, IL: Moody Bible Institute).
4. N. Micklem, cited in Leon Morris, *The Cross in the New Testament*, 381.
5. Gustaf Aulén, *Christus Victor* (New York: MacMillan Publishing Company, 1969), 102–104.
6. Leon Morris, *The Cross in the New Testament*, 359.
7. Some versions read *"teleō"* in Greek, meaning to make an end, completion, accomplishment.
8. Charles Spurgeon, "It Is Finished!" *The Power of the Cross of Christ*, 145.
9. John Calvin, *Institutes of the Christian Religion*, vol. 1, book II (Grand Rapids, MI: Wm B. Eerdmans Publishing Company, 1983), 440.
10. In the classic book *Christus Victor*, Gustaf Aulén tells how the early church and church Fathers clearly understood the victory of Christ on the cross. They saw Jesus as triumphing over "sin, death, hell, and Satan." Martin Luther revived a victorious theology of the cross during the Reformation, but eventually Protestant scholasticism clouded the clear revelation of the power and the victory of the cross (Gustaf Aulén, *Christus Victor*, 128–133).
11. Charles Spurgeon, "Christ Triumphant," *Spurgeon's Sermons on the Resurrection of Christ* (Grand Rapids, MI: Kregel Publications, 1993), 79.

12. Derek Prince, "The Cross at the Center," CD part 2, "Derek Prince Ministries," Charlotte, NC, 1990.
13. J. Rodman Williams, *Renewal Theology: Systematic Theology from a Charismatic Perspective* (Grand Rapids, MI: Zondervan, 1992), 363.
14. E. W. Kenyon, *What Happened from the Cross to the Throne*, 65, as quoted in Williams, *Renewal Theology*, footnote #30, 363.
15. Ibid., 89.
16. Wayne Grudem, *JETS* 34:1 (March 1991), 103–113, *Systematic Theology*, 586–587.
17. Hades is the place of the dead before Christ went to the cross. Abraham's Bosom, the holding place of the godly dead, is located in Hades, which Jesus described in Luke 16:19–31. Hell is called Gehenna, a place of torment and punishment. It was also the name of the garbage dump outside Jerusalem.
18. Derek Prince, "The Cross at the Center," CD part 2.
19. Ibid.

Chapter 11

THE CRIMSON TIDE

It's Time to Honor the Blood

LOOK UP NOW and see the blush of victory still glowing on Jesus' face as He shouts His last words from the cross: "Father, into your hands I commit my spirit" (Luke 23:46). At creation God rested on the seventh day; now with His seventh word He enters into His rest. And with this final word from the cross, He slowly bows His head. He doesn't slump it like a man out of control: "He bowed his head and gave up his spirit" (John 19:30). And now it happens.

THE DIVINE RUPTURE

His heart breaks. It ruptures, pouring out blood and water, which had separated and accumulated around the lining of the heart.

Indeed, nails didn't kill Him. Blood loss from scourging didn't take His life. He didn't die of asphyxiation or a soldier's spear. Jesus died of a ruptured heart from drinking His Father's cup. The final shreds tore when He cried the heart-piercing cry of dereliction, *My God, why have You forsaken me?* He had enough strength left to crush the devil's head and shout His last cries; but do you know what this means?

The Bible says, "At that moment the curtain of the temple was torn in two from top to bottom. The earth shook and the rocks split. The tombs broke open and many bodies of many holy people who had died were raised to life" (Matt. 27:51–52). This was not simply the severing of the thick veil that protected the way into the holy of holies in the temple. It was not only the tearing of the veil in heaven which separated God and humanity. It was not merely the cracking of rocks and tombs and earth.

137

Above all, it was the severing of the heart of the Son Himself, thus opening the way back into the presence and glory of God.

Watch now as a soldier lifts a heavy sledgehammer and prepares to smash Jesus' knees. This was usually done to hasten death by making it impossible for the victim to push down on the spike in his feet to lift his lungs for air. But long ago God told Moses, "Do not break any of the bones" of the Passover lamb (Exod. 12:46). Now, suddenly, the soldier drops the hammer. It's as though he hears God roaring from heaven:

Don't you dare break a bone of My Passover Lamb!

Look on now as a Roman soldier draws back his spear and aims it at Jesus' heart. See the young disciple, John, instinctively shielding Mary's view, but she refuses to tear her gaze from her Son. The soldier plunges his blade into Jesus' side, "bringing a sudden flow of blood and water" (John 19:34).

As a mother, I can imagine Mary breaking from John's arms and running, sobbing wildly, to the stone-cold feet of her Son. I see her pressing her lips against His bleeding feet, even as she did when He was her first-born. No one can know the anguish of this little mother as the prophet's words are fulfilled, "A sword will pierce your own soul too" (Luke 2:35).

As a soldier pulls her away, I'm sure she must have looked at her hands, now wet with the blood of her Son. The beauty and glory of each blood drop must have stunned her senses. For each sacred drop of Jesus' blood is precious: "It was not with perishable things such as silver or gold that you were redeemed…but with the precious blood of Christ, a lamb without blemish or defect" (1 Pet. 1:19).

My Salvation Story

I would like to tell you now my personal story of why the blood of the Lamb means so much to me. I stood in a crowd of thousands, utterly awestruck by what I was hearing. It was 1957 in Abilene, Texas; and as far back as I could remember, I had longed to know God. But my parents were atheists, and I knew nothing about Jesus Christ. Once, when I was barely able to talk, I looked up at my dad as he shaved and asked, "Daddy, who is God?" He quickly blurted, "Hush! We don't talk about that!"

Sometimes I would cry at night, yearning to know God; but no one ever told me how to be saved. I finally concluded that the only way to be a Christian is to try to live a good life. Then when I was thirteen, my friend, Martha Lyn, took me to a Crusade for Christ at Rose Field House on the campus of Hardin Simmons University. My heart trembled as I heard, for the first time in my life, the gospel being preached by evangelist Howard Butt, Jr. As I listened, I realized that Jesus Christ is the answer I'd been looking for all my life.

The altar call was given and I could feel my heart hammering hard in my chest. But I knew I couldn't answer the call and go forward because I was too sinful. My heart was too filthy to ever receive a holy God into my life. At that point I almost missed it. I came close to denying the answer I had sought because I knew I didn't deserve to be saved. My whole being longed to go forward; but I knew I wasn't clean enough, so I promised God I would go home and pray all day and try to get clean enough to go forward the next night.

Then suddenly I heard something. It was the words to a song the choir was singing. It was the second verse of "Just as I Am" that caught my attention:

> Just as I am and waiting not to rid my soul of one dark blot;
> To Thee whose blood can cleanse each spot,
> O Lamb of God, I come. I come.[1]

I thought, *What? I don't have to wait? His blood can cleanse each spot?* I could hardly believe it, and I didn't understand it, but I broke from the crowd and rushed forward, crying like a baby. I prayed with a counselor and repented earnestly and passionately for my sin. Then I invited Jesus Christ into my heart.

I was utterly undone. My heart felt clean! His blood really had washed me! At last I had found God. I found what I had looked for all my life. But it didn't come from an evangelist's sermon or a powerful altar call. My heart was drawn by a song, "Just as I Am," telling me of the Lamb of God "whose blood can cleanse each spot."

I learned later that the author of that song, Charlotte Elliot, was an invalid. She grieved deeply because she couldn't be out on the mission field like her brother. Yet thousands, probably millions, of people have been drawn to the Lord through that one song which honors the blood of the Lamb.

Oh, I tell you, I will never ever be able to thank God enough for the glory in one drop of blood. Every precious drop of that blood is sacred to me. I cherish it with my whole heart; as Spurgeon said, "His wounds distilled the richest balm that ever healed a sinner's wound."[2]

Yes, through His blood I found God. I found peace. I found victory over sin and the devil. I found purity. I found safety. I found purpose for my life. The blood of God, pouring from the wounds of the Lamb has captured my eternal devotion. I will never get over it.

Oh, Lamb of God, may I live for no other cause than to honor Your blood and bring You the reward of Your suffering. For through Your blood, my heart has been forever undone.

Jesus' Blood-Cry

During the French Revolution the emperor would ride his horse through the battleground, and wounded men would push themselves up on bloody appendages to pay homage to their king. Think of it—bloody people gave their lives to save their king, but we have a bloody King who gave His life to save His people.

You might wonder—why did God have to send His one and only Son to be the one to suffer? Why not an angel or a good man like Abraham or Moses or Paul? The answer is in the blood. You see, it couldn't be an angel because angels don't bleed. It couldn't be a great man because the blood of all men is polluted with sin. No, it had to be One who was perfectly holy. One who was uncreated. One who is self-existent and omnipotent. It had to be One who is God.

When a baby is conceived, the mother's blood never mixes with the blood of the baby in her womb. God planned it this way so that when His Son was conceived in the womb of a virgin, His blood could be pure and untainted. Now His pure and holy blood had to spill upon this earth to provide a way for our bloodstreams to be purified.

That's why He had to become a man—the God-Man—so that He could take our place as the punished Lamb and then wash us clean by "the precious blood of Christ, a lamb with out blemish or defect" (1 Pet. 1:19).

In the Old Testament God told priests to sprinkle blood seven times on the veil in the tabernacle: "And the priest shall dip his finger in the blood and sprinkle some of it seven times before the Lord before the veil of the sanctuary" (Lev. 4:6). But this veil in the tabernacle speaks of the veil of Jesus' flesh: for He opened the way "through the separating curtain (veil of the Holy of Holies), that is through His flesh" (Heb. 10:20, AMP).

As in the tabernacle, the veil of His flesh was actually sprinkled seven times: first, His own blood splotched His face in the garden; second, scourges drew His blood; third, thorns punctured His brow; fourth, spikes riveted His hands; fifth, a spike drove through His feet; sixth, His heart ruptured open; and seventh, the blood and water spurted out when a soldier's sword pierced His side. As in the tabernacle, His own blood sprinkled seven times on the veil of His own flesh.

Bob Sorge writes, "Look at His cross and all you see is blood. Blood on His scalp, blood on His face, blood on His neck, blood on His shoulders, blood on His arms, blood on His hands, blood on His back, blood on His chest, blood on His legs, blood on His feet, blood on His cross, blood on the ground. It was a spectacle of blood."[3]

Some would complain that the blood makes them uncomfortable. I say—we should have been uncomfortable about the sin that caused His blood to roll in the first place! Spurgeon said, "Sin is such a horrible thing that God has appointed blood to wash it away."[4]

That's why God showered the whole Old Testament with blood. Blood stained the priest's garments, blood splattered the altar, blood smeared the horns of the altar, blood spattered the veil, and blood sprinkled the mercy seat. Pools of blood splashed all through the outer court of the tabernacle, for God was proclaiming:

This is My Son—My eternal Lamb! His flesh will be bathed in blood so that you can be forgiven and draw near to Me!

Think what this cost the Father. In heaven no blood had ever existed. Before the creation of the world there was no such thing as human blood.

When the Holy Spirit impregnated a virgin with the seed of God, a tiny human heart began to pump the warm rich blood of God through an unborn child. The blood of bulls and goats and lambs had been sacrificed for centuries, but now God's blood was pulsing through a baby's arteries and veins.

Soon that sacred blood would pour out in sacrifice, for it took a wound to release that blood to earth. It took the piercing of a brow, a hand, a foot, a side before the blood of His heart could be released to us. But it took more than a piercing; it took a crushing: "He was crushed for our iniquities....It was the Lord's will to crush Him" (Isa. 53:5, 10). You see the heart of Jesus was crushed by an Almighty hand to squeeze out every last drop of the blood of God.

Now God looks down on this world, and He longs to see His Son's blood honored on earth as it is honored in heaven. The Father gazes on His Beloved, still looking "like a Lamb that has been slain" (Rev. 5:6). Continually He sees the wounds from which His sacred blood once streamed. Sorge writes, "Every glance at Christ's blood produces unfathomable emotions within the breast of God because it reminds Him of His Son's extreme devotion and the massive work of redemption that His blood purchased."[5]

In this day of political correctness, however, many Christians avoid any mention of the blood because it might be offensive. In an attempt to transform the culture or grow churches, we have presented a blood-drained gospel. It's like the story I told earlier of the father who ripped off his jacket and flagged away cars, crying, "Don't you see, you're traveling over the blood of my son!" His son's blood was precious to that father; but how much more is the blood of the Son of God precious to the Heavenly Father! He feels indescribable grief when "we have trampled the Son of God underfoot and treated as an unholy thing the blood of the covenant" (Heb. 10:29). Spurgeon said, "The sin of rebellion is vile, but the sin of slighting the Savior is viler still."[6]

God said to Cain when he killed his brother, "The voice of your brother's blood is crying to me from the ground" (Gen. 4:10). But you and I killed Jesus, for our sin crucified our elder Brother. If Abel's blood cried for vindication, how much more does Jesus' blood cry for vindication.[7] I believe the Father hears His Son's blood crying:

Father, when will My sacrifice be honored on earth as it honored in heaven? When will they honor the blood I poured out for them?

In heaven angels praise Him continually, crying, "Worthy is the Lamb!" But why is He so worthy? Do they sing, "You are worthy because of Your great miracles!" "Because of Your grand teachings!" "Because of Your virgin birth!" Is this why they say He is worthy? Do they say, "You are worthy because of Your resurrection!" "Because of Your ascension into heaven!" "Because of Your Second Coming!" No, millions upon millions of angels sing, "You are worthy...because you were slain and with your blood you purchased men for God" (Rev. 5:9).

THE BLOOD IN COMMUNION

But Jesus didn't bleed for angels. He bled for you and me. This is why I try to take the Lord's Supper every day if possible. I do it first to bring fresh sins before the Lord, confessing them and knowing that "if we confess our sins He is faithful and just and will forgive our sins and purify us from all unrighteousness," for "the blood of Jesus, his Son, purifies us from all sin" (1 John 1:9, 7).

But above all, I want to honor the blood of Jesus. On the night He transformed Passover into the Lord's Supper, Jesus said, "I have earnestly desired to eat this Passover with you before I suffer" (Luke 22:15). Now I "earnestly desire" to eat the Lord's Supper with Him *after* He suffered. For Communion is actually an encounter with Him. It is partaking of His body and blood.[8]

Paul said, "Is not the cup of thanksgiving for which we give thanks a participation in the blood of Christ? And is not the bread that we break a participation in the body of Christ?" (1 Cor. 10:16).[9] Spurgeon adds, "My Lord and my Master, I desire to meet with you. The bread alone will not satisfy me; I want to feed spiritually upon your flesh. The wine will not quench my soul's thirst; I want spiritually to receive your blood into my inmost soul."[10]

In fact, Ceil and Moishe Rosen in *Christ in the Passover* say that Jewish people heated water and added it to the wine in the Passover meal.[11] Not only would this dilute the inebriating effects of wine, but it reminds us of the warm red blood of our Savior, coursing out from His veins on the cross.

Smith Wigglesworth reverenced communion so deeply that he took it daily,[12] and Spurgeon pleaded with the church to take the Lord's Supper at least once a week.[13] "In the early church it is possible that they broke bread every day," he said. Then he added, "If there is any rule as to the time for the observance of this ordinance, it surely is every Lord's Day."[14]

He further wrote this word that we need to hear today: "Shame on the Christian church that she should put if off to once a month and mar the first day of the week by depriving it of its glory in the meeting together for fellowship and breaking of bread and showing forth the death of Christ till He comes."[15]

The beauty of daily Communion is that it keeps our hearts soft and tender. I like to dip the bread into the blood-red juice and look at it. It keeps the image of the Lord before me every day. Spurgeon suggested, "Use the blood and wine as a pair of spectacles. Look through them and do not be satisfied until you can say, 'Yes, yes, I can see the Lamb of God which taketh away the sin of the world.'"[16]

As Spurgeon said, in the bread and the juice I see Jesus. I see His body bathed in blood. I see His bloodshot eyes, bulging with tears and love. I see His back and shoulders beaten with the cruel lash. I see His hands and feet nailed up to a cross. I see the cup of wrath blazing down upon Him.[17] In the lovely and sacred act of the Lord's Supper, I look up at the Lamb and worship.

THE BLOOD AND THE FIRE

It is not enough, however, to preach about the blood, to pray about the blood, to think about the blood. We must *apply* the blood of the Lamb. Even as the Israelites applied the blood of the lamb to the frame of their doorposts, we must apply the blood to the frame of our lives and then the Holy Spirit will come.[18]

In his book *The Blood*, Benny Hinn says, "Years ago I discovered that when the blood is honored, the presence of God descends, and miracles take place. As we remember the work of the cross and recognize the power represented in the shed blood of Jesus, lives are touched and transformed by God's presence and power."[19]

Maxwell Whyte in *The Power of the Blood* wrote, "When we honor the blood of Jesus, the Holy Spirit immediately manifests His life on our behalf."[20] He tells the story of a church in Scotland which had become rather dry. But a brother came and urged them to honor the blood once again. "Immediately the power of God fell afresh and people were prostrated under the power of God."[21]

One morning our team popped in unexpectedly to an African church, but the pastor graciously asked me to preach for ten minutes. I began leading the people to behold the Lamb and call upon the blood of Jesus to wash us clean. "Wash me! Wash me! Wash me! Wash me..." I kept saying as they echoed my words in Swahili. I could sense something powerful happening in the hearts of the people as we prayed for cleansing by the blood. Then, with only a few minutes left, I led them to cry, "Fill me! Fill me! Fill me! Fill me..."

Suddenly, the power of God swept down on the people. A large lady in front began shaking intensely. "More, Holy Spirit," I said gently. Suddenly, she shot backwards, no one touching her, knocking down people and chairs with the impact of her fall. Time was up, so I sat down, but in just a few minutes the Lord had shown us how the power of His blood opens the way for the power of His Spirit.

Bob Sorge explains why honoring the blood is so powerful: "When you invoke the blood of Christ, you unlock the infinite passions of the eternal God." He continues, "Believe in Christ's blood and the heart of Abba Father turns seemingly inside-out as He eagerly lavishes on you His glorious favor. He opens the storehouses of heaven for those who look to the blood because He honors those who honor that which is most precious to Him."[22]

My pastor, John Kilpatrick, who pastored the Brownsville Revival in Pensacola and now pastors Church of His Presence and the Bay of the Holy Spirit Revival in Mobile, found this to be true. He said, "We took communion every single Sunday for five years before revival came. I believe God saw the sincerity of our hearts and our love for the blood. He sent revival because the Holy Spirit always kisses the blood."[23] This revival at Brownsville in Pensacola brought over four million visitors from around the world and led hundreds of thousands to salvation.

THE BLOOD IN AMERICA

I've seen the message of the cross received in Hong Kong, in Taiwan, in Bulgaria, in Peru, in Africa, in Mexico, in Scotland, in Germany, and in England and in other places around the world, but always one gnawing thought has ached in my heart. *What about America?*

Personally, I had tried to bring this message of the Lamb to America for almost thirty years, but it never seemed to make much impact. Then one night, Nathan Morris preached in our church and something happened that changed everything.

Before I tell this story, let me give a little background that is especially tender to my heart. One Sunday morning I was preaching about the piercing of the Lamb in Pastor Peter Morris' church in Wath, England. Pastor Morris sat on the front row sobbing openly as he heard the descriptions of Jesus engulfing His Father's cup. Sitting behind him was his twenty-two-year-old son, Nathan. Nathan had just gotten saved from a life of sin, primarily by watching videos of the Brownsville Revival and Steve Hill. Now, as he saw his own dad weeping, it grabbed his attention.

Suddenly I saw Nathan bending over, gripping his chest and groaning. I knew God was piercing his heart for the Lamb, so I went over and laid my hand on his chest. I was simply doing what I saw the Father doing as I asked God to pierce him for the Lamb. Nathan later told a group of our interns that he went home and wept the rest of the day.

Several years had passed and I had been hearing how God was using him in crusades in India and Africa with notable miracles happening in his ministry.[24] Now, ten years later, my pastor, John Kilpatrick, invited Nathan to preach in an Open Heaven conference at our church, the Church of His Presence. As he was preaching in our church, he began telling about his vision of a crimson tide rising and mounting and cresting and breaking through the walls of the church, sweeping multitudes into the kingdom and flooding through America.

The next night he started to preach; and out of nowhere, he felt something brush over the back of his legs. He turned to look and no one was there. He realized it was the Lord. Then suddenly, heaven's fire fell powerfully down upon him, and he was flattened to the floor. He tried to get up because he knew he needed to preach, but it was impossible. He lay there, his face flushed and red, sweating profusely, and trembling under the fire of God. When he got off the floor after lying under the power for at least twenty to thirty minutes, the glory of revival had completely consumed him.

In the next few months I saw with my own eyes more miracles than I had ever seen in my life. I saw blind people receive their sight; deaf people's ears pop open; brain cancer and other forms of cancer completely healed; a lady whose mother had died of lupus, who was already planning her own funeral, was healed. All of these people came back with medical reports verifying the healings. Soon the crowds had grown so large we had to move the revival to the Convention Center in Mobile.[25]

One of the greatest miracles was Delia Knox, a pastor's wife, who had been paralyzed from the waist down for twenty-two years. She was bound to a wheelchair with no feeling in her legs. Nathan prayed, and suddenly she cried, "I can feel your hands on my legs!" Pastor Kilpatrick and Nathan continued to pray and pray, not giving up but pressing through for her healing. The congregation stretched out our hands and supported them with prayer. All of a sudden, she pushed herself up from her wheelchair and began to walk! Though she still had to be assisted, she actually moved her legs and took huge lunging steps for the first time in twenty-two years.

But to me the most precious part was when she called her twin sister on her cell phone. I'm a mother of twin girls myself so I know how close twins can be. When her twin answered, Delia said, "Get on the Internet to watch the revival. I have a surprise to show you. I can walk!" As soon as her sister indicated she was watching on her computer, Delia said, "Look!" and she pushed herself up from her wheelchair and walked again.

Oh, I tell you, it was such a tender moment for everyone to watch. We were all sobbing. In a few weeks Delia was walking and dancing before the Lord, completely healed. After that, miracles abounded and still abound today as Nathan and Pastor Kilpatrick take the revival through

America. But Nathan Morris, the evangelist, stands boldly to proclaim over and over again: "This revival is not about miracles! It's not even about souls! This revival is all about the power of the cross! It's about the blood of the Lamb! It's the gospel of Jesus Christ."

The Lord told me that He had used Nathan and this revival to break the heavens open over America, making a way for the message of the cross and the blood. I weep as I write, for I know at last the way has been opened for the message of the Lamb. Yes, finally, the time has come for the blood of Christ to be honored on earth as it is honored in heaven. At last, God will set our hearts ablaze with the fire of the cross and people throughout this land will be undone by beholding a revelation of the Lamb!

CHAPTER 11 ENDNOTES

1. Charlotte Elliott, "Just As I Am."
2. Charles Spurgeon, "The Marvelous Magnet," *The Power of the Cross of Christ*, 20.
3. Bob Sorge, *The Power of the Blood*, 3–4.
4. Charles Spurgeon, *2200 Quotations from the Writings of Charles H. Spurgeon*, 352.
5. Bob Sorge, *The Power of the Blood*, 8.
6. Charles Spurgeon, "Mourning at the Sight of the Crucified," *The Power of the Cross of Christ*, Lance Wubbels, comp. (Lynnwood, WA: Emerald Books, 1995), 186.
7. Most commentators on this story of Abel's blood say that Abel's blood cries for vengeance but Jesus blood cries for forgiveness. This is true, of course, but I think there's a dimension of Jesus' blood-cry that we have overlooked. It's not a cry for vengeance, but a cry to be remembered for the magnitude of His eternal sacrifice.
8. "After our Lord's death was over," wrote Spurgeon, "the blood of animals was not the type, but the blood of the grape. That which was terrible in prospect is joyous in remembrance. That which was blood in the shedding is wine in the receiving. It came to him with a wound, but it comes to us with a blessing" (Charles Spurgeon, *2200 Quotations*, 121).
9. John R. W, Stott explains, "Thus they were not spectators of the drama of the cross; they were participants in it. They can hardly have failed to get the message. Just as it was not enough for the bread to be broken and the wine to be poured out, but they had to eat it and drink

it, so it was not enough for him to die, but they had to appropriate the benefits of his death personally. The eating and drinking were, and still are, a vivid acted parable of receiving Christ as our crucified Savior and of feeding on him in our hearts by faith" (John R. W. Stott, *The Cross of Christ*, 70).

10. Charles H. Spurgeon, "Fencing the Lord's Table," *Spurgeon's Expository Encyclopedia*, vol. 10 (Grand Rapids, MI: Baker Book House, 1977), 325. (I slightly edited this quote from Spurgeon.)
11. Ceil and Moishe Rosen suggest that the water was heated because the wine was warm, as stated in the Mishnah (Pesahim 7:13). The Mishnah is the earliest known rabbinical commentary, edited and compiled between A.D. 100 and 210. The Mishnah covers Jewish life, traditions, and customs at the time of Christ (Ceil and Moishe Rosen, *Christ in the Passover* [Chicago, IL: Moody Press, 1978], 50–51).
12. Perry Stone writes, "If the blood and body of an earthly lamb restrained the destroyer, how much more can the blood and body of Christ protect the believer!" (Perry Stone, *The Meal that Heals* [Cleveland, TN: Pathway Press, 2006], 43).
13. Charles H. Spurgeon, "The Object of the Lord's Supper," *Spurgeon's Expository Encyclopedia*, vol. 10 (Grand Rapids, MI: Baker Book House, 1977), 301–302. Spurgeon explained that we must have this sacred ordinance because we so easily "forget his sufferings." Then he cried, "Oh, that I could have the cross painted on my eyeballs, that I could not see anything except through the medium of my Savior's passion" (Charles H. Spurgeon, "The Lord's Supper, Simple but Sublime," *Spurgeon's Expository Encyclopedia*, vol. 10 (Grand Rapids, MI: Baker Book House, 1977), 352–353).
14. Charles Spurgeon, "The Object of the Lord's Supper 297.
15. Ibid., 297.
16. Charles Spurgeon, *2200 Quotations*, 121.
17. Perry Stone, *The Meal that Heals*, 41.
18. Apply the blood to your health. Apply the blood to your lost loved ones. Apply the blood to the difficulties you face. Jesus crushed Satan beneath His feet, but He gave you the weapon: "They overcame him (Satan) by the blood of the Lamb and by the word of their testimony" (Rev. 12:11). You have to apply the blood of Jesus in prayer. Do this daily and with authority and watch the miracles unfold in your life.
19. Benny Hinn, *The Blood* (Lake Mary, FL: Charisma House, 2006), xiv.
20. H. A. Maxwell Whyte, *The Power of the Blood* (New Kensington, PA: Whittaker House, 2005), 34.
21. Ibid., 60.

22. Bob Sorge, *The Power of the Blood*, 8–9.
23. John Kilpatrick, Church of His Presence, Daphne, AL.
24. See Nathan's website: www.shakethenations.org.
25. See the revival schedule and watch it live at www.churchofhispresence. org or on God TV. See "Bay of the Holy Spirit Revival" on You-Tube for clips of this healing and many others.

Chapter 12

A RIVER *of* GLORY

Streams of Revival from the Heart of the Lamb

Focus the eyes of your spirit again on that gash in the Savior's side. Watch the last precious drops of blood drip down. But now, squint the eyes of your spirit and see the color and texture of the liquid change. It looks like clear flowing water.[1]

John saw "a sudden flow of blood and water" (John 19:34), for Jesus' heart had literally ruptured. When the heart ruptures, red blood cells separate from the clear serum, accumulating in the pericardium around the heart. Now the clear serum pours from that open heart wound. It is just as the crucifixion Psalm says, "I am poured out like water,...my heart is like wax, it is softened (with anguish) and melted down within me" (Ps. 22:14, AMP).

Spurgeon said this is more than simply lymph oozing from His side: "In the state in which our Saviour was, blood and water might have been found naturally in his heart, but only in a very small and infinitesimal quantity. The fountain that flowed therefrom was miraculous, not natural but supernatural; or if natural, yet so exalted and so increased in quantity as to become supernatural."[2]

RIVERS OF LIFE

As drops of water drip down from His open wound, do you realize what this is? Long ago Moses struck the rock and a river spilled out, which quenched the thirst of millions of Israelites in their journey in the wilderness: "They drank from the spiritual rock that accompanied them, and that rock was Christ" (1 Cor. 10:4). And now that rock—the Lamb of God Himself—has been struck so that rivers could pour out.

Dutch Sheets, in his magnificent book *The River of God*, says that in studying the many scriptural references to water, "one truth emerges as critical and perhaps the most encompassing: *The water flows from Christ and was released at the* cross. He is the source. *The headwaters are found in Him.*...Yes, it looked like a trickle, but it was a river that has since quenched the thirst of millions. Truly, He is the fountain of life."[3]

You see, rich treasures must be mined. In Christ are hidden all "the unending (boundless, fathomless, incalculable, and exhaustless) riches" of God (Eph. 3:8, AMP). This treasure was dug open in the earthen vessel of Jesus' heart. When the soldier's spear pierced the lining of His heart, it struck a rich vein and out rolled a river of glory.

This piercing in His side makes me think of a story I heard about the great missionary, Amy Carmichael:

> For many years Amy had poured out her life as a missionary to India. She had a special love for Buddhist temple prostitutes, and she started a home to rescue them. But one girl was particularly hard hearted. Amy tried to reach her with the gospel, but she always refused.
>
> One day Amy sat, trying to explain to the prostitute how much she loved her. Then she took a long needle and poised it over her bare arm. With love and compassion trembling in her voice, she said to the prostitute, "I'm going to stab this needle into my arm to show you how much I love you!"
>
> Now with the needle aimed at her arm, she prepared to gouge it into her flesh. "Oh, no!" objected the prostitute. "That will hurt you too much!"
>
> "Not nearly as much as you are hurting me," Amy replied. Then she thrust the needle deep into her arm. The girl's heart was broken when she saw this demonstration of love. She threw her arms around Amy's neck and cried, "Oh, Amy, I never knew you loved me so much!"

In a far higher way, that's what Jesus did for us. He allowed His body to be pierced to show us how much He loves us. Now a river of love and life flows from His side, pouring out to all who are thirsty.

We illustrated this one night as I took a team of students to Harvest Vineyard Mission in Florida, which was filled with broken men and women. I talked with the people about the cup Jesus drank, which caused His heart to erupt and pour out a river. I held up a glass pitcher and poured water into it. "His heart was like this pitcher, containing the river of God," I said.

Then I lifted up the glass pitcher and began beating it with a hammer. As I pounded, I said, "It wasn't the scourge or the thorns or nails or spear that crushed His heart." Still hammering the pitcher, I raised my voice and cried, "It wasn't just our sin which ravaged His soul. It was when the Father abandoned Him, thundered His punishment upon Him, and He cried, 'My God, why have You forsaken Me?' That's what broke open His heart and released a pent-up river!"

At that moment, I took the hammer and smashed the pitcher as I held it. I cried, "When the wrath of His Father smashed down upon Him, His heart burst open and He poured out the first small trickle of the river of God!" As I slammed the hammer into the vase, the glass broke and shattered, spilling the water to the floor. Powerfully, this demonstrated the pent-up river of God, breaking out of Jesus Christ.

One time I was giving this same illustration when a sliver of glass cut my finger. It made the illustration more poignant. I held up a piece of glass, now covered with blood, and said, "Jesus was broken so His blood for cleansing and His waters for revival could pour out on you!"

That night at the mission I further illustrated what happened by showing a clip from *The Passion of the Christ* film. As Jesus' side was pierced, out burst volumes of blood and water, spraying the centurion's face and driving him to his knees. "That was the first release of the river!" I shouted. "Now God wants you to come to the river and drink. Many of you have probably been drunk on alcohol," I said, and they all nodded in agreement. "But this river will make you drunk on God, like on the day of Pentecost!" (See Acts 2:1–13.)

We formed two lines for a prayer tunnel and the room erupted in glory. Men and women of all ages walked through the two lines of prayer. One young woman, who had attempted suicide that week because of the pain she carried over the death of her baby, fell to the floor, pouring out

UNDONE: BY A REVELATION OF THE LAMB

her grief. I bent over her and whispered, "Honey, cry it all out on Jesus." She wept and sobbed and screamed until finally the tears subsided.

Then we prayed for the Holy Spirit to fill her back up, and the Lord showed her a vision of her baby in the arms of Jesus. Peace flooded over her, and in moments she overflowed in laughter. She laughed and laughed, and when she tried to walk, she toppled over, completely inebriated in the Lord. It was wonderfully refreshing as the Holy Spirit filled her with hope and renewed her purpose for living.

As the prayer tunnel continued, all I could do was stand back and worship; for I knew this river was flowing through the room all because of Jesus' pierced open heart. Only a trickle broke forth at Calvary, but at the resurrection the power increased. At the ascension and outpouring of the Holy Spirit at Pentecost, the river roared forth in mighty waves of glory.

Indeed, I believe this water flowing from the Lamb is the pent-up river of God which had been treasured up in the heart of Christ since the closing of the Garden of Eden. And even as a flaming sword blocked the way to the Garden of Eden, now a soldier's sword has been plunged into the side of the Lamb, releasing this pent-up flood. It is just as the Scripture says, "And he shall come like a pent-up flood that the breath of the Lord drives along" (Isa. 59:19).

Dutch Sheets said, "There is a powerful, cleansing, thirst-quenching river that flows from the cross even today."4 God has been releasing streams of His river, for this river is real. It is a river of revival. Resurrection glory fills the streams, and everything the river touches springs to life.

WATERS OF REVIVAL

Oh, I tell you, I feel like I cannot bow low enough as I meditate on the wonder of this river of glory, released from the side of the Lamb. Ezekiel saw this river and he said that wherever this "river flows everything will live" (Ezek. 47:9). As streams of living water tumble down to earth, everything the river touches bursts into life. Waters gleam. Trees blossom. Fruit matures, and leaves heal. This is the same river David saw: "There is a river whose streams make glad the city of God" (Ps. 46:4).

In John's heavenly vision, he wrote, "Then the angel showed me the river of the water of life, as clear as crystal flowing from the throne of

154

God and of the Lamb" (Rev. 22:1). Yes, this river flows from the throne, but it comes from the One upon the throne. Jesus—the Lamb of God—is the source of the river of God. He is the fountainhead. He is the headwaters. He is the reservoir. He is the container of all true revival flowing down from heaven to earth.

Sadly, today some people try to dismiss the idea of a genuine heaven-sent revival by labeling it "revivalism," as though revival is a force to dismiss.[5] But revival is not a force or a power. Revival, says Robert Coleman of Wheaton College, "is breathing in the breath of God." Revival means "to wake up and live."[6] Revival is the presence of Christ Himself. It is the fullness of His Spirit in our midst. Revival is His arrival.

Martyn Lloyd-Jones describes revival as "a consciousness of the presence of God literally in the midst of the people....Suddenly those who are present in the meeting are aware that someone has come amongst them, they are aware of a glory, they are aware of a presence." He continues, "Sometimes they describe it as 'days of heaven on earth'....God has come down amongst them and has filled the place and the people with a sense of his glorious presence."[7] That's why I say, "Revival is His arrival."

Sometimes, however, people can get so caught up with revival that they forget the source of revival. We enjoy the feeling, but we fail to focus on the One from whom the glory flows. In heaven the Lamb of God is the central focus, the shining lamp (Rev. 21:23), the source of this rushing river (Rev. 22:1). May we never forget—revival flows down from the side of the Lamb. That's why it's the message of the Lamb and the cross that will keep the river flowing and the winds and fires of revival burning.

JONATHAN EDWARDS AND REVIVAL

I want to take you back to a time in America's history when revival broke out in Jonathan Edwards' church. This is the story of how it all happened.

Showers of divine blessings broke over the little church in Northampton like a refreshing spring rain. Jonathan Edwards, the pastor, had just preached a sermon as though standing in the presence of God. When he finished his sermon, what he saw took his breath away. He wrote, "Then it was, in the latter part of December (1734) that the Spirit of God began extraordinarily to set in, and wonderfully to work among us."[8]

God seemed suddenly to open people's eyes to the fullness of Christ, and they broke into laughter or tears "issuing like a flood and intermingling with a loud weeping." They sometimes cried out loud for sheer joy at a view of the glory of God's sovereignty. The conversion of lost souls was "astonishing," said Edwards, as people flocked to Jesus Christ. When the story of a sinner's conversion was heard, it was as though a dart of conviction pierced people's hearts and they too were saved."[9]

"The whole town seemed to be full of the presence of God," said Edwards, and soon the revival began spreading to several small towns around Northampton. Taverns emptied and people thronged the church or the pastor's home. One lady, though she knew the Bible well, became overwhelmed by a sight of what Jesus did for her on the cross. She wept and wept over her own ungratefulness for what Jesus did on the cross until people thought she was dying. Others had a view of the excellency of His dying love, seeing Christ on the cross with the blood flowing down from His wounds.[10]

Edwards told the story of a four-year-old girl, whose mother heard her crying out loudly in her closet, praying for her own salvation. Finally, she ceased crying and came out smiling, "Mother, the kingdom of heaven is come to me!" After that, she would often burst into tears, praying for the salvation of her sisters, fearing they would go to hell. During family prayers she would often cry out about her love for Christ and God and how much the Lord loved her. She was eager to go to church "to hear Mr. Edwards preach," she told her mother.[11]

Revivals of this intensity were practically unheard of in those days, and Edwards knew it was important to record the story of the revival for others to read. He told the story in a little book called *A Faithful Narrative of Surprising Conversions*, which had a tremendous impact around the world and prepared the way for the Great Awakening in America and Great Britain.[12]

GOD IS ALWAYS MOVING

I've already mentioned the time when the river was receding from the Brownsville Revival, and the Lord said to my broken heart: "My river still rushes!" Those four words spoke volumes. They told me that God is still pouring out His river of revival from heaven, even when revival seems to be ending in a certain local. They reminded me that indeed there is a river flowing down from the heart of the Lamb and His river will never run dry.

His words took me back to Ezekiel's ever-rushing river. The river of God in Ezekiel's vision doesn't grow shallower as it pours out; it flows deeper until it streams "ankle deep," then "knee-deep," then "up to the waist," and finally it becomes "deep enough to swim in—a river that no one could cross" (Ezek. 47:3–5). I believe this speaks of the river of revival, flowing down from the side of the Lamb, which will someday flood the whole earth with the glory of the Lamb as the waters cover the seas.

And yet, because so many revivals have had false starts or shaky foundations, many people today have become disillusioned with revival. I do not believe it is ever God's perfect will for the river to cease or the fire of revival to smoke out. Ezekiel's vision of the river deepened as it flowed. And looking at the metaphor of fire, God said, "The fire must be kept burning on the altar continuously; it must not go out" (Lev. 6:13). In my book *The Unquenchable Flame* I wrote:

> God doesn't tease us with His glory; He urges us to move from "glory to glory" (2 Cor. 3:18). His glory doesn't decrease, it increases for "of the increase of His government and peace there shall be no end" (Isa. 9:7)….God doesn't send the dove of His Spirit down to quickly flit away. He wants His Holy Spirit to remain like He did on Jesus: "I saw the Spirit come down from heaven as a dove and remain on Him" (John 1:32). Indeed, it is not God's will for His river to cease, His glory to depart, His fire to burn out, or His dove to take wing. God intends for revival to come down and remain.[13]

Because of those four words, "My river still rushes," I realized that God doesn't shut down revival. People do, but it's not because God has quit moving. Jesus said, "My Father is always at his work to this very day, and I, too, am working" (John 5:17). Yes, God's river still rushes, regardless of what we humans do about it.

That's when I decided to keep on lifting the Lamb, keep on pouring this message into hungry students, and keep on taking teams to the nations. I have never regretted that decision, for God has never stopped pouring out His river of glory and revival. And when God's river is allowed to freely flow, nothing can keep the fruit from growing along the river.

FRUIT FLOURISHES BY THE RIVER

Through the years I've watched tremendous fruit produced from students who clung to the cross and soaked daily in the river. It's just like Ezekiel said:

> Fruit trees of all kinds will grow on both banks of the river. Their leaves will not wither nor will their fruit fail. Every month they will bear, because the water from the sanctuary flows to them. Their fruit will serve for food and their leaves for healing
> —EZEKIEL 47:12

Some beautiful fruit happened in young Sophie's life. Sophie was only seventeen when she came from England to our Glory of the Lamb Internship in Alabama. Shy and somewhat reserved, she began to see the depths of what Jesus endured for her on the cross, and she was undone. She began pressing into God with all her heart and soul and strength. Sometimes I would see her laid out on the carpet in our chapel, crying out to God, asking Him to take the sword of the cross and cut the scales that veiled her eyes. Soon Sophie was taking this passion for the Lamb into Kenya, East Africa.

One day Sophie walked up a hot dusty road in Kisumu, Kenya, when she saw a group of boys sniffing glue near the garbage dumps. She began telling them about God's Son who hung on a cross. She told them how He took their pain and shame and guilt. She described to them Jesus, taking their punishment for sin, drinking the Father's cup of wrath and hell which they deserve. Then she offered them the greatest gift she could give them. She asked them to pray and receive Jesus Christ into their hearts. Right there beside a stinking garbage dump, these boys began to pray and repent and receive Jesus. It was hearing about the Father's cup—about a Savior who took their place and was punished for them—that opened their hearts. This is what I call fruit.

But Sophie is just like you. A few years ago she was shy and introverted; but when the Lamb pierced her heart, out flowed a river of passion. You see, rivers that don't pour out become swamps. When we receive the gospel but never give it away, something inside us stagnates. We must share Jesus with others if we want the river to keep on flowing. It's just like Ezekiel wrote, "Where the river flows everything will live," but wherever the river doesn't flow, everything turns to "swamps and marshes" (47:9, 11).

HEAR THE SOUND

I stood one day at the closest point possible to the overflowing waters of Niagara Falls. The waters crashed down with sublime and magnificent force. In fact, this is why natives originally named the falls *Onguiaahra,* meaning "great thunderer of waters."[14]

As I soaked in the spray of the falls, I thought of the river of God rushing down from the side of the Lamb. Powerful. Majestic. Indescribably beautiful. Yet the waters never cease flowing. Even now the river of life tumbles from the heart of the Lamb, rushing out through the courts of heaven, coursing down to planet earth.

So listen. Can you hear it? Can you see the moisture dancing in the air? Can you feel the warmth on your face or in your hands? Can you sense the electricity charging the atmosphere? It's the radiant river of God that flows from the heart of the Lamb. For Jesus is the source, the reservoir, the divine container of the river of God. Drink your fill of these refreshing streams; but with every touch of His power, with every sip of the stream, every taste of joy, never forget—it all flows down from the wounded heart of the Lamb.

You see, this is the open secret. This is the mystery of the cross: that God would pour His cup of wrath upon His Son until His heart ruptured open and poured out a river. Now this river of God rushes down to those who are thirsty for Him.

So drink your fill of this ever-rushing river. Soak your theology, your teachings, your understanding of Scripture in these refreshing streams. Let streams of His glory wash over your heart until it is fully undone by a revelation of the Lamb.

CHAPTER 12 ENDNOTES

1. Spurgeon said, "Oh the kindness in the heart of Christ, that did not only for a blow return a kiss, but for a spear thrust returned streams of life and healing!" (Charles Haddon Spurgeon, "On the Cross after Death," *Spurgeon's Expository Encyclopedia*, vol. 4 (Grand Rapids, MI: Baker Book House, 1977), 361). In another beautiful sermon he writes, "If all the rivers of love did run together, they could not fill such an ocean of love as was in the heart of Jesus the Saviour....The pierced heart of Christ is a load-stone (magnet) to draw all other hearts" (Charles Spurgeon, "Marvelous Magnet," *The Power of the Cross of Christ*, 20).

2. Charles Haddon Spurgeon, "The Water and the Blood," *Spurgeon's Expository Encyclopedia*, vol. 4 (Grand Rapids, MI: Baker Book House, 1977), 345.

3. Dutch Sheets, *The River of God* (Ventura, CA: Renew, 1998), 38.

4. Ibid., 33.

5. Beware when you hear critics tag "ism" on the end of something from God (for example, revivalism). This has a way of belittling God's work in an attempt to use the age old trick called "label and dismiss."

6. Robert E. Coleman, "What is Revival?" *Accounts of a Campus Revival*, Timothy K. Beougher and Lyle Dorsett, eds. (Wheaton, IL: Harold Shaw Publishers, 1995), 13–14.

7. Ibid., 306.

8. Jonathan Edwards, *A Faithful Narrative of Surprising Conversions: Jonathan Edwards on Revival* (Edinburgh: The Banner of Truth Trust, 1995), 12.

9. Ibid., 12, 14–15.

10. Ibid., 21, 23, 51.

11. Ibid., 64–66.

12. You'll read how *A Faithful Narrative of Surprising Conversions* influenced John Wesley and the Evangelical Awakening in Britain in the next chapter. From 1737–1739 Edwards' little book went through three editions and twenty printings, which was remarkable for that day.

13. Sandy Kirk, *The Unquenchable Flame*, 20.

14. Joan Colgan Stortz, *Niagara Falls* (Markham, ON: Irving Westorf and Company, Ltd., 1994), 2.

Chapter 13

THE RISEN LAMB

The Glory of Christ Floods the Tomb

PAUSE NOW TO take in the scene at Calvary. It will take your breath away. Jesus hangs lifeless upon a cross. Rain drizzles down across His body. The crowd has thinned except for the soldiers and a few of Jesus' followers. Mary, His mother, stands weeping in the arms of the young disciple John.

GOD'S MASTERPIECE

Look up at Jesus. This is God's Masterpiece, painted in blood and floodlit with glory. Oh, I can't get over it, and I pray I never will! From omnipotence to impotent weakness on two slabs of wood. From omnipresence to being spiked to one spot on a hill. From omniscience to not knowing why He was forsaken. From eternal, undying, uncreated self-existence, to dying as a Man. From being clothed with divine glory, to the bloody shreds of wounded flesh.[1]

That's why we may spend a lifetime in a seminary library, searching for deep insights into the attributes of God, but never will we see them more simply and eloquently revealed than at Calvary. Words could not express the inexpressible so God displayed them on a hill called Golgotha. He demonstrated them on two strips of timber. He inscribed them on the tablet of His own Son's flesh. Spurgeon said, "O heart of God, I see you nowhere as at Golgotha, where the Word incarnate reveals the justice and love, the holiness and tenderness of God in one blaze of glory."[2]

Yes, here on this windswept hill called Calvary, it's as though the Father dipped His brush into the blood of His own Son. With tender touches of mercy and blazing strokes of judgment, He painted His love on the canvas of His own Son's flesh. He raised Him up on the easel of the cross. Displayed Him in the gallery of Golgotha. Pulled back the veil and thundered,

> *"This is my son! Behold the one who laid down his life as a lamb! He is forever my masterpiece!"*[3]

THE EMPTY CROSS

Watch now as soldiers pry the spikes from His hands and feet, then lower His body to the arms of Joseph of Arimathea. Suddenly the drizzle stops. Black clouds scatter. Golden shafts of light streak across the western sky. A hush settles over the land.

A soft breeze drifts over the hillside. The pungent scent of the earth after a fresh rain permeates the air. The smoky aroma of the evening sacrifice at three o'clock wafts through the vale. A bird sings. A snake slithers out from under a rock, as though it's been in hiding.

Jesus' body has been removed for burial, but there in the distance, rising like a sun-splashed mountain peak against a velvet blue Jerusalem sky, is the empty cross. The cross is the place where the most monumental work of all time has now been accomplished. This is indeed God's Masterpiece. It is the quintessence of God's redemptive plan on earth, for this is where the Son laid down His life as a Lamb.

However, it's not about two stakes of wood. It's about a Person. It's about the risen Lamb, still bearing wounds from His sacrifice.

So let's go now to that garden where Jesus has been buried. Let's dare to look inside the tomb at the corpse of Jesus laid out on the slab. Imagine now what the Father would feel as He looks down on His Son.

DIVINE ANTICIPATION

This is His one and only precious Son, laid out on a cold stone slab. This is the One He held in face-to-face communion in *"the bosom of God"* (John 1:18, KJV) through all eternity. This is the One whose glory flooded infinitude, around whose throne angelic beings worshiped and adored.

With tender emotion He recalls when He turned to His Son before the creation of the world and said, "Son, I want a family! I want to give

You a bride!" Then He paused, holding back deep emotion. "But this will require a fathomless sacrifice. Son, You must lay down Your life as a lamb!"

Then one day His Beloved laid aside His robes of glory and turned to leave His presence in the Triune Godhead. The Father must have reached out and held Him closely, never wanting to let Him go. Then He stood back and watched as His Son walked right out of His glorious throne room and into a virgin's dark womb.

Now as the Father looks down on His dead Son, His body stiff and cold in a borrowed tomb, I'm sure He trembles with anticipation. A raw ache pulses in His heart from the grief of pouring His undiluted wrath and judgment upon His innocent Son. Nothing so wrenched the Father's heart as those three hours of absolute horror when the Son bore His Father's wrath against sin.

Even more, Abba's heart still throbs from the pain of His Son's tortured cry, *"My God, my God, why have you forsaken me?"* No human mind, no angel in heaven, no seraph or elder or created being can ever comprehend what it meant to the Father to rip open His heart and give His own Son as a Lamb. This cry of terror from the lips of His Son, wounded His heart forever.

And now, as He looks down on His Beloved, holy expectancy fills Him, for He knows He is getting ready to raise His Son from the dead. Surely the prayer of Jesus pounds in His heart: "Now Father, glorify me in your presence with the glory I had with you before the world began" (John 17:5). Oh, how the Father yearns for His Son to return to His eternal glory in the Triune Godhead. Most of all, He longs to hold Him close once more.

But it's not just the Father. It's the Holy Spirit, too, who looks on with deep emotion. The feelings of the Holy Spirit run deep, for He is not a force. He is a Person. He is God, equal with the Father and the Son. He is the One in the Godhead who especially possesses such extravagant tenderness. His feelings are exquisitely delicate. The Bible compares Him to a dove because He is gentle, and sensitive, and easily grieved.

Can you imagine the emotion the Holy Spirit must feel? This is the One He has always loved. Infinitely, eternally, everlastingly He has loved the Son with a love beyond human comprehension.

He was there at the covenant of redemption before creation, so He has always known that the Son would lay down His life as a Lamb. He filled Him at His baptism and walked with Him through the days of His flesh. He watched as the soldier's scourge gutted His human body and left Him in bloody shreds. He saw the precious blood of God streaming from His wounds. How He longed to run to Him, to embrace Him, and to protect Him from this excruciating pain, but He could not.

He looked on as soldiers crushed thorns into His brow, spit in His face, and mocked Him. He saw them hammer His hands and feet to two strips of timber and then lift His naked body before the eyes of strangers. How He wanted to draw near and shield Him from their leering eyes. How He yearned to wipe away the blood and spit and tears from the face of the One He had always loved, but He could not.

And when He saw the filthy sin of all humanity pouring down upon Him…When He saw the heavens open and the Father roar down His violent wrath upon Him, He was shattered. As the Son hung writhing in horror on the cross, the Holy Spirit stood back moaning and weeping, rolling and convulsing in unthinkable grief.

Even more, when He heard that hideous cry, "My God, my God, why have you forsaken me?" He was utterly *undone*. He knew that cry was not only for the Father. It was a cry of forsakenness meant for Him as well. He is the Comforter. He is the One who comes alongside and protects and shields and loves. Oh, how He longed to run to His Beloved and wrap Him in His comforting arms, but He could not. This was a mission planned in the great covenant of redemption before the world's creation. But now, at last, the time has come for the Son to return to the glory He had before creation. With a heart full of joy, the Father turns to the Holy Spirit and commissions Him to go and raise His Son from the dead.

GLORY FLOODS THE TOMB

In the early hours of the third day,[4] while darkness still pervades the land, suddenly the leaves of the almond trees begin to rustle. A wind blows into the garden. Olive leaves stir and gleam in the brightness of this supernatural current, for it's not a wind at all. It's the Person of the Holy Spirit, breezing into the garden like a gust of heavenly wind.

Toward the rock-hewn grave He rushes. Reaching the boulder which blocks the entrance, He whiffs through the rock and enters the tomb. Now He hesitates, looking down on the corpse of the One He loves, laid out on the stone slab.

Hovering over the bruised and broken body of Jesus, He waits. Even as He hovered over Mary like an overshadowing "haze of brilliancy" (see Luke 1:35), now He overshadows the corpse of Jesus.

There lies Jesus, stiff and lifeless. No breath in His body. No blood flowing through His veins. No heartbeat in the chest of this One He loves. Now the Holy Spirit—the *Rûach Ha Kodesh*, the breath or wind of God—trembles over the body of the Lamb. He has ached for this moment. Closer He draws to the body of the Son, waiting for the Father's command...

"Now, Holy Spirit!" shouts the Father, with emotion bursting in His heart. "Raise My Son to life!"

With a mighty rush, the Holy Spirit sweeps into the lifeless frame of the Lamb. His presence floods Jesus' spirit, then His soul, then His body. Glory pumps through every vein. The breath of God fills every part of His being.

Now Jesus' heart begins to beat. He catches His breath and air fills His lungs. Oxygen surges through His body. Strength pours into His muscles. His eyelids flicker and He opens wide His eyes. Slowly now He rises, lifting out of the grave clothes that wrapped His body. These clothes, deprived now of their body, sink in as if by the suction of a vacuum.

Jesus stands upright, for now the "Dayspring from on high" (Luke 1:78, NKJV) sheds forth His brilliant rays. The "Sun of righteousness" rises "with healing in His wings and His beams" (Mal. 4:2, AMP). Now the "Light of the world" (John 8:12) spreads His radiance through the rock-hewn grave.

The rarefied air in the tomb is thick with the presence of God. Jesus' face shines like the morning sunrise. Because the veil of Jesus' body has been torn on the cross, the glory behind the veil of His own flesh has been released. He simply breathes out and glory floods the whole tomb.

Omnipotence now flows from these hands once riveted to a cross. Omniscience streams from this "sacred head sore wounded." And from this heart once ruptured at Calvary, pours floods and floods and floods of resurrection power. Like the spray of an erupting geyser, like a spring of living waters, bubbling and rising from the heart of the earth, resurrection glory erupts from the heart of the Lamb.

Yes, like the rock struck by Moses' rod to pour out rivers of water, the Rock of Christ has been struck by the rod of God's wrath, pouring out rivers of life. The river was released from its reservoir at Calvary, but now the floodtide pours out. It is the river of God, filled with resurrection power, issuing from its source in the heart of the Lamb. Now the *glory of the Lamb* floods the atmosphere of the tomb.

I can envision the angels attending the glory falling backwards, trembling under "the power outflowing from His resurrection" (Phil. 3:10, AMP). They surely must cover their eyes from the brilliance, for this is the resurrection power of God, now released from its storehouse in the heart of the Lamb.

When at last the angels recover, they quietly roll away the stone. This is not so Jesus can come out, for He could walk right through the stone; it's for the women and the disciples so they can see that the tomb indeed is empty. Jesus Christ has risen!

UNDERSTANDING THE RESURRECTION

The resurrection of Christ shines floodlights on the work of the Lamb. It is the grand display of His finished work on the cross. Though some mistakenly say, "The cross is the place of defeat; the resurrection is the place of victory," John R. W. Stott corrects this misconception. In his book *The Cross of Christ,* he writes, "We are not to regard the cross as defeat and the resurrection as the victory. Rather, the cross was the victory won, and the resurrection the victory endorsed, proclaimed and demonstrated."[5]

Bob Sorge, one of my favorite authors, explains, "His shed blood purchased the provision of redemption. His resurrection released those provisions to this earth."[6] Another of my favorites, John Piper, says, "The resurrection was the *reward* and *vindication* of Christ's achievement in death." "It was the public declaration of God's endorsement. This He gave by raising Him from the dead."[7]

Leon Morris, a profound scholar of our day, writes, "Some modern writers put such emphasis on the resurrection that the cross appears as little more than a necessary preliminary. The two should not be separated. They should appear together. But we should not forget that if they are separated, the New Testament puts the emphasis on the cross."[8] This is why Paul said, "God forbid that I should glory save in the cross of the Lord Jesus Christ" (Gal. 6:14, KJV).

Yes, the resurrection is the greatest demonstration of glory ever released upon this earth. It is the most magnificent display of the power of the cross ever shown upon this planet. It is God's grand announcement, for He "was declared with power to be the Son of God by his resurrection from the dead" (Rom. 1:4). Through the glory of the resurrection, the Father was indeed declaring:

> *This is My Son! He has always existed by My side! He is My eternal Lamb, and I have raised Him from the dead!*

Often I've heard preachers, after telling a mythical story about Christ suffering in hell, proclaim with booming conviction, "Jesus conquered death and the devil by rising from the grave!" The congregation always bursts into applause, and my heart sinks, for the Bible says, "By His death he might destroy him who holds the power of death—that is, the devil" (Heb. 2:14). And again, "Having disarmed the powers and authorities, he made a public spectacle of them, triumphing over them by the cross" (Col. 2:15).[9]

Thus a more biblical way to say it would be, "Jesus *proved* that He had conquered death and the devil on the cross when He rose from the grave!"[10] John Stott explains, "The resurrection did not achieve our deliverance from sin and death, but has brought us an assurance of both."[11]

The reason, however, that so many preachers today don't fully understand the power of the cross is because they haven't looked into the Father's cup. But once we've gazed with trembling heart at the judgment of God roaring down like a fire on the Lamb, our eyes open and we understand that the work was done on Calvary.

Erich Sauer writes, "The cross is the greatest event in the history of salvation, greater even than the resurrection. The cross is the victory, the resurrection is the triumph, but the victory is more important than the triumph, although the latter necessarily follows from it."[12]

Indeed, we will never understand the heights of the resurrection if we don't know the depths of the crucifixion.[13] This is why the New Testament writers put such emphasis on the cross. This was John the Baptist's highest message: "Behold the Lamb of God who takes away the sin of the world" (John 1:29, KJV). The apostle Paul boasted in the cross above all else: "May I never boast except in the cross of our Lord Jesus Christ" (Gal. 6:14). The apostle John, after gazing into heaven and seeing the Lamb twenty-nine times, gloried above all else in the slain Lamb of God (Rev. 5:6). And the holy angels are so captivated by the slain Lamb that all they can do is cry, "Worthy is the Lamb!" (Rev. 5:9, 12).

Some, however, may argue, "But Jesus isn't still on a cross!" Your response to them is simple: No, He's not still on the cross, but He's the risen Lamb on the throne, still bearing wounds from His sacrifice.

This is why, when we speak of "the Lamb," we mean both the crucified and resurrected Jesus. But the reason God reveals Him twenty-nine times as a Lamb, who still bears scars, is because He wants us to remember what He did for us. He wants us to always keep focused on the risen, wounded, glorious Lamb of God!

RESURRECTION POWER FOR MINISTRY

What then is this resurrection power, which Paul speaks of in the Bible? Paul said, "I want to know Christ and the power of his resurrection and the fellowship of sharing in his sufferings" (Phil. 3:10). What is this "power of his resurrection," or the "power outflowing from his resurrection," as the Amplified Version puts it?

Resurrection power is first of all—the power to overcome sin, purchased in the finished work of the cross. It is also the power to overcome Satan in Christ's completed work. And it is the power for ministry. Grudem explains:

> This new resurrection power in us includes power to *gain more and more victory over remaining sin* in our lives—"sin will have no dominion over you" (Rom. 6:14; cf. 1 Cor. 15:17)—even though we will never be perfect in this life. The resurrection

power also includes *power for ministry in the work of the kingdom.* It was after his resurrection that Jesus promised his disciples, "You shall receive power when the Holy Spirit has come upon you; and you shall be my witnesses in Jerusalem and in all Judea and in Samaria, and to the end of the earth" (Acts 1:8). This new, intensified power for proclaiming the gospel and working miracles and triumphing over the opposition of the enemy was given to the disciples after Christ's resurrection from the dead and was part of the new resurrection power that characterized their Christian lives.[14]

And this "power outflowing from his resurrection" (Phil. 3:10, AMP) is for all believers. It should not be relegated to a certain segment of the church. Jesus died to give it to us and the whole New Testament proves it.

Through the years, I've seen many students carrying this power for ministry. They were not high powered evangelists, just humble young adults who loved Jesus and believed His Word. It's like the time I sat in church in Peterborough, England, watching Sophie, Jessie, and Whitney pour out their passion for the Lamb, preaching from the depths of their being. Earlier that day we had joined Pastor Jon and Kisha Featherstone's Rock Church in feeding the homeless and preaching the cross to them.

Twenty men prayed to receive Jesus, but most were immigrants from Slovakia, unable to speak English. Yet they sat on the edge of their chairs, drinking in every word as these young women preached passionately in a language they didn't know. They couldn't understand English, but they did understand the language of the heart, streaming out with burning passion. When we concluded with a prayer tunnel, these broken men stumbled through the tunnel, with tears washing down their faces. The resurrection power of God exploded through the sanctuary, and one young man, in severe pain from a freshly broken arm, said in broken English, "Arm feels nice!"

Fourteen-year-old Candice and sixteen-year-old Gisell spent a month of their summer at our Internship in Alabama. When they returned to their youth group in California, they both preached on the power of the cross and the cup. Their youth leader told me, "The power of God came down on everyone like a blanket. Youth and parents were weeping over the cross!"

Mary and I were preaching in a conference in Taiwan where the people were desperately hungry to hear about the cup. Dr. Chan, leader of the huge Asian network, was deeply impacted by the message of the Father's cup. He urged the people to receive, and when we prayed, the resurrection power swept in so hard that people were knocked back, one man sliding backward up the aisle.

A few years later, we were preaching in a similar Taiwanese meeting with Dr. Chan in California. With only five minutes to minister (because several baptisms had already been scheduled to follow), we urged the people to call upon God and ask for His fire to fall. And believe me it did! People began shaking and crying out as the fire hit them without anyone touching them.

One day twenty-four-year old Sophie accompanied a few Kenyan pastors into the village where they all preached the power of the blood, the fire of the cross, and the depth of the Father's cup. People ran to the altar to get saved, and the fire of God began falling on them. Sophie emailed me:

> Oh, Doccie [my nickname], it's EXPLODING here in Kenya! We preached the cross and people started giving their lives to the Lord with MASS deliverance taking place. People began running away from the service because they were demon possessed. We called FIRE on the people who were running away, and they began falling to the ground, manifesting demons until they were set FREE!

This fire we are talking about is "the power outflowing from His resurrection." It is the resurrection glory. It pours from the heart of the Lamb opened up on the cross. It's not weird or flakey. It's real and it brings people into a genuine encounter with God. These are only some of the stories, and I cannot express to you the joy this gives me as Jesus receives the reward of His suffering.

God wants to use you in this way as well. I'm sure you already have this resurrection power, but He wants to give you a greater intensity. This is what is meant by a baptism of "the Holy Spirit and fire" (Luke 3:16). It's the fire that comes from the finished work of the cross. And it comes from allowing the cross to do a deep, deep work inside you. It comes from meditating on the Father's cup until God ignites your heart and you are absolutely undone by a revelation of the Lamb.

Chapter 13 Endnotes

1. Jesus laid down the independent exercise of His transcendent attributes—His omnipotence (which means all powerful), His omnipresence (which means being all places at all times), His omniscience (which means all knowing), His self-existence (which means eternally existing within Himself). He lay these glorious perfections aside to become a Lamb!
2. Charles Spurgeon, "Mourning at the Sight of the Crucified," 192.
3. This section was taken from my book *The Masterpiece*, (Hagerstown, MD: McDougal Publishing, 2005).
4. How can I say "the third day"? Let me explain: The Jewish day ends at sunset and a new day begins, so Jesus was placed in the grave while it was still daylight on Friday—*Day One*. As the sun set and the Sabbath began, this was *Day Two*, which ended at sunset on Saturday. As the sun went down on Saturday, *Day Three* began. Jesus rose sometime between sunset on Saturday and sunrise on Sunday, which was the *Third Day*. In fact, the reason Christians celebrate the Lord's Day (Sunday) instead of the Sabbath on Saturday, is because Jesus was in the grave all during the Sabbath. This was the end of Saturday as our day of worship.
5. John Stott, *The Cross of Christ*, 235.
6. Bob Sorge, *The Power of the Blood*, 109.
7. John Piper, *Fifty Reasons Why Jesus Came to Die*.
8. Leon Morris, *The Cross in the New Testament*, 382, fn.
9. When Jesus rose from the dead, He had a new kind of human body, a body which reveals what our new bodies will be like. Wayne Grudem explains: "Christ's resurrection was not simply coming back from the dead, as had been experienced by others before, such as Lazarus (John 11:1–44), for then Jesus would have been subject to weakness and aging and eventually would have died again just as all other human beings die. Rather, when He rose from the dead, Jesus was the "first fruits" (1 Cor. 15:20, 23) of a new kind of human life, a life in which his body was made perfect, no longer subject to weakness, aging, or death, but able to live eternally" (Wayne Grudem, *Systematic Theology*, 608–609). The reason "it was impossible for death to keep its hold on

him" (Acts 2:24) was because He had already destroyed the power of
death on the cross.

10. John Stott, *The Cross of Christ,* 239.

11. Erich Sauer writes, "The cross is the greatest event in the history of
salvation, greater even than the resurrection. The cross is the victory,
the resurrection is the triumph, but the victory is more important than
the triumph, although the latter necessarily follows from it. The resurrection is the public display of the victory, the triumph of the Crucified
One. But the victory itself was complete. 'It is finished!' (John 19:30)."
(Erich Sauer, *The Triumph of the Crucified One,* [London: 1951], 32);
cited in Leon Morris, *The Cross in the New Testament,* 383 fn).

12. But please—never underestimate the power of the resurrection of
Christ. It is the hope of every Christian. It is proof positive that Jesus
Christ is alive forever. It also proves that, like His body, our own
bodies will be raised from the grave: "Christ has indeed been raised
from the dead, the first fruits of those who have fallen asleep....For as
in Adam all die, so in Christ all will be made alive" (1 Cor. 15:20, 22).
The grand hope is this: Christ has risen so that we can live with Him
eternally!

13. Wayne Grudem, *Systematic Theology,* 614–615.

Chapter 14

RESURRECTING *the* LOST LAMB

"They Have Taken Away My Lord."

DARKNESS STILL SHROUDS the land as she rises from her pallet, slips out of the house, and steals up the pathway to the garden where her Lord is buried. Incredibly, the greatest Man who ever lived, who healed the sick, raised the dead, and was followed by multitudes, had only a few attending His funeral. Her heart aches heavily with grief. How she will roll away the stone, she doesn't know, but she must get there to anoint His body.

Finally, she reaches the tomb, but what she sees causes her to gasp. The stone is already rolled away! Cautiously, fearfully, her heart hammering with heavy strokes, she tiptoes into the tomb and her heart sinks. The tomb is empty!

As fast as she can run, she races to the house where Peter and John sleep. Banging on the door, she bursts into the room and cries, "They have taken the Lord out of the tomb, and we don't know where they have put him!" (John 20:2).

Peter and John run to the tomb, but when they don't find him, they return to the house. Mary Magdalene, however, won't give up. She comes back to the garden again, still looking for Jesus. She stands outside the tomb, weeping: "As she wept, she bent over to look into the tomb and saw two angels in white, seated where Jesus' body had been, one at the head and one at the foot. They asked her, 'Woman, why are you crying?'" She responded again, "They have taken my Lord away...and I don't know where they have put him" (John 20:11–13).

Something about these words, spoken from a desperate, yearning, sincere heart, must have drawn the Lord's attention; for the Bible says, "At this, she turned around and saw Jesus standing there" (John 20:14–15). Then He whispered her name—*Mary*—and she knew at last she had found Him. "Rabboni!" she cried and fell on her knees at His feet. In that moment of awe and wonder, while weeping at His nail scarred feet, I'm sure Mary Magdalene was undone by a revelation of the Lamb.

However, please notice this—of all the people who followed Jesus, of all His disciples, of all the other women—it was Mary Magdalene who was allowed to see Him first. How could this be? Not only was she a woman, but she came from a scarred and sordid past. In fact, she was so steeped in sin that Jesus had cast seven demons out of her (see Luke 8:2). Yet, she was the one, above all others, whom Jesus chose as the first to announce the glory of the resurrection! She was the first herald of the risen Lamb!

Why was she chosen? I believe it's because she wouldn't give up. She refused to stop seeking Jesus. She had to find the Lamb. Love compelled her. She couldn't let Him go, and Jesus saw her hunger. She found Him when He saw her heart as she cried with deep emotion, "They have taken my Lord away…and I don't know where they have put him!"

THEY'VE TAKEN AWAY THE LAMB

I think I know a little of what Mary Magdalene felt, for I have often felt: "They have taken away the Lamb, and I don't know where they have laid Him!"

For almost three decades now I've been teaching and writing on the cross, the Father's cup, and the Lamb. For years the response of many leaders in my own Charismatic and Pentecostal realm seemed to be, "It's time to move beyond the cross, on to resurrection power!" Because I had sunk my roots deep into the works of Jonathan Edwards and the Puritans, with their rich biblical theology, and because I had experienced such a deep encounter with God at the cross, I knew something about this wasn't quite right. My heart ached with an indescribable longing to see Jesus glorified as the Lamb.

One of my first disappointments was when a potential publisher of my first book sat me down, looked in my eyes, and snarled, "You made me sick! You made me look at the blood and wounds of Jesus, and I'm repulsed!" I was devastated, but I refused to quit. I couldn't imagine how the Father could allow His Son's sacrifice as the Lamb, which is so honored in heaven, to be so neglected on earth. I felt: "They've taken away the Lamb and I don't know where they've laid Him."

I began working on a master's in theology and then a Ph.D. It's not that I craved a title or a higher degree, but I thought maybe then people would listen to my heart's cry for the Lamb. Like Mary Magdalene, the men wouldn't listen to her because she was a woman, and in my generation that is sometimes still true.

In seminary, however, I had some interesting experiences. I've already told you about the professor who said, "It wouldn't have mattered if Jesus had died of a heart attack!" At the time, once again, I felt: "They've taken away the Lamb and I don't know where they've laid Him." I was desperately hungry to see the Son glorified as the Lamb.

There were, of course, some professors at Fuller Seminary who were brilliant on the cross. One day one of my professors, Dr. Collin Brown, beautifully described the wrath Jesus endured on the cross, and then he humbly said, "I guess I swim upstream against the current of most liberal theologians today." I raised my hand and cried, passion trembling in my voice, "No Sir, you swim in the stream of the apostle Paul who said, 'May I never boast except in the cross of our Lord Jesus Christ' (Gal. 6:14)' who said, 'I resolved to know nothing while I was with you except Jesus Christ and him crucified!' (1 Cor. 2:2); and who said, 'The message of the cross...is the power of God' (1 Cor. 1:18)!" The whole class burst into applause, affirming my words and the professor's teaching.

Yet, still my heart ached to see the atonement of Christ central again. I continued to feel: "They've taken away the Lamb and I don't know where they've laid Him." During this time I felt so alone in my pursuit of the cross; but one day I walked into a renewal meeting at Harvest Rock Church in Pasadena. Jill Austin was preaching on the cross, and I was stunned. I hadn't heard anyone preach the cross in years. I sat there weeping as I heard Jill say these striking words:

> The best kept secret in the universe is the mystery of the cross.
> If you understand the mystery of the cross, you understand the
> mystery of the outpouring of God....By understanding the blood
> and the cross, it's an entryway to the Lord. As soon as you talk

about the cross and the blood, glories come, angels come, heaven opens because they love the cross.

Years later I received a note from Jill's assistant, telling me that she keeps my little book *The Glory of the Lamb* on her night stand by her bed and weeps over it as she reads. Jill has gone on to be with the Lord, but her memory will always be with me as one who encouraged me in the cross when I really needed it.

After seminary, as I've mentioned, I uprooted from Texas and started a revival camp near the Brownsville Revival in Pensacola. Soon I was teaching seven courses at the Brownsville Revival School of Ministry (BRSM); but still, the ache in my heart continued. Often I would walk through the prayer garden at our camp, crying out to God:

> *Oh, Father, this is Your Son! When will You unveil to Your people the magnitude of Your Son's sacrifice? I feel it so deeply, but I know Your heart must ache so much more! Please honor Your Son as a Lamb on earth even as He is honored in heaven!*

Once, while I was teaching in a Bible college, one of the leaders of the school called me into his office and said, "I don't want you teaching anymore on the cross." It was true that I made the cross of Jesus the foundation of every course I taught, but I was teaching a New Testament survey course at the time. I didn't know how I could teach the class without telling about the sacrifice of Jesus. My heart broke, and I knew the Holy Spirit was grieved. Once again, I felt: "They have taken away my Lord—the Lamb of God—and I don't know where they've laid Him!" Yet still, I refused to give up.

Another time a leader said, "There's no new revelation of the Lamb!" He didn't say it to my face, so I couldn't respond, but I wanted to say, "Of course there's no new revelation of the Lamb. This is not new at all, but as old as the Bible." Actually the revelation of the Lamb is older than time itself, for Jesus offered Himself as a slain Lamb before the creation of time and space. In fact, the word *revelation*, *apokalypsis*, means "an unveiling of what has already been revealed in Scripture."[1] So a revelation of the Lamb is simply an unveiling of Jesus from the Bible.

That's why it meant so much to me when, years later, I was teaching in Scotland, and Pastor Peter Cochrane, the retired superintendent of the Assemblies of God of all Scotland, sat down beside me. With tears in his deep blue eyes, bloodshot now with age, he said, "Lass, in my sixty-five years of ministry, I have never heard such sound doctrine mixed with such fire of the Spirit. I've seen the anointing and I've heard sound doctrine, but I have never seen the two combined like this!"

Oh, I tell you I was broken by his words. I said, "Sir, that means so much to me because this message has often been rejected in America." He smiled and said, "You go for it, Lass!" At the time I couldn't help but think of Mary Magdalene, who wouldn't give up until she found the Lamb.

THE SIGNS OF FRUIT

Meanwhile I wrote books.[2] I wrote about the Father's cup from every possible approach. I wrote about it to the fatherless generation in *The Cry, The Pain,* and *Rivers of Glory.* I further wrote *America Ablaze, The Glory of the Lamb, The Masterpiece, A Revelation of the Lamb for America,* and *The Unquenchable Flame* with its emphasis on revival and the cross. I even wrote a little book for Africans called *The Pain in an African Heart* and then a Christmas book entitled *Bethlehem's Lamb,* hoping to stir a hunger for the Lamb.

Then in 2006, after Brownsville Revival School of Ministry had been closed for over a year, I invited young adults to a Revivalists of the Cross Internship at our camp. After pouring out twenty-five in-depth lessons on the crucifixion and resurrection in our Glory of the Lamb course, I began to see the message take root. The young adults grabbed hold of the message like a thirsty man in a desert. The truth bore witness in their hungry hearts, and they knew the message of the cross and the glory of the Lamb was what had been missing in the church. Their young hearts exploded with passion when they learned that Jesus drank down every drop of the Father's cup of judgment for them.

We had another class called Finding Your Preaching Voice; and we began to see some passionate young preachers arise. Not only could they preach with passion, but they preached the cross with fire. Soon we were taking teams all over the world, telling about the Lamb. Now, at last, I'm seeing fruit, real, genuine fruit in the lives of young adults. These are, as John Wesley said, "my living witnesses."

I see young men and women ablaze with the message of the Lamb, leading youth groups, pastoring churches, preaching about His sacrifice, writing, painting, making video, ministering in power, pouring out their lives in other nations, ministering in rehabs, praying for healing and seeing genuine miracles, testifying on the job, healing racial wounds, receiving songs from heaven, preaching in crusades, witnessing on college campuses and in the streets—and it's all with the central message of the cross of Christ.

I see older adults and pastors, experiencing increased fire and miracles in their ministries, mentoring the young generation, healing mother and father wounds, preaching with more anointing than they dreamed possible. But it's all because they preach about the cross and the cup and the blood of the Lamb.

And now, as we launch our new Behold the Lamb School of Revival, many of these same ones, burning for the Lamb, will be helping make it happen. Through it all, I see Jesus, the Lamb who was slain, receiving His reward. At last I can honestly say, the message of the Lamb is rising. The cross is being resurrected and restored to the center of the church.

Yes, Mary Magdalene wouldn't give up, and I pray you will be just like her. She didn't let her scarred past stop her; she didn't care if she looked like a fool. All she wanted was to find the Lord. Will you be like her and excavate the Lamb from the rubble in the church?

Honor Your Pastor

Please don't blame the pastors and leaders for rarely preaching the cross, except perhaps once a year at Easter. They would preach their hearts out if they were given an opportunity to look into the Father's cup. Remember how you loved Jesus, but you hadn't seen the Father's cup. You had never wept over the cross. You needed to look deeply at the cup before you understood the magnitude of His sacrifice.

Sometimes I've seen fiery young men and women, full of zeal; but it's zeal without wisdom. They charge into their churches, expecting to change their pastor and the people, and they only divide and alienate. Please, please don't be arrogant and puffed up about your knowledge of the cross. If you can't walk with a humble, lamb-like heart, people will never hear your message.

So keep your heart at Calvary. Gaze upon the Lamb until your selfish ambitions are undone, your pride is undone, and He fills you with a Lamb's heart.[3] Support and honor your pastor; and when God opens the door for you to preach, then you can preach the cup and the Lamb and watch the fire fall.

But I assure you there will be times you will feel: "They have taken away my Lord—the Lamb of God—and I don't know where they've laid Him!" Your message may be resisted at first; but keep on loving and keep on taking the message to those who will receive it. Keep on lifting the risen Lamb and you will see at last—the day will come when the glory of the Lamb is revealed in all the earth.

SPURGEON'S SALVATION

I want to tell you now the story of the salvation of Charles Spurgeon. This story reveals the power of beholding the Lamb of God, but it also shows a man who wrestled with the theological errors that were slipping into the church of his day. For him it also seemed they have taken away the Lord and he didn't know where they had laid Him.

> Icy winds blew against the boy's face, pelting him with snow and rain as he trudged toward the Baptist church in the village. This desperate teenager knew he was unsaved, but somehow, he must find God.
>
> Finally, he realized he couldn't make it to the village, so he decided to stop in at a little Primitive Methodist chapel along the way. He had heard about these Methodists. They shouted so loudly it made one's head ache, but he didn't care. He had to find an answer to his heart's hungry quest. He slipped into the back pew and waited for the service to begin.
>
> It was the first Sunday of January, 1850, in England, and the regular minister of the church was snowbound. An old country layman filled the pulpit, speaking crudely in broad English Essex. "The Bible says, 'Look to me and be saved, all the ends of the earth,'" the old man began in a feeble voice. "It says, 'Look.'

Now lookin' don't take a deal of pains. It ain't liftin' your foot or your finger; it is just 'Look.' Well, a man needn't go to College to learn to look. You may be the biggest fool, and yet you can look...."

Then he said, "Many of ye are lookin' to yourselves, but it's no use lookin' there. You'll never find any comfort in yourselves.... Look to Christ. The text says 'Look unto Me.'" Then he continued, "Look unto Me, I am sweatin' great drops of blood. Look unto Me; I am hangin' on the cross. Look unto Me; I am dead and buried. Look unto Me; I rise again. Look unto Me; I ascend to Heaven. Look unto Me; I am sittin' at the Father's right hand. O poor sinner, look unto Me! Look unto Me!"[4]

Then the old man leaned over his pulpit and pointed directly to the fifteen-year-old boy on the back pew. "Young man, you look very miserable, and you will always be miserable—miserable in life and miserable in death—if you don't obey my text, but if you obey now, this moment—you will be saved." Then lifting up his hands and shouting as only a Primitive Methodist can do, "Young man, look to Jesus Christ. Look! Look! Look! You have nothin' to do but look and live."

Suddenly the boy felt an arrow shoot into his heart and his spiritual eyes flew open. With the eyes of his spirit he looked up and saw the crucified Lamb of God. In that moment, young Charles Spurgeon was saved!

This encounter with God remained forever engraved on Spurgeon's heart. He said, "That happy day, when I found the Savior and learned to cling to his dear feet, was a day never to be forgotten by me....That precious text led me to the cross of Christ....I thought I could have sprung from the seat on which I sat and called out with the wildest of Methodist brethren....'I am forgiven! I am forgiven!'" And when he told about his conversion, he often quoted this line from his favorite hymn, which is engraved on his tombstone: "E're since, by faith, I saw the streams Thy flowing wounds supply, Redeeming love has been my theme, and shall be 'till I die."[5]

At the age of nineteen, Spurgeon pastored a large Baptist church in

London, and for thirty-seven years he preached in this city, growing the largest evangelical church in the world of his day, with 3,800 of his sermons published. He was known as the "Prince of Preachers."

As I told you earlier, I soon discovered that Charles Spurgeon, who wrote magnificently about the cross, wrestled with the same issue in his day. Spurgeon's central theme, which he fought for until the day he died, was the doctrine of "penal substitution," which is just another way of saying, "the Father's cup."[6] Spurgeon said, "Substitution is the very marrow of the whole Bible, the soul of salvation, the essence of the gospel.[7] We ought to saturate all our sermons with it for it is the life-blood of the gospel."[8]

But liberal theology had slithered into the Bible schools and churches in England. That was in the late 1800s so that by the turn of the century, the subject of a bloody cross and a punished Savior had become unpopular. "Surely God is too loving to pour wrath on His Son," the higher critics said. Again I quote Spurgeon, who said, "If you put away the doctrine of the substitutionary sacrifice of Christ, you have disemboweled the gospel, and torn from it its very heart."[9]

Spurgeon went to his grave still fighting for the truth of the gospel and the substitution of Christ. Though the theology of his day was calling for this so called gospel of love, which omitted the truth of Jesus' enduring the judgment of hell, Spurgeon said that to remain silent in order to keep love is to "betray our Lord with a kiss."[10]

Because I admire Spurgeon so deeply, I was encouraged to know he fought the same battles over the cross, especially over propitiation, substitution, and the Father's outpoured wrath. He died in his fifties, worn down by the "Downgrade Controversy." I find it interesting that this one, who so defended the gospel, is still remembered and quoted by thousands, while other contemporaries of his day have faded into "the twilight dust of history."[11] His sermons and books are still in constant demand; as German theologian Helmut Thielicke advised young preachers, "Sell all and buy Spurgeon."[12]

EXCAVATING THE SON

The Father looks down on earth and He sees how His Son has been covered beneath the rubble of popular subjects in the church today. He will not remain silent much longer. He will honor the sacrifice of His Son and keep His word to Him. This story about a father during an earthquake in Armenia in 1989 which killed 30,000 people helps illustrate the Father's heart.

> When the 8.2 earthquake struck a city in Armenia, a young father rushed to his son's school only to find it completely flattened. He saw parents screaming over their children who had been crushed to death beneath the rubble. He stood in shock until he remembered his promise to his son: "Armand, no matter what, I'll always be there for you!"
>
> Racing around to the part of the school where his son's classroom once stood, he began digging. For eight hours he dug with his bare hands, stone by stone, handful by handful. People came and said it was hopeless. The fire chief told him to stop, for fires were breaking out everywhere. But he refused to quit. He kept gouging and scooping until his hands were torn and his fingers bleeding.
>
> On through the night he dug, twelve hours, twenty-four hours, thirty-six. His hands ached and bled, but he wouldn't give up. Finally, in the thirty-eighth hour, he lifted a heavy boulder and thought he heard his son's voice. "Armand?" he shouted. "Dad? Dad, I knew you'd come!"[13]

Yes, that day a boy was excavated by a father who was determined to keep his word: "Son, I will always be there for you!" How much more will God the Father keep His word to His Beloved Son!

The Father promised that His Son will receive the reward of "the suffering of His soul and be satisfied" (Isa. 53:11, MT). He will be exalted on earth as a Lamb even as He is exalted in Heaven. God will excavate His Son from the rubble in the church. He will dig out the debris of greed; the stones of materialism; the mudslides of religion, pride, and legalism; and the boulders of humanism that have blocked our vision. He won't give up until His Son receives the glory He deserves for giving His life as a Lamb.

So now I ask—where are those who will shoulder the shovel and dig out the rubble that covers God's Son as the Lamb? Would you be that man or woman? Will you bring a revelation of the Lamb to your generation? Will you please the Father's heart by honoring His Son's sacrifice? If so, then reach up to heaven and cry out to Him:

> *O God, for the sake of Your Son, I will preach the blood of the Lamb! I will tell of the fire of the cross. I will spread the glory of the gospel. I will live to bring the Lamb back to the center of Christianity. With every breath that I take I want to bring Jesus, the Lamb who was slain, the reward of His suffering. I will live to resurrect the message of the Lamb, for my heart has been undone by the glory of the Lamb!*

CHAPTER 14 ENDNOTES

1. J. Rodman Williams says, "If there is to be knowledge of God, He Himself must grant it. It must come from His side, out of His mystery, across the chasm of finitude and sin" (J. Rodman Williams, *Renewal Theology*, 32).
2. I learned this from the apostle Paul. When he was locked away in prison he wrote most of the books of the New Testament!
3. For the best book I've ever read on humility, read Greg Violi's *The Lamb's Heart*.
4. Lewis Drummond, *Spurgeon, Prince of Preachers* (Grand Rapids, MI: Kregel Publications, 1992), 22–23.
5. Ibid., 24.
6. The reason I use the "cup" is because that's what Jesus called it as He prayed in the garden, and that is also what it was called in the Old Testament. But in seminary the term "penal substitution" would be more commonly used.
7. Spurgeon said, "If you proclaim the death of the Son of God, but do not show that He died the Just for the unjust, you have not preached the blood of the Lamb. You must make it known that the chastisement of our peace was upon Him...or you have not declared the meaning of the blood of the Lamb....Sin must be punished: it is punished in Christ's death. This is the hope of men" (Drummond, *Spurgeon, Prince of Preachers*, 294).
8. Charles Spurgeon, *22000 Quotations from the Writings of Charles Spurgeon*, 200.
9. Ibid., 200.
10. Lewis Drummond, *Spurgeon, Prince of Preachers*, 692, 665.

11. Ibid., 769.
12. Ibid., 25.
13. Jack Canfield and Mark Victor Hansen, *Chicken Soup for the Soul* (Deerfield Beach, FL: Health Communications, Inc., 1993), 273–274.

Chapter 15

THE TRIUNE REUNION

The Wounded Son Comes Home

MARY MAGDALENE BANGS on the door of the upper room where the disciples are still in hiding. "I have seen the Lord" (John 20:18), she shouts, crying and laughing ecstatically. I'm sure her words exploded like fire in John's heart. Though the others doubt, he knows it's true because of what he has already seen.

Earlier that morning, when Magdalene awakened them all, wailing, "They have taken away my Lord" (John 20:2), the young disciple didn't hesitate. He tucked his tunic into his girdle and dashed toward the tomb. The boulder was rolled away, so with trepidation he cautiously entered the tomb.

Here lay the empty grave clothes. Just like Jesus would do, they were folded and placed neatly on the stone. The Bible says that John believed; but I think there was more than simply the folded grave clothes that stirred his faith. I believe John could sense something in the atmosphere. The Holy Spirit had flooded the body of Jesus; and when He arose, the glory of the Lamb had infused the whole tomb.

I believe a residue of glory still hung in the air, and John could sense it. He could smell His fragrance drifting through the tomb like a sweet musky perfume. He could feel the life of God everywhere, for Jesus' presence still lingered behind Him.

John had returned to the upper room, puzzled but believing. Now Magdalene's words "I have seen the Lord!" had confirmed what he believed with all his heart: Jesus Christ has risen!

He Still Bears Wounds

The day passes quickly. Then suddenly, the room where John is staying fills with the heavy presence of God. John's heart almost stops. The disciples gasp. John looks up quickly to see what causes this stir.

Without a twist of the bolt or a creek of the locked door, the Lord Himself walks into the room. "Shalom!" He says. His smile splashes glory over everyone.

John springs to his feet. His heart pounds hard in his throat. Tears wash his face as he sees Jesus reach out with open hands, exposing the gaping holes. Then He pulls back His robe and shows them "his hands and side" (John 20:19–20).

The young disciple's eyes widen. His knees weaken as he looks into these deep, shining wounds. "Master!" breathes John, falling to his knees. Jesus lifts His nail-scarred hands and breathes out upon them all. "Receive the Holy Spirit" (John 20:22), He says, His eyes sparkling with love.

John breathes in the life of Christ. He drinks and drinks of the sweet presence of God. His body trembles as his whole being floods with weighty glory. He knows this is the glory which Jesus died to give him. It's free to receive, but it cost God everything. It's the resurrection glory of the Lamb.

One week later, Jesus walks back into the room. He looks straight at Thomas. This disciple had not yet seen the Lord, insisting he would not believe unless he saw His wounds. Looking into the disciple's eyes, Jesus says, "Put your finger here; see my hands. Reach out your hand and put it into my side. Stop doubting and believe" (John 20:27).

When Thomas looks into the wounds of his Lord, he is undone, crying, "My Lord and my God!" (John 20:26). Oh, do you see? Nothing so stirs one's faith, humbles our pride, ignites passion in the heart as beholding a revelation of the Lamb! Thomas was forever gripped by a view of the Lamb, eventually even giving his life as a martyr for Christ.

So let me encourage you—when you feel discouraged, fearful, or weak in faith, focus the gaze of your heart on these blessed wounds. Spurgeon said, "Whenever your unbelief prevails, follow in this respect the conduct of Thomas, and turn your eyes straightway to the wounds of Jesus.

These are the founts of never-failing consolation, from which, if a man doth once drink, he shall forget his misery, and remember his sorrow no more."[1]

Nothing so clears one's vision as a long deep look at the wounds of the Savior. Spurgeon added, "My hearer, when your soul is clouded, turn to these wounds which shine like five bright stars. Look not to your own wounds, nor your own pain, or sins, or prayers, or tears…but gaze intently upon your Redeemer's wounds if you would find comfort…. Christ's wounds pour life into the church by transfusion: the lifeblood of the church of God is from Jesus' wounds."[2]

But you might be wondering—after more than 2,000 years, does Jesus still bear wounds? Yes! We know He still bore wounds in His flesh after He was seated on the throne because John saw Him "looking like a slain Lamb" (Rev. 5:6). I believe the reason He was so intent on showing His wounds in His post-resurrection appearances, was so we would know that He still bears these wounds in His body. Furthermore, the Bible says "they shall look upon me, the one they have pierced" (Zech. 12:10), which implies that His piercings are still evident.

You may have heard about the little boy named Colton who became deathly ill from a ruptured appendix. Infection set in and the doctors couldn't save him. He died but then he was resuscitated and his spirit returned to his body. One day after his recovery, he began telling his dad about seeing Jesus in heaven. He said, "Dad, did you know Jesus has markers?" His dad didn't pay much attention, so he said again, "Jesus has markers." Then Todd, who is a pastor, said, "Son, where are the markers?" Colton dropped his toys and pointed to his hands and top of his feet. "These were where He has markers," he said matter-of-factly.[3]

WOUNDS TELL THE STORY

Indeed, Jesus' wounds give a vivid reminder of the sacrifice He made on the cross. His wounds tell a story without words. I want to tell you now this amazing story of Pastor Richard Wurmbrand, which illustrates how wounds tell the story.

When Russian communist troops swept into Romania after World War II, the secret police kidnapped Richard Wurmbrand, a Jewish believer in Jesus, and threw him in prison where he suffered unspeakable torture. He was brutally beaten over and over again, his torso carved with deep torture wounds. For three years he was held in a cell thirty feet below ground in solitary confinement. Finally in 1965, some Christians in Norway paid his ransom to release him from prison.[4] Here's the rest of the story:

> Wurmbrand visited America during that time, but few were interested in his story. Then one day as he was preparing to leave the country, he found himself swept into a crowd of 60,000 people who had gathered for a pro-left rally. A Presbyterian pastor took the mic and began praising communism.
>
> These words, coming from a fellow minister, horrified Wurmbrand. Without hesitating, he jumped to the podium, pushed the speaker aside and cried out over the microphone: "Your Christian brethren suffer under communism, and you, a minister, instead of praising their Christian martyrdom, you praise their torturers! You are a Judas! You know nothing of communism. I am a Doctor in Communism!"
>
> The startled pastor retorted sarcastically, "There's no such thing as being a 'Doctor in Communism.'"
>
> Richard Wurmbrand responded with humble authority and confidence, "I will show you my credentials." Then he took off his shirt to show the deep torture wounds, the result of years of suffering under communism. His scars spoke more than a thousand words. Finally he said, "Do you think it is right for communists to inflict such pain and scars upon a fellow minister?"
>
> With this powerful demonstration of his "credentials," Wurmbrand amazed the crowd and took over the rally. Police came and made him cover his wounds with his shirt, but nothing could stop the sympathetic support he received that day. His wounds told the story.[5]

In an even greater way, Jesus' wounds still tell the story of what He did for us. So let's follow Him now up the Mount of Olives as He rises into heaven, still bearing the scars on His flesh.

THE WOUNDED ONE ASCENDS

For forty days Jesus has walked with His disciples, telling them all about His Father's kingdom, which is coming down to this earth. But now He is about to ascend back to the side of His Father, and I'm sure He is breathless with excitement.

I can imagine Him climbing the mount with His disciples. It is a warm day in late spring. A light breeze tosses the Master's hair. Lilies bloom in the fields and red and yellow anemones dot the hillside as Jesus and the men climb the rocky pathway up the mount.

This same Mount of Olives is where Jesus had made His triumphal entry into Jerusalem; now He is about to make His triumphal exit from this earth and His triumphal entry into heaven.

He leads them to the Bethany side of the mount (see Luke 24:50).[6] Here in Bethany Jesus had raised Lazarus from the tomb; now from the Bethany side of the hill, Jesus is getting ready to raise Himself from the tomb of this earth.

Finally, Jesus stops, turns to face them all, and raises His hands to bless them. Look closely at those hands as blessings spill from the wounds dug out in His flesh. As Charles Spurgeon said, "The hands that bled now bless."[7]

Jesus pushes down on His feet and begins to rise. As He mounts upward, He still stretches out His hands, shedding blessings as He ascends. The Bible says, "He lifted up his hands and blessed them. While he was blessing them, he left them and was taken up into heaven" (Luke 24:50–51). Like a high priest coming out of the holy of holies and lifting his hands to bless the people, Jesus, our heavenly High Priest, lifts His hands and blesses the people as He enters the holy of holies above.

When the high priest in the tabernacle ministered in the holy place, he wore a breastplate embedded with gems. On these jewels the names of the tribes of Israel were engraved. But our High Priest, Jesus, says, "See, I have engraved you on the palms of my hands" (Isa. 49:16). As Spurgeon said, "Those wounds, those scars of our Lord, were the memorials of his love to his people."[8]

As He breezes now above the trees, olive leaves glisten and rustle. Higher and higher He rises until a cloud covers Him and He ascends out of sight. Closer to heaven He draws, anticipation building in His heart. Imagine with me the scene when the King of Glory enters back into heaven.

HOME AT LAST

"Who is this King of glory, asks one of the angels as the Lord draws near the gates above. "He's the LORD, mighty in battle," shouts a cherub guarding the gates. "Lift up your heads, O gates; be lifted up you ancient doors that the King of glory may come in!" (Ps. 24:7–8).

Now the wounded Son strides through the gates and into the open court. Angels stand aghast, awed that One so holy would wear a robe "dipped in blood" (Rev. 19:13). His wounds shine like medals of honor pinned upon His flesh.

Jesus is unaware of the stares, for His eyes are fixed on a goal. He sees the One for whom He's been longing. There stands the Father up ahead, waiting with outstretched arms. Love and adoration beam from the Father's face. Tears sparkle in His eyes.

With purpose and passion the Son heads straight for His Father's arms. Excitement so fills His heart that He almost stumbles. Seraphim stand aside as He reaches the throne and falls into His Father's arms. At last the wounded Son is home.

And now the wave bursts over the shores of their hearts. It's as though the loneliness of separation, the agony of suffering, the horror of drinking the cup, the relief of completing the work of redemption, the joy of the resurrection, and the love of reunion have all rolled together in one swelling wave of emotion. They weep and weep in each other's arms. Sweet relief from a painful job well done sweeps over them and unites their hearts again. At last, God embraces God.

All heaven hushes. Not a sound. Not a breath. Only the muffled sobs of Father and Son, weeping in each other's arms. "Abba, My Abba!" the Son weeps. "Son, My Beloved," cries the Father, holding the Son with all the devotion and passion of His heart. Their tears mingle together, flowing on and on.

And overshadowing them is the Holy Spirit, weeping and rejoicing with ineffable love. He knows how this sacrifice tore open the Father's heart. He too had wept and convulsed with sorrow over the Son. Now at last, they are all reunited in the union of the Triune Godhead. Now Father, Son, and Holy Spirit hold each other, weeping as the love of God floods the infinite realms of eternity.

Timeless moments pass. Then finally the Father opens His arms and stands up straight. The Holy Spirit slips back, hovering around the Son. I can almost imagine the Father wiping His eyes and clearing His throat. He steps to the side and points toward His Son. With bursting heart, He bellows through infinitude:

> *Behold the Lamb, Slain from the creation of the world!*
> —REVELATION 13:89

PASSION FOR THE SON

Now the Father looks down upon this earth and He sees the divorce rate rising, suicides increasing, drug use soaring, pornography intensifying, child prostitution mounting, poverty swelling, street children multiplying, and terrorism advancing. In the midst of it all He shouts,

This is My Son!

And though we in the church pursue many peripheral causes, through it all, He roars,

This is My Son!

Even as the earth shakes and darkness encroaches, He says,

> *If you'll honor what He has done on the cross, you will find the answer to the suffering of humanity! If you'll reveal the depths of the hell He endured, you will give hope where there is no hope!*

People everywhere are covered with shame and guilt because they don't understand the shame He already carried for them. They know they have sinned and deserve hell, but they don't know that One already endured their hell so they wouldn't have to go there.

The reason they don't know what Jesus did for them is because we haven't told them. We've been too preoccupied with our programs, the latest spiritual bandwagon, the hottest new revelation, trumpeting every other subject from our pulpits. We've also been chasing after other goals in life. We've lost sight of the greatest purpose in life: living to bring Jesus, the Lamb who was slain, the reward of His suffering. Reinhard Bonnke said the following:

> New religions offer us gods who bear no Calvary scars. New songs give no hint of a heart burst open with the spear of Divine Judgment, and new preaching all charm, sweetness and light. Are our feelings too delicate to contemplate a bloodstained cross? It is when they see the face marred more than any man's, and the hands with wounds and the side riven open that doubters cry out like Doubting Thomas, "My Lord and my God!"

Again, I plead, do not blame your hard-working pastors. We have all forsaken the Lamb, but God is saying that no longer will His Son's sacrifice be neglected. Now the Father looks down on this planet and cries,

> *This is My Son! He will be celebrated for His great sacrifice! He will receive the reward of His suffering as a lamb!*[10]

So let me ask you, as I did in the introduction of this book, have you wept over the cross? Does your heart tremble over the cup He drank for you? Do you burn for the Lamb of God? Has He become the supreme focus of your life, the energizing passion behind all you do?

Once I lost my passion for the cross. I had been teaching and preaching and writing about the cross at that point for over ten years. One day I watched a video in which I was speaking about the Father's cup on television. I was devastated to see that I could talk about it without a trace of a tear. I even smiled slightly as I explained the horror of God's wrath and the hell the Lamb endured.

It broke me when I saw that. I fasted and prayed and wept for three days in repentance. I was horrified that I could take the cross so lightly. At the end of those three days, my heart was forever tenderized. I felt like I had been through the meat grinder with Jesus; and since then, I have never lost my tears and passion for the cross. I've never been a very emotional person, but I am deeply emotional over the cross, and I make no apology. If He would drink down every gruesome drop of the Father's cup for me, then at least may I be unashamed to let my heart shake and my tears fall.

Now I know I have a mandate from God to tell about the Father's cup. He has created me for this cause. I can't get over the wrath which He absorbed into Himself. I don't want to ever get over it! I intend to spend the rest of my life, to my last dying breath, exalting the Lamb and telling about the Father's cup.

A MAN'S DYING WORDS

I want to tell you now about a young man who did just that—he honored the Lamb with his last dying breath.

Nicolas wasn't a pastor or a profound speaker, but he had a heart for souls. When we sent the pastors into the streets to preach in our preaching class in Kenya, the crowds gathered quickly. Nicolas weaved through the people, leading them to Jesus. Everywhere he went he told people about the cup Jesus drank and the hell Jesus endured for them.

A week after we returned to America, I received a phone call from Kenya in the middle of the night. Nicolas had been hit by a car, and he was rushed to the hospital. Even in the hospital, all he could do was tell people about the glory of the Lamb. Doctors tried to save him, but he went to be with Jesus. Just before he died, he said, "Bring me my Bible and my *Glory of the Lamb* book. I must set this hospital ablaze with the glory of the Lamb! Victory! Victory! Victory!" then he died.

But Nicolas did not die in vain. His life was not wasted. He lived it to the full, bringing Jesus the glory He deserves even with his last dying breath. Oh, this is what we need! We need a fresh passion kindled within us. We need a revelation of the Lamb in our hearts. We need a revolution to gather in a young generation, compelling them with one driving purpose. We need a reformation in the church, energized by the passion to bring Jesus the reward of His sacrifice. We need a generation who will arise, pick up the eternal torch of the cross, and ignite the next generation.

Now, with a heart full of understanding, won't you be like the apostle Paul when he said, "I resolved when I was among you to know only

Christ and him crucified" (1 Cor. 2:2)? Like Paul, will you resolve to take up this one great cause for your life? Again, as John Piper said, "Christ is the glory of God. His blood-soaked cross is the blazing center of that glory….And thus a cross-centered, cross-exalting, cross-saturated life is a God-glorifying life—the only God-glorifying life. All others are wasted."[11]

Please don't waste your life. Don't drift through life without a great purpose. With your eyes on the glory of His wounds, live to bring Jesus, the Lamb who was slain, the reward of His suffering for you. Let this single passion compel you for the rest of your life, for your heart has been tenderly undone by a revelation of the Lamb.

CHAPTER 15 ENDNOTES

1. "Look soul and live by the proofs of His death! Come and put thy finger, by faith, into the print of the nails, and these wounds shall heal thee of unbelief. The wounds of our Lord are the tokens of His love" (Charles Spurgeon, "Cries from the Cross: Evidence of Our Lord's Wounds," *Spurgeon's Sermons on the Death and Resurrection of Jesus*, 432).
2. Ibid., 437.
3. Todd Burpo with Lynn Vincent, *Heaven is for Real: A Little Boy's Astounding Story of His Trip to Heaven and Back* (Nashville, TN: Thomas Nelson, 2010).
4. "The Story of Richard and Sebina Wurmbrand," www.persecution.com; cited in "The Story of Richard Wurmbrand, *Israel, My Glory*, September/October 2010, 19.
5. Soon a door opened which no man could shut for Pastor Wurmbrand. He immigrated to the United States, starting the "Voice of the Martyrs" which now reaches around the world, ministering to persecuted Christians (Michael [Mihai] Wurmbrand, "Snapshots: A Son Remembers His Father," 2009, www.torturedforChrist.com; cited in "When God Opens a Door," *Israel, My Glory*, September/October, 2010, 20).
6. In Acts 1, we see the disciples returning from the Mount of Olives; but in Luke 24, we see Jesus leading them over the hill to the Bethany side of the mount: "When he had led them to the vicinity of Bethany" (Luke 24:50). This is because one side of the Mount of Olives leads to Bethany, the other side to Jerusalem.
7. Charles H. Spurgeon, "Our Lord's Attitude in Ascension," *Spurgeon's Expository Encyclopedia*, vol. 4 (Grand Rapids, MI: Baker Book House, 1977), 419.

8. Charles Spurgeon, "Evidence of Our Lord's Wounds," p. 433.
9. Also see 1 Peter 1:19–20.
10. Spurgeon said, "Glorified spirits can never cease to sing, 'Worthy is the Lamb that was slain'; for every time they gaze upon Him they perceive His scars. How resplendent shine the nail-prints! No jewels that ever gemmed a king can look one-half so lustrous as these" (Charles Spurgeon, "Cries from the Cross: Evidence of Our Lord's Wounds," 434).
11. John Piper, *Don't Waste Your Life*, 59.

Chapter 16

THE GLORIFIED LAMB

Beholding the Glory of the Exalted, Omnipotent God-Man

ENVISION HIM NOW, standing next to His Father. Joy exudes from His heart and His laughter ripples through the courts. He smiles and glory drenches eternity. His eyes wash heaven with love.

Now He slowly lifts His arms. Streams of splendor shine out from the glorified Lamb. His glory illumines all of heaven like a bright chandelier. He looks like a fountain of light.

Can you see Him? See the One whose eyes once spilled teardrops of sorrow, now sparkling with holy fire. See the face, once swollen and raw from patches of His beard torn out, now radiating brighter than the light of the sun. See His body, once stripped naked and bathed in blood, now bathed in eternal majesty (see Rev. 1:12–16).

Narrow your focus and look at His hands and feet. See the hands that bled from nail holes, bleeding with infinite splendor. See the feet once spiked to a stake of timber, now gleaming like polished brass (see Rev. 1:15). See His side, once stabbed with the blade of a sword, now releasing rivers of revival to this earth. Most of all, look at His heart from which this resurrection glory flows. These shining streams will someday fill the whole earth as waters cover the seas.

Yes, the glorified Lamb is the generating force, the source of God's eternal light. He is the headwaters, the well-spring, the fountainhead of glory. He is "the sole expression of the glory of God [the Light-being, the out-raying or radiance of the divine]" (Heb. 1:3, AMP).[1] He's the central sun of the universe, the lamp of all heaven, the daystar from on high. As Spurgeon said:

He is the sun of our day; He is the star of our night; He is our life; He is our life's life; He is our heaven on earth; and He shall be our heaven in heaven.[2]

Now at last Jesus' own prayer is answered: "Father, glorify me in your presence with the glory I had with you before the world began" (John 17:5). Even as the glory of the Lamb flooded on and on through infinitude before the creation of the world, now the sweet light of the Lamb fills eternity once again: "For God who said, Let light shine out of darkness, has shone in our hearts so as [to beam forth] the Light for the illumination of the knowledge of the majesty and glory of God [as it is manifest in the Person and is revealed] in the face of Jesus Christ (the Messiah)" (2 Cor. 4:6, AMP).

BLAZING IN GLORY

Draw in closer now to gaze upon the Lamb. Slip beyond the outer court, filled with tens of thousands of worshiping angels. Enter into the holy place with the worshiping elders. Dare to come even further, into the very holy of holies through the blood of the Lamb.

See multicolored radiance filling the realms above. Hear rumbles of thunder and watch bolts of lightning flashing around the throne. Breathe in the atmosphere. The very air of heaven floods with glory. Describing this heavenly glory, Bob Sorge writes in *Glory, When Heaven Invades Earth:*

> Just as our sun radiates energy and light, God exudes Glory. God is such a dynamically blazing inferno that the radiation of His person is called Glory. Glory imbues and sustains all of heaven. It is the air of heaven. The reality of God's Glory in the heavenlies is more real than the seat you're sitting in right now. His Glory is the ultimate reality. It is the tangible manifestation of the infinite beauty and splendor of His magnificent face.[3]

Worshipers bask in this glory. Seraphim breathe it in and all they can do is cry over and over, "Holy, holy, holy!" They cover their faces because they stand so close to His shining wounds. They cannot bear to look with unveiled eyes upon the brilliance and holiness streaming from these rips in the veil of His flesh.

Look carefully at these "burning ones." The reason they burn with holy fire is because "our God is a consuming fire" (Heb. 12:29), and these seraphim stand so close to the blazing inferno Himself, they catch fire. They derive their glory from Christ, for He ignites them. He derives His glory from no one. He *is* glory. His glory is innate. He flames with fire and glory because that is who He is.

So look closely now at Jesus, the glorified Lamb of God. See the robe of majesty now draping over the Son. When Isaiah saw the coronated Christ, "the train of His robe filled the temple" (Isa. 6:1). R. C. Sproul describes "the robe that Isaiah saw furled down from the shoulders of the king, spilling out over the sides of the throne, and then in gigantic folds came down into the sanctuary, moving across the floor and up the sides of the wall, completely engulfing the whole of the heavenly temple."[4]

But think about this—if just the train of His robe filled the whole temple, what about the magnificence of the robe itself. But far more, think of the One inside the robe—the full radiant glory of Christ, the Lamb of God Himself. As Piper says, "Christ is the glory of God....His blood-soaked cross is the *blazing center* of that glory."[5]

It is my conviction that the reason the cross is the "blazing center of glory" is because, on the cross, the heart that contained the radiant splendor of God's glory, ruptured. When this divine rupture occurred, the glory within Him was released. It spilled forth with a rushing surge at His resurrection, filling the tomb with His glory. But when He ascended on high and returned to His beloved Father, the glory within Him burst out through His wounds, filling eternity once again with the glory of the Lamb.

Now every wound bleeds glory. Light beams burst from His hands. Bright shining rays spill from His feet. Swift flowing rivers stream from His side. Glory pours from His whole being. Habakkuk wrote, "And His brightness was like the sunlight; rays streamed from His hand and there [in the sunlike splendor] was the hiding place of His power" (Hab. 3:4, AMP). Malachi wrote, "The Sun of Righteousness" shall "arise with healing in His wings and His beams" (Mal. 4:2, AMP).

Look at His face. That face once coated with human spittle and stained with His own blood now shines like a million suns. Now fire burns in His eyes and His tears blaze like shooting sparks. This is why John saw Him with eyes "like blazing fire" (Rev. 1:14). In fact, the glorified Christ describes Himself as "the bright Morning Star" (Rev. 22:16). He is indeed a fountain of light, for "The city does not need the sun or the moon to shine on it, for the glory of God gives it light, and the Lamb is it's Lamp" (Rev. 21:23).

Isaiah said, "The moon will be abashed, the sun ashamed" in comparison with the glory of Christ (Isa. 24:23). Do you know what this means? Think about the sun. The luminosity of the sun is four hundred septillion watts. That's four hundred trillion-trillion watts.[6] Explosions of helium and hydrogen leap 100,000 miles from its surface, each explosion having the force of one billion hydrogen bombs. Yet the brilliance of the solar sun, which is one million times the size of the earth, seems dark in comparison with the glorified Lamb of God.

No wonder Jesus said, "I am the light of the world" (John 8:12). He used the Greek word *phōs* for light, which is a light that was never kindled and never quenched. This is His uncreated glory, which existed eternally and blazed on and on through infinitude. Spurgeon said, "Jesus is the sun that never had a setting, always shining, always progressing in His mighty course."[7]

Yes, now at last the Lamb of God has returned to His glory beside His Father where He dwells in "unapproachable light" (1 Tim. 6:16). Commenting on this verse, Bob Sorge in *The Fire of God's Love* writes: "Wow! What a gripping description of God! God dwells in a light that's so bright that we can't bear to get close to it. This light is unapproachable because it's also a fire. It's a fiery inferno that emits an unapproachable light, and it's God's home."[8]

Look up now as He unveils His divine attributes which meet together in one convergence of glory. See His omnipotence, His omniscience, His omnipresence, His immutability, His self-existence, and His sovereignty exuding from the Lamb in one shimmering blaze. "The radiant, bright God illumined in the complexity and perfection of all His attributes unveils Himself to the objects of His affection," writes Allen Hood in *The Excellencies of Christ*. "He is wrapped with the luster of all His attributes as they work in perfect harmony and perfect potency."[9]

Spurgeon said, "Even eternity will not be too long for the discovery of all the glory of God which shines forth in the person of the Word made flesh."[10] Paul Washer says, "You will spend Eternity chasing down the beauty and splendor of the revelation of God in Christ."[11]

THE GOD-MAN ON THE THRONE

Billows of excitement now roll through the halls of heaven, for at last, the exalted Lamb of God takes His seat next to His Father on the throne. This is called His "session."[12] "The climactic stage in the exaltation of Christ is called His session," writes systematic theologian J. Rodman Williams. Allen Hood writes, "Jesus' session is where He sits and waits for all His enemies to be made a footstool underneath His feet."[13] Though His enemies were already defeated on the cross, now the church must subdue them and bring them under His feet through the power of His blood. Williams adds:

> He who humbled himself to the depths has now been exalted to the heights....The fullness of power has now come to the one who gave up all power.....He who claimed nothing has now been awarded everything.[14]

This is heaven's highest glory: that He who sits on High would stoop so low! That He who was "in very nature God...humbled himself and became obedient to death—even death on a cross!" (Phil. 2:6, 8).

> Therefore God exalted him to the highest place and gave him the name that is above every name, that at the name of Jesus every knee should bow, in heaven and on earth and under the earth, and every tongue confess that Jesus Christ is Lord, to the glory of God the Father
>
> —PHILIPPIANS 2:9–11

You see, though He was on the throne of the Father, shining in glory, before the creation of the world, now something is different. Now, since His incarnation, humiliation, resurrection, ascension, and exaltation back to the throne,[15] something has changed—tremendously!

Now the Son has a different image. He's a *Man*. He's the *God-Man* on the throne. He has human flesh. And furthermore, He has a name. Before time and space, He was called Son of God, the Lamb of God, and other meaningful titles; but now He has a human name. The name of *Jesus*.

Whisper that name *Jesus* and your heart will warm, your eyes will fill with tears, and your face will feel the light of His presence. You could roll the term "Lamb" or "Son" over your lips but it will not satisfy the tender longing inside. It will not touch the sensitive nerve in your soul like the name of Jesus. The Lamb is His eternal title; the Son is His eternal position; but His human name is *Jesus*. It's the name that is "above every other name," at which "every knee should bow, in heaven and on earth and under the earth, and every tongue confess that Jesus Christ is Lord, to the glory of God the Father" (Phil. 2:9–11).

WHAT THE FATHER SEES

Through all eternity, before the creation of time and space and earth, God the Father delighted in His beloved Son. Greaves describes this as "God enjoying God, God stunned by the beauty of God, God searching out God."[16] Because "the Son is the radiance of God's glory and the exact representation of his being" (Heb. 1:3), He was like a mirror image of the glory of the Father. So when the Father looked at the Son, He saw the beauty and glory of God shining brightly before Him.[17]

But now He sees something different. He sees the wounded One— the God-Man who looks like a Lamb. Spurgeon said, "Centuries have gone by and yet He looks like a Lamb that has been slain." We know this because when John gazed into heaven, he said, "Then I saw a Lamb, looking as if it had been slain" (Rev. 5:6). Furthermore, this is how millions of angels see Him as they continually sing, "Worthy is the Lamb who was slain" (Rev. 5:12).

So if John saw Him as a slain Lamb, and angels still see Him as a slain Lamb, this tells us that Abba Father sees Him as a slain Lamb. He sees His Son with deep gashes plowing His flesh, nail holes gouging His hands and feet, a gaping wound carving His side.

But I believe it's the wound in His Son's heart that moves the Father most profoundly. That sacred wound in the heart of the Lamb didn't come from thorns or scourge or spikes or spear. It came from a ruptured heart, from drinking the Father's cup. I believe that every time the Father looks at His Son, His heart turns over, for He recalls what this cost His Beloved.

He remembers the loud pleading of His Son that caused Him to sweat blood in the garden; He remembers the lashes of the Roman scourge that tore His Son to shreds; He remembers the spikes, boring holes into His healing hands; He remembers the darkness of sin poured down upon the pure and holy One; He remembers, most of all, the cup of eternal wrath and judgment which He tumbled down upon His innocent Son.

And even more, He remembers the earsplitting cry that tore from Jesus' lips, "My God, my God why have you forsaken me?" (Matt. 27:46). When that cry burst out from the Savior's lips, it blazed up through earth's atmosphere, penetrating the gates of heaven, soaring into the third heaven and up to the throne, then goring into the heart of the Father.

Now the Father's heart is raw and sensitive to every reminder of His Son's sacrifice. When this "cry of dereliction" pierced into God's heart, it left a wound that still pulses raw and aching within Him. That is why the infinite passions of the Godhead open when His Son's sacrifice is remembered. The sight must be heart wrenching for the Father, except for one thing.

Now, from these very wounds, waves of divine glory billow out through eternity. Yes, He shines even more brilliantly than before, for now His glory blazes through the wounds in His human flesh. I believe with all my heart that when the Father looks at His wounded but glorious Son, His heart is undone by a revelation of the Lamb.

THE OMNIPOTENT LAMB

My prayer is that the Holy Spirit will bring this revelation of the Lamb to an entire generation. To His whole church! You see, when heaven unfolded like a scroll before the eyes of the apostle John, he didn't see the Lamb as a weak, wimpy Lamb. He saw Him as a mighty Omnipotent Lamb of God.[18]

Sometimes I hear it said, "It's not about the Lamb; it's all about the Lion!" But God gave Him the title "the Lamb" before the creation of the world (1 Pet. 1:20; Rev. 13:8), proving how He values this title for His Son.

God shows this clearly when you look into the Book of Revelation, which is a window into heaven. Here you will see that Jesus is called the "Lion of the Tribe of Judah" *one* time (Rev. 5:5), the "Word of God" *one* time (19:13), the "King" *three* times (15:3, 17:14, 19:16), the "Morning Star" *one* time (22:16).

But He is unveiled as "the Lamb" *twenty-nine* times! This reveals how deeply the Father feels about His own Son's sacrifice. No other view holds such infinite passion as does this view of His Son, wounded like a slain Lamb.

I've sometimes heard people say, "He's not coming as a weak, wimpy Lamb; He's coming as a mighty, majestic Lion!" Respectfully, I want to say, if He is a "weak, wimpy Lamb," then why do "the kings of the earth, the princes, the generals, the rich, the mighty, and every slave and every free man" hide themselves and cry out to the rocks and mountains, "Fall on us and hide us from the face of him who sits on the throne and from the wrath of the Lamb!" (Rev. 6:16)? As Leon Morris says, "The wrath of the Lamb is regarded as something greatly to be feared."[19]

If the Lamb is so impotent and enfeebled, than why do the ten kings and the beast try to make war against the Lamb? And why can't they overcome Him? The Bible gives the answer: "They will make war against the Lamb, but the Lamb will overcome them because He is Lord of lords and King of kings" (Rev. 17:12–14). You see, the Lamb of God is the great Lord of all earthly lords. He is the great King of all other kings He is not a weak, anemic, wimpy Lamb but a powerful, triumphant omnipotent Lamb!

Furthermore, when John the Apostle "saw a Lamb, looking as if it had been slain....He had seven horns and seven eyes" (Rev. 5:6). Seven eyes speak of the seven Spirits of God or perfect and complete revelation. But horns in the Bible always speak of power. The reason the Lamb is depicted with seven horns is because He has perfect and complete power. Morris says, "A horned lamb is the symbol of a conqueror,"[20] for He is victorious, mighty, and undefeatable. Yes, He is the conquering Christ! The victorious God-Man! The mighty omnipotent Lamb upon the throne!

I heard one well-known preacher insist that Jesus sits as a Lion in heaven, but He's only a Lamb from our earthly point of view. This simply isn't biblical. The Bible doesn't say that He is a Lion, looking as if it has been slain. No, the Bible says He's "a Lamb, looking as if it has been slain" (Rev. 5:6). It doesn't say that angels in heaven cry, "Worthy is the Lion who was slain!" No, it says they cry, "Worthy is the Lamb who was slain" (5:12).[21]

Furthermore, the Bible doesn't say we are invited to the Wedding Supper of the Lion; it says we're invited to "the Wedding Supper of the Lamb" (Rev. 19:9). It doesn't say we are the wife of the Lion; it says we are "the wife of the Lamb" (21:9). It doesn't say that our names are written in the Lion's book of life; it says our names are "written in the Lamb's book of life" (21:27; 8:13). And the river of life doesn't flow down from the side of the Lion; it's "the water of life, clear as crystal, flowing from the throne of God and of the Lamb" (22:1).

However, I must be quick to add, it is not the form of a Lamb who will be coming again for His church. Nor is it the form of a Lion. Jesus is coming back as a Man, the God-Man. He is coming for His bride as an omnipotent Bridegroom Lamb. And make no mistake about it—He will be a Man, with wounds still carved in His flesh like a Lamb.

You see, when John the Baptist (in John 1:29), Peter (in 1 Peter 1:19), and John the Beloved (twenty-nine times in Revelation) called Jesus "the Lamb," this term encompassed much more than just the cross. His title "the Lamb" implies the eternal span of His existence from before creation, to His incarnation, crucifixion, resurrection, ascension, exaltation to the throne, His ultimate return for a bride, and on into His sovereign reign through the endless ages of eternal glory.

Professor Leon Morris explains that today's Christians "have lost the key" to the interpretation of the Book of Revelation, which "is the cross of Christ." Then he makes this shocking but eye-opening statement: "The result is that the book becomes the happy hunting ground of all sorts of religious cranks."[22]

Morris explains, "They make it foreshadow all sorts of strange pro-phetical schemes," confidently claiming to "have the only correct inter-pretation." This throws Christians into confusion, causing them to leave the book alone, "which is a great pity, for, while much of the symbolism of the book is obscure, a very great deal of its teaching is both plain and valuable."[23] The "plain and valuable truth" in the Book of Revelation is a revelation of the Lamb![24]

Yes, we need a revelation of the Lamb restored to Christianity. But again, I insist—this is not a new revelation. It's not some deep mystical truth that has suddenly been revealed. It has always been there, weaved like a scarlet thread through the entire Bible. We've just overlooked it, but the time at last has come to reveal this golden key to the whole Bible. The time has come to honor the Son as the Lamb of God. Even as John saw Him "in the center of the throne" in heaven, it's time to restore Him to the center of His church on earth.

And oh, what strength and stability this message of a conquering Lamb will bring! The church world is shaking because God is bringing back His Son's reputation. He is bringing back the cross and restoring the Lamb to the center of His church. He is shaking everything loose that is not founded on the solid rock foundation of Calvary. A human-istic, materialistic, off-centered "gospel" has caused many contemporary churches to be built on shifting sands.[25] But Jesus warned about a house built on the sand: "The rain came down, the streams rose, and the winds blew and beat against that house, and it fell with a great crash" (Matt. 7:27).

Yes, Jesus Christ deserves to be honored as the Lamb on earth as He is honored in heaven. This is why I believe the final world sweeping revival will shine forth with a revelation of the Lamb. Even as the last book of the Bible, the Book of Revelation, unveils a revelation of His Son as a Lamb, I believe the last move of God will unveil to the church a revelation of His Son as a Lamb. Then, through the church, God's Son will be revealed to all the nations of this earth.

How could it be any other way? How could God the Father rip open His own heart and give the gift of His own Son and remain casual about it? How could He pour His eternal wrath upon the Darling of His heart and let us remain aloof and oblivious to the depth of such a price? How could He allow His glory to flow from His pierced One and His church remain blind to it? Impossible!

This is why God is reaching down from above and piercing the veils that have blinded His church. He is digging through the rubble and causing us to behold His Son as the Lamb. For the glory of His kingdom won't fully come on earth until the church honors the blood of the Lamb, until she lifts high the cross of Christ, until she preaches the fire of the gospel, and until she worships the Lamb with all her heart.[26]

As we face the trembling and shaking of this earth, we need the solid foundation of the cross of Jesus Christ. As the whole world shakes, may we lift our gaze to a far distant hill called Calvary where the blood of the Lamb dripped down.

Then may we raise our eyes still higher to the Lamb upon the throne. As we "Behold the Lamb" (John 1:29), He will "baptize us "with the Holy Spirit and fire" (Luke 3:16), enflaming us with revival that never burns out.[27]

And then we can know—our lives will never be wasted. We will be motivated with a compelling passion to bring Jesus, the Lamb who was slain, the reward of His suffering. For our hearts have been undone by a revelation of the omnipotent, glorified Lamb of God!

CHAPTER 16 ENDNOTES

1. Spurgeon writes, "This is the first and this is the last; the bleeding Lamb slain from before the foundation of the world, and yet living and reigning when earth's foundations shall dissolve. That blessed Lamb of God in the midst of the throne, and His people shall all be with Him, forever triumphant. He is the Alpha and Omega, the beginning and the ending, the foundation and the headstone. O Saviour of sinners, glory be to Thy name" (C. H. Spurgeon, "Silver Sockets, or Redemption the Foundation" Twelve Striking Sermons, 139).
2. Charles Spurgeon, 22,000 Quotations, 111.
3. Bob Sorge, Glory, When Heaven Invades Earth, 10.
4. R. C. Sproul, audio message: "Blazing in Glory," Ligonier Ministries, Sanford, FL.
5. John Piper, Don't Waste Your Life, 32, 59.
6. "Power of the Sun," Glenn Elert, editor, http//hypertextbook.com/facts/1999/MatthewTsang.
7. Lewis A. Drummond, Spurgeon, Prince of Preachers, 645.
8. Bob Sorge, The Fire of God's Love (Greenwood, MO: Oasis House, 1996), 165.
9. Allen Hood, The Excellencies of Christ, 3.
10. 10. C. H. Spurgeon, "The Glory of God in the Face of Jesus Christ," Twelve Striking Sermons, 141.

11. Paul Washer, "Romans 14:17," www.sermons.com, sermon preached at Radford Fellowship, Radford, VA.
12. The word *session* was once an English word which meant "the act of sitting down" (Wayne Grudem, *Systematic Theology*, 618).
13. Allen Hood, *Excellencies of Christ*, 135.
14. Williams says, "He is now the Father's co-regent, and on His behalf exercises total dominion" (J. Rodman Williams, *Renewal Theology*, vol. 1, 395, 403).
15. Jesus' incarnation, humiliation, resurrection, ascension, and exaltation are known in theology as the "states" of Christ (see Grudem, *Systematic Theology*, 620).
16. Stuart Greaves, *The Existence and Majesty of God*, 46.
17. John Piper says, "God himself takes full pleasure in the radiance of his Son. He reveals him in blinding light and then says, 'This is my delight!'" (John Piper, *The Pleasures of God*, 27).
18. John the Apostle did not see the Lamb standing off in the shadows, where we have kept Him. He saw Him "standing in the center of the throne" (Rev. 5:6). If the Lamb of God is the center of the church above, should He not be the center of the church on earth?
19. Leon Morris, *The Cross in the New Testament*, 355.
20. Ibid.
21. And though many today still dismiss the power of the Lamb, the Bible doesn't say we overcome Satan by the blood of the Lion; it says, we overcome Satan "by the blood of the Lamb" (Rev. 12:11). It doesn't say our garments are made white in the blood of the Lion; it says, our garments have been "made white in the blood of the Lamb" (Rev. 7:14).
22. Leon Morris, *The Cross in the New Testament*, 354.
23. Ibid.
24. This is why I keep sounding a trumpet for sound biblical doctrine. We must not be afraid of solid biblical theology. We must have theology ablaze! Charles Spurgeon told his students, "Be well instructed in theology, and do not regard...those who rail at it because they are ignorant of it" (Lewis Drummond, *Spurgeon, Prince of Preachers*, 614).
25. That's why John the Baptist didn't cry, "Behold the angelic!" "Behold the apostolic!" "Behold the prophetic!" "Behold the sons of God!" "Behold the kingdom of God!" "Behold the end times!" John the Baptist cried with all the conviction of his heart, "Behold the Lamb of God!" This should be our central cry as well.
26. "It is crucial that the revelation of the knowledge of God found in Christ Jesus be the premier focus and top priority of our lives," writes Stuart Greaves (*The Existence and Majesty of God*, 13).

27. Charles Spurgeon said, "There is about Calvary and its infinite stoop of divine love a power that never dies out and never will while the world stands"(Spurgeon, "The Marvelous Magnet," 19).

Chapter 17

THE BRIDEGROOM LAMB

Preparing a Bride with Unquenchable Love

JESUS LOOKS DOWN on His beloved friends and disciples and sees them praying in an upper room in Jerusalem. "Father, can I send Him now?" Jesus asks. He had promised: "I will ask the Father and He will give you another Counselor to be with you forever" (John 14:16).

He longs to give them the "Promise of the Father"—the wonderful Holy Spirit. Most of all, He knows the Holy Spirit will prepare a church to become His bride. No wonder the Son is so anxious to send Him to His people.

Finally the Feast of Pentecost dawns, which commemorates the giving of the Law engraved by the finger of God on tablets of stone.[1] Now the Holy Spirit will come, engraving a love wound, by the finger of God, on the fleshy tablets of human hearts.

"Now, Son!" the Father finally shouts. "Send the Holy Spirit to prepare for yourself a bride!"

This was indeed God's promise to His Son before the creation of the world in the eternal covenant of redemption. This was why the Son must bleed and suffer and drink the Father's cup—to prepare for Himself a bride. Now at last the time has come for a bride to be prepared for her Bridegroom Lamb.

Down, down, down the Holy Spirit descends. Breezing into the upper room where 120 followers of the Lamb are praying: "Suddenly a sound like the blowing of a violent wind came from heaven and filled the whole house where they were sitting" (Acts 2:2). The fire of God burns down onto each head and into every heart and they are all filled "with the Holy Spirit and fire" (Luke 3:16).

Like the day when God the Son breathed life into Adam's lungs, now the breath of God rushes into every person. You see, at Calvary a bride was taken from the side of the Lamb, but here at Pentecost she has taken her first breath. They all inhale deeply of the *Rûach Ha Kodesh*, the wind of the Holy Spirit pouring down from the Lamb of God. As they do, I'm sure their hearts are utterly undone.

UNQUENCHABLE LOVE

When I was first filled with the Spirit more than forty years ago, I'm sad to say that I was taught to follow Jesus for what I could get from Him, for His gifts and blessings. I didn't really love Him as He deserves.

Then the Lord, in His grace and mercy, opened up a fathomless well of the cross, the Lamb, the cup, the cry—and my heart began to flood with an unquenchable love. I began to understand what Jesus meant when He prayed to His Father "that the love you have for me may be in them" (John 17:26).

Now today, over and over again I hear the Father pouring down these words from heaven:

> *My Son will have a bride who loves Him as I love Him! He will have a bride who lives to bring Him the reward of His suffering as a lamb! He will have a bride who loves Him as He deserves to be loved!*

The following story of a father and a son helps describe what I believe the Father feels as He looks down on the earth today.

> "Dad, she doesn't love me," said the young man solemnly. His face was flushed and tears filled his eyes. "Since the day I returned from the war with only one arm, she has looked at me with contempt." He buried his face in his hand, ashamed to even look at his father.
>
> "I know, Son," the father said softly.
>
> "I honestly think she never loved me. She just wanted the wealth and the blessings I could give her as your son."
>
> "I know," the father nodded, for he was a very wealthy man

and he had always suspected the motives of the girl his son wanted to marry.

"But now, what am I to do? The guests have already arrived and filled the wedding chapel. My bride is clothed in an expensive wedding gown and she is waiting to walk down the aisle." Even as he spoke, the soft strains of wedding music could be heard through the door of the little room which opened on to the sanctuary. The fragrance of gardenias and roses wafted through the air. Already the groomsmen had taken their places, and the mother of the bride had been escorted to her seat.

"What do I do? Should I marry her anyway, knowing she doesn't love me, and be miserable the rest of my life?"

"No, Son. She's not ready to love you. She is selfish and immature, and you would be foolish to take her as your wife."

The father looked sadly at his despondent son. He would never forget the night he received the call that his son had been severely wounded on the battlefield. When the young man was flown to a hospital in America, this loyal dad had rushed to his son's side, praying and standing beside him as he slowly recovered.

But the son's future wife never even bothered to come. Now whenever the father looked at his son, his heart swelled with pride, mingled with deep sadness for the sacrifice his son had made.

"But, Dad, her family would be so humiliated. She will be furious. The bridesmaids will be hurt. The guests will be disappointed. We have already spent a fortune on this wedding. I just don't know what to do."

"Don't worry, Son. I'll take care of it." The father hugged his boy, then stepped out of the room onto the platform in the front of the church. He cleared his throat and looked out over the vast crowd.

People gasped. Why, this was not according to wedding protocol. The groom's father does not open a wedding ceremony.

The father looked out, his eyes glazed with tears but his jaw set with firm resolve. "Ladies and Gentlemen," he began. "We have gathered today to celebrate a wedding. But I think you would all agree—there can be no marriage where love is not the foundation. Love must not be unequal but mutual."

The people began to squirm and look around, mumbling under their breaths. The bride's family looked shocked, but everyone knew they had manipulated and pushed for this marriage. It was obvious this girl was marrying, not for love, but for the blessings he could give her.

The father paused, took in a deep breath and continued. "As you all know, my son has paid a great price for all of us, fighting for freedom and coming home as a wounded hero. I'm sure you would all agree that he deserves a wife who will love him with all her heart."

People nodded, tears filling many eyes.

"So I am here to announce: there will be no wedding at this time, for my son will have a bride who loves him as he deserves!" And with those words, most of the crowd broke into applause, knowing the son deserved to be honored for his great sacrifice.

That's a shocking account, but it reminds us of another wounded Hero. On the battlefield of Calvary, He fought for our freedom, returning home to His Father, still bearing wounds and scars. Now He awaits His wedding day, looking for a bride who will love Him, not for the gifts and blessings that come from His Father's vast resources of wealth, but who will love Him as the Father loves Him—with a deep, sacrificial, unquenchable love.

Do you remember in Job what Satan said to God? "Does Job love you for nothing?...You have blessed the work of his hands." Then he tells God that if He removes the blessings, Job "will surely curse you to your face" (Job 1:9–11). In other words, Satan implies that Job loves God for what He can give him, but without the blessings, he will not really love Him.

Do you see why I say we have been falsely taught to follow Him for what we can get from Him— for His gifts and blessings—rather than sheer burning love?

The bride described in the Song of Solomon loves her bridegroom with a love that "burns like a blazing fire, like a mighty flame" (8:6). It's an unquenchable love, for "many waters cannot quench love; rivers cannot wash it away" (8:7). She loves Him like the Father loves Him, just as Jesus prayed "that the love you have for me may be in them" (John 17:26).

Jonathan Edwards said, "God created the world to provide a spouse and a kingdom for his Son: and the setting up of the kingdom of Christ, and the spiritual marriage of the spouse to him, is what the whole work of redemption" is all about. "All other works are to be looked upon either as parts of it or as appendages to it....So all the decrees of God some way or other belong to that eternal covenant of redemption which was between the Father and the Son before the foundation of the world."[2]

Do you see what Edwards is saying? The entire purpose for the creation of the world was to provide a bride for the Son. Indeed, the purpose of Christ's massive sacrifice on the cross was for His bride. This was the reason for the eternal covenant of redemption transacted in the Godhead before creation.

Now the Father looks down and searches for a bride for His Son who will honor His profound sacrifice. She will weep over the cross with a heart full of wonder. She will tremble with amazement over the cup of wrath He drank for her. A love wound for Jesus will throb in her soul. She will burn with a passion to bring Him the reward of His suffering as a Lamb. She will ache with the Father over His Son's cry of God-forsakenness from the cross. The Father will have a bride for His Son who loves Him as He deserves to be loved.

THE LOVE WOUND

So look up now at the One whose flesh was undone there on a bloody cross. See the One whose heart was undone for those He loves. Look at Him until the Holy Spirit carves a love wound into your heart. "Behold the Lamb" (John 1:29) until all other wounds are washed away in His blood and only one wound remains. Let Him scar your heart with a love wound for Him alone.

I want to make it clear that I'm not talking about a grievous, sorrowful wound. It is not something painful and hurtful. It is a glorious wound of unprecedented affection. It is a scar of love sickness, a piercing sweet passion for Jesus. This is what a deep revelation of the Lamb will do.

Like those at Pentecost, you'll be "cut to the heart" (Acts 2:37). Like

213

Mary, when Simeon said, "A sword will piece your soul" (Luke 2:35), the sword of the cross will pierce your very soul. Like Paul, your heart will be circumcised (Rom. 2:29), for the veil that covers the eyes of your heart will be cut away.

Stuart Greaves in *The Existence and Majesty of God* writes, "Out of the nations of the earth, the Father is fashioning a bride who will be equally yoked to the Lamb of God. Christ will marry a bride who will be prepared in the way He was prepared, and that is through the reality of the cross."[3] I don't believe this means that she will be prepared by suffering in sickness and pain, as was believed in the Middle Ages. I believe it means that a *love wound* will brand her heart. The cross will be seared into her soul.

Saint John of the cross describes this piercing as a "wound of fire." He said that medicine won't heal the wound, for the very instrument that wounds, which is the cross, is the instrument that heals. "The more wounded the lover, the healthier he is," he said.[4]

Kevin Wells points out that "when one is wounded by love the only cure is more of Jesus' love. It's a paradox. As hunger begets hunger, a love wound begets more love." He further said, "When a wound heals, a scar seals over the wound. The Bridegroom in the Song of Solomon said, "Set me as a seal on your heart" (8:6). "This seal," suggests Wells, "is the scar of a love wound imparted through the wounding of the cross in the heart."[5]

Yes, when the cross is engraved deeply on our hearts, a bride is fashioned whose heart is wounded with love just like her Bridegroom's heart. On the cross of Calvary, His heart ruptured for the sake of His bride.

This love wound carved in the heart of His bride causes a passion that never burns out. It causes her to be so flooded with unquenchable love that she is "besotted with God," as the Puritans put it. Indeed, by allowing the cross to penetrate deeply into the heart of the church, a bride will be prepared for her Bridegroom Lamb.

God has been pouring "the Father's love" down upon His church in extraordinary measures, soaking us in His presence and healing our wounds. As Toronto's Fred and Sharon Wright say in *The World's Greatest Revivals*, the Father has been "pouring out His love on us so that we are able to love the Son passionately."[6] His highest desire is to see a bride who loves His Son with the same unquenchable love which He has for Him. Again, we know this because Jesus prayed "that the love with which you loved me may be in them" (John 17:26). With divine pathos and fervent passion, the Father desires to see Him honored on earth as He is honored in heaven.

And He will see it!

KNOWN BY THE FATHER

Shortly before Jesus went to the cross, He told a parable of the ten virgins. There's a part of this story now that I would like to highlight.

The virgins went out to meet the Bridegroom, but only five had enough oil in their lamps. The other five were not prepared. Their lamps were dimming and they had to go buy more oil. They came late to the wedding and the door was already shut. Then urgently they cried, "'Sir! Sir! Open the door for us!' But he replied, 'I tell you the truth, I don't know you'" (Matt. 25:11). Notice that He didn't say, "*You* don't know *Me*," but He said, "*I* don't know *you*!"[7]

So the question is not do *you* know Him, but does *He* know you. How then does He know us? I believe He knows us when we share in His own tender heart for His Son. If I have wept over the Father's feelings for His Son; if I have felt the mingled joy, the bittersweet pain, and the trembling emotion heaving in His heart when He looks at this beautiful wounded One; if I have fellowshiped with the Father over what He experiences every time He looks at His Beloved; if I have felt the displeasure of His heart for the neglect of His Son's sacrifice—then the Father knows me.

I further believe He means, if I have wept at the feet of Jesus, repenting to Him for being cold hearted over His cross; if I've cherished the body and blood of Christ in the Lord's Supper; if I've looked at the depths of His suffering when He drank the Father's cup; if I've let the cry of abandonment, "My God, why have You forsaken Me?" penetrate my heart; if I've felt His agonizing grief over being separated from His Father; if I've rejoiced in their reunion when He rose and ascended back into His arms, then I know Him and Jesus knows me. I may know Him partially, but I'm seeking to grow in communion with Him over that which is deepest in His heart.

The glory of the Son is the Father's highest desire; so if I love the Son like the Father loves Him, then the Father and the Son know me. If I have communed with the Father and experienced His heartbeat for His Beloved, then I know Him and He knows me. If I have taken the time and the effort to experience the "fellowship of sharing in His sufferings" (Phil. 3:10), then I know Him and He knows me. If I have fallen on my face in gratitude to the Father for giving such a profound gift to the world, if I have thanked Him with all my heart and soul for the anguish it caused Him when He poured wrath on His Son instead of me, then I have known Him and He has known me.

How could it be any other way? How could God crush His only Son with the full force of His wrath for us, and then allow us to take it lightly? How could the punishment of hell swallow up the innocent Son on the cross, and then we rarely, if ever, share it with others or mention it in the church? How could He sacrifice the Son of His heart and not expect us to feel what such a sacrifice meant to Him? This is the One who lived in the "bosom of God" (John 1:18) through all eternity! This is His One and only Son who laid down His life as a blood soaked Lamb!

How could other issues—other subjects and programs and messages— be more vital to the Father's heart? This is the greatest feat of all time! The most monumental work, the most colossal accomplishment, the highest achievement in the universe, and this is what is uppermost on the Father's heart. If we want Him to know us, we must feel His heart. We must commune with His emotions of deep love and appreciation for His Son.

I see no other way. If I'm wrong, when I look into the eyes of Jesus at the end of my life, I will hear Him say, "Sandy, you were wrong about the Father's love for Me. Furthermore, you were over the top about My cross, My blood, My gospel!" But when I think about that, it seems absurd to me. Jesus wouldn't say that, and I'm sure the Father wouldn't say that either.[8]

If you are reading these pages and wondering, "Is it too late for me?" Please know—it is not too late. The hour was late for the virgins, and indeed the hour is late for us. But if you are still breathing, there is still time. You can begin right now. Furthermore, the fact that you have been willing to read through this book, though at times I know it has hurt to look so deeply at Jesus, this shows your heart is hungry to know Him and to be known by Him.

Please understand, I am not talking about one's salvation. I am simply saying there is a place of knowing the Father's heart for His Son and the Son's heart for His Father. I believe this is how He knows us—by fellowshiping with Him in that place of tender communion and piercing sweet love. It's beyond description but I think you can sense what I mean.

I believe this is how He knows us—by the seal of love on our hearts. By the tender love wound for the Lamb pulsing inside. God knows us when our hearts have truly been undone by beholding a revelation of the Lamb.

CHAPTER 17 ENDNOTES

1. The Feast of Pentecost, sometimes called the Feast of Weeks, occurs fifty days after the Sabbath of Passover week (Lev. 23:15–16).
2. Jonathan Edwards, *A History of the Work of Redemption: The Works of Jonathan Edwards*, vol. 1, 616.
3. Stuart Greaves, *The Existence and Majesty of God*, 34.
4. Thomas Dubay, *Fire Within* (San Francisco, CA: Ignatius Press, 1989), 47.
5. Kevin Wells, preached in a message at Camp America Ablaze, Lillian, AL, 2008.
6. Fred and Sharon Wright, *The World's Greatest Revivals* (Shippensburg, PA: Destiny Image Publishers, Inc., 2008), 266.
7. He said the same thing in Matthew 7:22–23: "Many will say to Me on that day, 'Lord, Lord, did we not prophesy in your name, and in your name drive out demons and perform many miracles?' Then I will tell them plainly, 'I never knew you. Away from Me you evil doers!'"
8. People sometimes ask me, "Dr. Sandy, why do you so relentlessly teach and preach and write on the cross and the Lamb?" All I can do is answer with a verse from the Song of Solomon: "Because 'Many waters cannot quench love!'" (8:7). It's like that story I told in an earlier chapter about Amy Carmichael, saying to the Buddhist prostitute, "I'm going to stab this needle into my arm to show you how much I love you!" Then, when the girl saw her plunge the long needle into her arm, she cried, "Oh, Amy, I never knew you loved me so much!" When I saw how much He loved me on the cross, all I can say is, "Oh, Jesus, I never knew You loved me so much! Now I want to live my whole life for Your reward!"

SECTION FOUR

A REVELATION *of the* LAMB *to the* NATIONS

Chapter 18

A BLOOD DRAINED GOSPEL

Rediscovering the Glorious Gospel of Christ

A BLIND MAN, WITH disheveled hair, unkempt beard, and rumpled clothes shuffles to the door and slowly opens it.

"Brother Saul, I am Ananias," a young disciple says nervously. His face flushes with fear, for he has heard stories of this murderer who is bent on destroying the church. "The Lord has sent me here to pray for you."

Saul throws open his arms, tears rushing down his cheeks, as he hugs the young disciple. "My brother, my brother, come inside," he motions.

Ananias breathes a sigh of relief. He sits down and listens to Saul's amazing story. This sightless man, his face aglow with the glory of God, begins telling him about the flashing light from heaven and the vision of Jesus Christ.

Tears moisten Saul's eyes and his lips tremble as he speaks. "I heard a voice from heaven say to me, 'Saul, Saul, why do you persecute Me?' I asked, 'Who are you, Lord?' He responded, 'I am Jesus, whom you are persecuting!'" (See Acts 9:5–6.)

"Oh, Ananias, I tell you—I am shattered! I have seen the Lord and in these three days, in the pitch blackness of my blindness, a revelation of Jesus Christ has filled my soul. I may not be able to see but I know the Torah almost by heart. I've been thinking back through the first five books of the Old Testament, realizing now that 'Christ redeemed us from the curse of the law by becoming a curse for us, for it is written "cursed is everyone hung on a tree"' (Deut. 21:23; Gal. 3:13).[1]

"Brother, do you know what this means?" Saul cries, his voice mounting with excitement. "Jesus Christ, the crucified Messiah, became a curse for me! For me! After all I've done to persecute His people. Oh, I tell you I haven't stopped crying for three days. I have seen the Lord, and like Isaiah, I am utterly undone!"

Ananias smiles and places his hands gently on Saul's head. Then he says boldly, "Brother Saul, the Lord—Jesus, who appeared to you on the road as you were coming here—has sent me so that you may see again and be filled with the Holy Spirit" (Acts 9:17).

Color rushes to Saul's face and he takes a deep breath as the Holy Spirit floods his whole being. The Bible says that suddenly, "something like scales fell from Saul's eyes and he could see again. He got up and was baptized" (Acts 9:18), and now, at last, he can see like he has never been able to see in all his life.

Now, all over Damascus Saul talks about the Lord Jesus Christ. In the synagogue he preaches that Jesus is indeed the Son of God. He cannot stop talking about the grace the Lord has poured out on him through the power of the cross. To him this means that Jesus absorbed God's curse into Himself, taking his place and receiving the punishment he deserves for sin.[2]

Because of this great act of redemption, by sheer grace, Saul has received salvation through faith in the crucified and resurrected Christ. He sees this vast truth encompassed in one word—the *gospel*.

PAUL'S PURE GOSPEL

Saul is so astonished by the sheer power—the divine power—in the gospel that he tells the message everywhere he goes. He clearly defines his gospel, which the Lord Himself has given him, as the death, burial, and resurrection of Christ:

> Now, brothers and sisters, I want to remind you of the gospel I preached to you....For what I received I passed on to you as of first importance: that Christ died for our sins according to the Scriptures, that he was buried, that he was raised on the third day according to the Scriptures.
>
> —1 CORINTHIANS 1:3–4

Saul, now called Paul, realizes that there is innate power in the message of the gospel. He writes, "I am not ashamed of the gospel because it is the power [*dúnamis*] of God that brings salvation to everyone who believes" (Rom. 1:16). This Greek word *dúnamis* means "the almighty energy of God." Paul understands that it is the dynamic energy of God, contained within the seed of the gospel, which leads a soul to salvation.

Paul knows that only the light of the gospel transforms. God designed it this way on purpose, so that we would know it is nothing of ourselves but only the light of the gospel that saves: "We possess this precious treasure [the Divine Light of the Gospel] in [frail, human] vessels of earth, that the grandeur and exceeding greatness of the power may be shown to be from God and not from ourselves" (2 Cor. 4:6, AMP).

Charles Spurgeon said, "I am persuaded that light will penetrate" a person's conscience when the gospel is heard. "There is such force, such energy in Christ, it must and will pierce through some crevice and convince."[3]

Armed with this gospel, Paul sets out with Barnabas to spread this glorious message. His story amazes us. He sails first to Cyprus and then travels up through Galatia, preaching the glorious gospel. As he goes, the Jews begin to stir up persecution against his message and soon he is beaten, imprisoned, stoned and left for dead.

But what does he do? Does he quit? No! He simply rises, shakes himself, and goes to the next town to preach the gospel. Nothing can stop the wild determination of this man, aflame with God, compelled to bring the gospel to the entire known world.

PERVERTING THE GOSPEL

As the years pass, and Paul pours out the gospel of Christ, false brethren come in and began twisting the truth of the gospel. He says to the Galatians, "I am astonished that you are so quickly deserting the one who called you to live in the grace of Christ and turning to a different gospel—which is really no gospel at all. Evidently some people are throwing you into confusion and are trying to pervert the gospel of Christ" (Gal. 1:6–7).

Paul warns the Corinthians,

> I am afraid that just as Eve was deceived by the serpent's cunning, your minds may somehow be led astray from your sincere and pure devotion to Christ. For if someone comes to you and preaches a Jesus other than the Jesus we preached, or if you receive a different spirit from the Spirit you received, or a different gospel from the one you accepted, you put up with it easily enough.
>
> —2 CORINTHIANS 11:4

But sadly, this is what is happening today in the Western church! We are sometimes hearing a "different gospel!" God help us![4]

For example, in a popular book today, entitled *Love Wins*, the author summarily dismisses the blood of Jesus, calling it an outdated "metaphor." He writes, "There's nothing wrong with talking and singing about how the 'Blood will never lose its power' and 'Nothing but the blood will save us.' Those are powerful metaphors. But we don't live any longer in a culture in which people offer animal sacrifices to the gods." He continues:

> People did live that way for thousands of years, and there are pockets of primitive cultures around the world that do continue to understand sin, guilt, and atonement in those ways. But most of us don't. What the first Christians did was look around them and put the Jesus story in language their listeners would understand.[5]

First of all, the Holy Spirit breathed the Bible: "All Scripture is God-breathed" (2 Tim. 3:16), and it is heretical to say the New Testament writers "put the Jesus story in language their listeners would understand." This implies that they made up a story themselves instead of receiving it by divine inspiration from the Lord.

Secondly, the author implies that only primitive, ignorant people would believe in such a concept as the saving blood of Jesus. The blood of Jesus is not a metaphor. His blood is the substance which our Lord poured out from His own veins to cleanse our sins (see 1 John 1:7–9), to prepare a bride (see Rev. 7:14), and to overcome Satan (see Rev. 12:11). If we throw out the blood of Jesus, we must give up our salvation, allow

Satan to run rough shod over us, dismiss the only means of preparing a bride for the Lamb, deny the eternal covenant of redemption, and jettison the Lord's Supper.

As we've seen, the primary reason lambs were slain all through the Old Testament was to reveal the blood of God's own Son which would be shed on the cross. If we brush aside the blood, we must abandon the cross and throw out the entire message of the gospel which the apostles Paul, Peter, John, Philip, and others preached. To negate the message of the blood is exactly what Paul meant when he warned about "perverting" the gospel. He said, "If anybody is preaching to you a gospel other than what you accepted, let him be eternally condemned!" (Gal. 1:9).

If we dismiss the blood, we must also deny what angels sing about constantly in heaven, "Worthy is the Lamb...because you were slain and with your blood you purchased men for God" (Rev. 5:9). And most of all, if we neglect the power of the blood of Christ, preaching a bloodless gospel, rigor mortis slowly sets into the church. As Russell Moore writes, "If you drain the blood out of the church, all you are left with is a corpse."[6]

That's like the story I told you in the first chapter of this book about a soldier who lay dying in a pool of his own blood. Suddenly he stopped breathing and his heart went into cardiac arrest. A defibrillator charged his heart and caused it to beat again, but it took a blood transfusion for him to fully revive.

Now do you see why I said, "The church is like that dying soldier. The blood has drained from her gospel and she has almost slipped into cardiac arrest. She's been riddled with subtle forms of materialism, humanism, and mysticism until her senses have dulled and the life has slowly and imperceptibly oozed out." Do you see why I concluded, "The church needs electrodes applied to her heart. She needs her soul defibrillated. She needs her veins infused with a fresh transfusion of the blood of Christ."

Another example of watering down the gospel describes a "split gospel," which divides the message into a gospel of salvation and a gospel of the kingdom. This view encourages Christians to bring in the kingdom, but don't offend people with the gospel of salvation. The gospel of the kingdom is the gospel of salvation and it cannot be separated. Paul would ask us: "Why do you put up with it?" "Why are you allowing them to throw you into confusion by perverting the gospel?"

A similar view says that we should lead people to Jesus with our good lives, rather than by preaching the gospel. Those who hold this view quote St. Francis of Assisi: "Preach the gospel, and if you have to, use words." This concept suggests that our lives, not the divine power of God contained within the gospel, can save a soul.

Paul would be indignant, for he believed that only the gospel—not our good lives—transforms. Again, he writes, "We possess this precious treasure [the divine Light of the Gospel] in [frail, human] vessels of earth, that the grandeur and exceeding greatness of the power may be shown to be from God and not from ourselves" (2 Cor. 4:6, AMP).

Though Christ-like love and kindness is part of the Christian life, our own goodness may influence, but it cannot save. The following true story illustrates how a gospel of love alone cannot change people:

> John Richard Green left Oxford University determined to reform the squalid, sin ridden slums of London, not with the power of the gospel, but with love and the kindness of his own life. His view was—like the current popular book—*Love Wins*. For ten years he labored earnestly but finally in despair he said, "It's no use. These men will go on drinking and gambling until doomsday!" In defeat he left the slums and returned to Oxford to write his history of England.
>
> Down into these same slums went William and Catherine Booth, armed with the gospel, their hearts aglow with love. They brought both the power of the gospel and the love of Jesus Christ. They preached "the power of God unto salvation to everyone who believes," and lives were transformed. Men and women, once ruined with sin, were born again and were gloriously delivered from the wreckage of their past lives. While John Richard Green's work was based on his own efforts, he failed. The Booths based their efforts on the glory of the gospel, combined with God's love, and after 150 years, the Salvation Army still thrives.[7]

You see, "In the gospel...there is real light and real glory, and it is manifestly divine," says John Piper in *God is the Gospel*.[8] The gospel doesn't derive power from another source; it has its own inherent power. Indeed, as Paul said, "In the whole world [that Gospel] is bearing fruit and still is growing [by its own inherent power]" (Col. 1:6, AMP).

What happened in Germany during the Holocaust should serve as a striking warning to us today. It was a blood-drained gospel which actually weakened the church in Germany and subtly opened the pastors to Hitler's deception. As Timothy J. Keller wrote in the foreword of Dietrich Bonhoeffer's biography, "How could the church of Luther capitulate to Hitler in the 1930s? The answer is that the true gospel, summed up by Bonhoeffer's 'costly grace,' had been lost."[9] This lost gospel led to a spiritual blindness in the churches of Germany, which allowed Hitler to gain power and ultimately to annihilate six million Jewish people in the Holocaust.

Obviously, Satan utterly hates the divine light inherent in the true gospel and he does everything in his power to blind our eyes from seeing it: "For the god of this world has blinded the unbelievers' minds [that they should not discern the truth], preventing them from seeing the illuminating light of the Gospel of the glory of Christ (the Messiah)" (2 Cor. 4:4, AMP).

Do you see why the devil fights so hard against the message of the cross and the glory of the gospel? Piper explains, "Satan does not want us to 'see' this light. Seeing 'the light of the gospel of the glory of Christ' is what liberates people from his power"[10]

Sadly, however, a gospel of personal happiness, selfish ambition, and material gain has replaced the one true gospel of Jesus Christ. Instead of the central message of the cross and the risen Lamb, which is the essence of the gospel, we have replaced it with a self-centered gospel of prosperity and wealth.

As an African pastor told me bluntly, "Preachers today want to get rich from their people so they preach a message of prosperity. You know how it goes—'plant your seed into my ministry and God will bless you!' But," he said with firm resolve, "that's manipulation and it's wrong! The message that will change lives and change this land is the message of the cross!"

THE MORAVIAN'S SECRET

One day a young nobleman wandered into a museum in Germany to admire the paintings. Suddenly, he caught a glimpse of a powerful painting of Christ, with blood from the thorns and the scourging running down His body. It struck his heart so deeply that he stood gazing at it for hours.

Then he read the caption engraved beneath the painting: "I did this for thee; what wilt thou do for Me?" He fell to his knees, sobbing. With all his heart he promised God that for the rest of His life he would glorify the Lamb for what He suffered on the cross. This young man was Count Nikolas Ludwig von Zinzendorf. Because of his love for the Lamb, he provided refuge on his Hernhutt estate for a persecuted Christian group known as the Moravians. The watchword of the Moravians became this: May the Lamb who was slain receive His due reward for what He suffered on the cross!

This heart cry impelled the Moravians into one of the greatest missionary movements in history. The Holy Spirit fell upon them in what was known as the Moravian Pentecost; and for the first thirty years, says Arthur Wallis, "Moravian evangelists, aflame for God, carried the gospel not only to nearly every country in Europe, but also to many pagan races in North and South America, Asia, and Africa."[11]

But eventually, some of the Moravians laid the golden key aside and began to neglect the message of the gospel. Charles Spurgeon tells the story of a group of Moravian missionaries who went to Greenland to convert the natives. Using "great prudence," they thought, "These people are in such darkness that it cannot be of any use to preach Jesus Christ to them at first." Instead, they reasoned, they would show the heathens the difference between right and wrong as well as the rewards of the righteous and the punishment of the lost.

Years passed and there were no converts. The missionaries became discouraged, and no one seemed to realize what was wrong. "Jesus was being locked out of the Greenlanders' hearts by those who wanted Him to enter," said Spurgeon. Then one day one of the missionaries started reading to a Greenlander the story of the bleeding Savior and the gift of eternal life offered to all who receive Him. The man said, "Would you read me that again? What wonderful words! Did the Son of God die for us poor Greenlanders that we may live?"

The missionary nodded, and then the Greenlander began clapping his hands and crying, "Why did you not tell us that before?"[12] He gave his life to Christ and soon his wife and children followed. Many Greenlanders came to Christ after that, but it was all because the power of the gospel had finally been preached in the land.

Spurgeon said, "Let us start with the Lamb of God that takes away the sin of the world. 'For God so loved the world that He gave His only begotten Son, that whosoever believes in Him shall not perish but have everlasting life' (John 3:16). To my mind, that is the point to begin with and that is the point to go on with."[13] Indeed, the gospel is the only message that will save, and when we leave it out, there is no true and lasting salvation.

The Tragedy of a Bloodless Gospel

Spurgeon said, "There is no true, deep, tender, living conversion except through the cross."[14] This is why we dare not attempt to lead people to salvation without giving them a true sight of the gospel. Oh, I've done it, and I'm heart sick about it, because the inherent power to bring a soul to genuine repentance and salvation is contained within the gospel—in the message of the crucifixion and resurrection of Jesus.

Only the gospel has heart-cutting, life-changing power. Beholding Christ and Him crucified is what changes us from within. Perhaps this is why, in our day, so many slide back into sin or get stuck in dry religion. Maybe it's because we haven't given people a true revelation of the Lamb—a revelation that pierces the veil that covers our hearts and helps us really see.

But we are so afraid to offend. We don't want to make people feel bad; and yet, without conviction of sin, followed by genuine repentance, no true salvation results. People who think they are saved still struggle with sin and see little change in their lives. They wonder why they can't change, and yet it's because they never received the pure gospel. This heart-breaking story illustrates what we've done when we leave the gospel of Christ out of our churches:

No one noticed when the toddler wandered out the back door, which had been left ajar. Friends had gathered to celebrate the christening of the child on the following morning. Distracted guests chatted merrily and sipped their cocktails while the baby slipped into the swimming pool and sank to the bottom.

Suddenly, the mother, aware that her child was missing, ran to the back door, looked out, and screamed. There was her baby, floating face down on top of the water. The next morning headlines read, "Baby Drowns at His Own Christening Party!"

That's what has happened in the midst of the American church today! We all love the Baby, but we have become so distracted with our programs, our church growth efforts, our attempts to please people, or the hottest revelation of the hour that we've left the door ajar. Now the Baby has gone missing. In the midst of His own celebration, we've forgotten the gospel and we've let God's Baby drown!

THE ETERNAL GOSPEL

Now the Father looks down on this earth and thunders:

This is My Son! His gospel will be preached in all the world!

You see, this gospel did not just begin with Peter or Paul; nor did it even begin when Jesus came to earth. This gospel is eternal: John saw an "angel flying mid air, and he had the eternal [*aiōnios*] gospel to proclaim to those who live on earth—to every nation, tribe language, and people" (Rev. 14:6). The Greek *aiōnios* means without beginning or end, for this gospel has always existed in the heart of God. It dates back to the eternal covenant of redemption before the creation of the world.

Spurgeon asked, "Do you know...what God's estimate of the gospel is? Do you not know that it has been the chief subject of his thoughts and acts from all eternity? He looks on it as the grandest of all his works."[15]

Sometimes we simply don't understand the magnitude of the gospel.[16] This gospel is eternal and God will be unveiling its vastness in heaven forever.[17] As one preacher says, "You will be in the eternity of Eternities in heaven and you will not even reach the foothills of understanding the gospel. Heaven will be tracking down the glory of God in the Person of Christ and the cross of Christ. We will forevermore revel in this one thing: He shed His blood for my soul!"[18]

Can you imagine how you will feel when you get to heaven and gaze on the glorified, exalted, shining Lamb of God? As He unfolds before you the mysteries of the eternal gospel, your heart will be forever undone by a revelation of the Lamb.

CHAPTER 18 ENDNOTES

1. For example, we know he understands that "the Rock was Christ," which followed the children of Israel through the wilderness and poured out endless spiritual rivers (1 Cor. 10:4). He realizes that "Christ our Passover" (1 Cor. 5:7) fulfills this sacred feast of Passover.
2. Paul never used the term "the Father's cup," which Jesus used in His prayers in the garden. He used instead words like "propitiation" or the "curse of God" or the "wrath of God" (11 times in Romans) when speaking of the Father's cup. Whether we use the term Father's cup, propitiation, substitution, or bearing the curse, these all speak of Christ standing in our place and bearing the Father's eternal wrath.
3. Charles Spurgeon, *22000 Quotations*, 84.
4. Paul Washer asks, "Do we have a Gospel worth exporting, or should it be quarantined so that it doesn't infect other nations?" (Paul Washer, "A Gospel Worth Exporting," Missions Conference 2009, www.sermonaudio.com).
5. Rob Bell, *Love Wins* (Toronto, Ontario: Harper Collins, 2011), 128.
6. Russell Moore, "The Blood Drained Gospel of Rob Bell," March 11, 2011, accessed from the Internet, 4.
7. Walter B. Knight, *Knight's Master Book of 4,000 Illustrations* (Grand Rapids, MI: William B. Eerdmans Publishing Company, 1956), 255.
8. John Piper, *God is the Gospel*, 81.
9. Timothy J. Keller, in the foreword to Eric Metaxas, *Bonheoffer, Pastor, Prophet, Martyr, Spy: A Righteous Gentile Verses the Third Reich* (Nashville, TN: Thomas Nelson, 2010), xv.
10. Piper points out that blindness does not stop the light from shining but it stops us from seeing the light (Piper, *God is the Gospel*, 59–60).
11. Arthur Wallis, *In the Day of Thy Power* (Columbia, MO: Cityhill Publishing, 1956), 88. "This small church in twenty years called into being more missions than the whole evangelical church has done in two centuries," wrote German historian Dr. Warneck (Arthur Wallis, *Day of Thy Power*, 88). In Wallis' day, when subtle forms of racism affected

men's thinking, the term "pagan races" would have been common language. But I think it would be better to say "pagan people" because "pagan races" is far too sweeping, implying that certain races are pagan and other races are not pagan. This is not true.

12. Charles Spurgeon, "The Marvelous Magnet," 16.

13. Ibid., 16.

14. Ibid., 21.

15. Tom Carter, *22000 Quotations of Spurgeon*, 85.

16. Jesus said, "This gospel of the kingdom will be preached in the whole world as a testimony to all nations and then the end will come" (Matt. 24:14). If in fact the gospel is not being preached many places, than perhaps we should be placing more emphasis on preaching the gospel than preaching "End Times." Maybe we are putting the cart before the horse.

17. Paul Washer says, "You will cut your teeth on the Gospel, but you will be chewing on it through all Eternity" (Washer, "He Drank Your Hell," www.sermonaudio.com).

18. Paul Washer says, "The Gospel is not Christianity 101. The Gospel is *everything* in Christianity! It is not some beginning truth. It is not a tract. It is not four spiritual laws. It's *everything*! It is the greatest revelation of God, and we grow and we are revived to the degree we understand who Christ is and what Christ did for us on that Tree" (Washer, "The Lost Gospel," Revival Conference, 2009, www.sermon-audio.com).

Chapter 19

THEOLOGY ABLAZE

A Plea to Combine Sound Doctrine with Revival Fire

W ITH A HEAVY heart, the apostle Paul trudges up the road toward Corinth, lost in thought. I can see him now, burdened with a sense of failure. He had tried his hardest in Athens. He had studied the culture, planned eloquent and persuasive words, and carefully articulated his culturally relevant sermon. He even had the honor of preaching on the famous Mars Hill to the most brilliant Greek philosophers of his day. But the Bible says, that when he left Athens, only "a few men became followers of Paul and believed" (Acts 17:34).

Many tout this Mars Hill sermon in Acts 17 as a model sermon, but I am sure that Paul was broken by his failure. Somewhere along that forty-four mile journey from Athens to Corinth, light must have dawned on his soul. He realized that he never even mentioned the cross or the blood of Jesus Christ one time in his Mars Hill sermon. Allen Hood, in *The Excellencies of Christ*, writes:

> When Paul went to Mars Hill, he preached the gospel and tried to make it relevant to the culture. Afterwards three people came to Christ. This was a defeat compared to the response in the other towns he had just visited; it was not an effective crusade. Once in Corinth, he went back to preaching the simple message of the cross, and God birthed a whole church.[1]

WHERE ARE THE APOSTLE PAULS TODAY?

Learning from his mistake, Paul makes a fresh resolve to God. We know this is true because of what he writes to the Corinthians. He said that Christ sent him "to preach the gospel—not with words of human wisdom, lest the cross of Christ be emptied of its power. For the message of the cross is foolishness to those who are perishing, but to us who are being saved it is the power of God" (1 Cor. 1:17–18).

Here in Corinth Paul soon had 25,000 converts and he established a powerful church.[2] What made the difference? As he explained in his letter to the Corinthian church, "God was pleased, through the foolishness of what was preached to save those who believe. Jews demand miraculous signs and Greeks look for wisdom, but we preach Christ crucified" (1 Cor. 1:23). He had learned his lesson in Athens, thus he wrote, "When I came to you, brothers, I did not come with eloquence or superior wisdom as I proclaimed to you the testimony about God. For I resolved to know nothing while I was with you except Jesus Christ and him crucified" (2:1–2).

Now I want to ask—where are the apostle Pauls today? Where are those who will stop trying to be so "politically correct" and relevant to the culture and will preach the pure gospel of Christ? Where are those who will seek to please God rather than people? Where are those who will preach the message that transforms human lives?

Sometimes I wonder—is the reason we rarely preach the cross anymore because we think there's no power in this message? Do we think the solid biblical teaching on the cross is dry and lifeless? That's not what Paul said: "The message of the cross…is the power of God" (1 Cor. 1:18).

We say we want revival and we pray for it earnestly, but where are those, like Paul, who will preach the message of revival, which is the message of the cross? As Andrew Murray said, "At all times of revival, when the Spirit of God is poured out, it is in connection with the preaching of the cross."[3] Selwyn Hughes asks, "Can there be any movement of the Holy Spirit in which the cross is not made prominent? Such a thing is unthinkable. It is as impossible as a river without a source, or a day without light."[4]

Furthermore, where are those who will get on their faces before God and weep for the sins of the American church? Of the Western church? Who will grieve over our neglect of the Father's cup? How could the Father pour out the horrors of eternal wrath upon His beloved Son, and our pulpits remain silent about it? We've hardly even thanked Him for it! We've rarely shed a tear over it! Oh, God, help us!

Where are those who will repent for following hard after the latest revelation or hottest new spiritual fad rather than preaching Christ and Him crucified? The subject is fathomless, yet we thought we knew all there was to know about it. Our pride and ignorance have blinded us from wanting to understand the depths of His sacrifice.

I know I was ignorant until I started reading Jonathan Edwards and then plunged into a deep study of the Father's cup.[5] Not only was I ignorant, but my pride blinded me. I thought I knew all there was to know about the cross. Jesus was scourged, nailed, thrust with a spear and died. What else is there to know? But even worse—when I realized that I didn't want to preach the cross because it won't draw a crowd, I wept and wept in repentance. When I saw this selfish ambition in my heart, I was undone.

> *Oh, God, forgive us for our pride, our negligence, our apathy, our disregard for Your sacred bloody cross! Forgive us for our spiritual pride and selfish ambition which thwarts us from preaching the Lamb! Please, Father, let a spirit of repentance come on those reading these pages. Let us weep over the sin of neglect and pride and selfish ambition in ourselves and in this country. Let repentance go deep. Let it wash and purge like Peter, when he denied the Lord and "went outside and wept bitterly" (Luke 22:62).*

Paul said, "Godly sorrow brings repentance" (1 Cor. 7:10), so let repentance wash like rivers through your whole being. This is what will prepare you to be set ablaze by God. "Repent then and turn to God, that your sins may be wiped out and times of refreshing may come from the Lord" (Acts 3:19). Repentance means to turn. It brings change. And once we've repented for neglecting God's Son, everything changes. The heart is prepared to allow the message of the cup, the cry of dereliction, and the cross to engulf you. Then, a once smoldering fire in the soul suddenly bursts into flames of revival.

Again, I'm pleading with you not to blame your pastor if he doesn't preach the cross. Honor your pastor, but please don't hop on the latest bandwagon, which comes from those who travel around preaching a "different gospel." As Paul warned, don't blindly follow after those who "distort the truth in order to draw away disciples after them" (Acts 20:30). Why must we allow them to scratch our "itching ears" with false doctrine? Paul told us to beware, "For the time will come when people will not put up with sound doctrine. Instead, to suit their own desires, they will gather around them a great number of teachers to say what their itching ears want to hear" (2 Tim. 4:3).

Paul further warned of "false apostles, deceitful workers, masquerading as apostles of Christ" who do not preach the gospel (2 Cor. 11:14). Today we have many ministers claiming to be apostles; but my question is—if they are true apostles, why don't they preach the apostolic message of the cross? Why do they preach a "different gospel?"

I often hear Spirit-filled people mock the idea of doctrine and theology, calling it "all that theological stuff." I believe they say this out of insecurity and their own lack of knowledge. Actually, theology is simply a study of God (*Theos*: God, *ology*: study of), and what could be more wonderful than learning more about Him? Theology ablaze can be thrilling.

I say this especially to those of us in the Charismatic and Pentecostal arena. Oh, how we love the Holy Spirit and His work; but please, let's not forsake solid biblical doctrine. Let's bring the cross back to the center of Christianity and place the Lamb back in the center as He is in heaven. Let's rediscover the power of sound theology and burning doctrinal truth, and keep the blood central in our preaching. Charles Spurgeon points out that "the doctrine of the precious blood, when it gets into the heart, drives error out of it and sets up the throne of truth."[6]

THE BLAZING THEOLOGY OF JONATHAN EDWARDS

In *The Supremacy of God in Preaching*, John Piper tells about a seminary professor who encouraged him, rather than studying a smattering of many theological views, to find one great theologian and sink his shaft down deep into his thought. He writes, "The theologian I have devoted myself to is Jonathan Edwards. I owe him more than I can ever explain. He has fed my soul with the beauty of God and holiness and heaven…. He has shown me the possibility of mingling rigorous thought about God and warm affection for God...Above all, he is a God-besotted preacher."[7]

My experience was much like Piper's. As I said earlier, when I was a young Bible teacher in 1984, a wise pastor challenged me to dig into the works of Jonathan Edwards.[8] I did; and soon I was devouring his works, planting down deep into the soil of his tremendous writings. I was over-awed by the depth and breadth of Edwards' understanding of redemption through the Bible; his wisdom in defense of revival, which offered warnings to opponents and proponents; his urgent call to unified and "extraordinary prayer" for an outpouring of the Spirit; and his descriptions of the sovereignty of God and the glory of Christ. He left me breathless with awe and reverence.

Edwards is considered one of the greatest theologians America has ever produced. His preaching and writing could be described as theology ablaze. "He embodies the truth that theology exists for doxology," says Piper.[9] Piper said, "Our people are starving for God. My guess is that one great reason why people sometimes doubt the value of God-centered preaching is because they have never heard any. And so many of them are tragically starved for the God-entranced vision of that great old preacher Jonathan Edwards."[10]

One of the greatest treasures I found was Edwards' *The History of the Work of Redemption*, a compilation of thirty sermons he had prepared which plowed the ground for America's First Great Awakening. Though it was tedious to read, straining my eyes because of the small print, it caused my heart to burn.

In this massive work Edwards described the glory of God filling all eternity before the creation of the world. He told of the grand condescension of the Son when He agreed to purchase our salvation in the eternal covenant of redemption before the world was made. He explained the crimson thread of redemption running through every page of the Bible; but He also unveiled the golden cord of the glory of Christ weaving through the types and prophecies of the Old Testament. Not only was his vision full of the glory of God in eternity, but he revealed a latter day of glory coming to this earth to prepare a bride for the Son.

As I read, I felt my whole being suffused with truth and light. At the time I was teaching an Old Testament survey course in a Bible institute, so this great work of Edwards was helping me prepare for my course. As I said earlier, I later went to Fuller Theological Seminary in Pasadena, California, completing a Ph.D. in Theology of Missions (Intercultural Studies). I soon became a teacher of systematic theology as well as Old and New Testament; but Edwards' work was foundational to all my teaching. It is clearly the theological underpinning of this book.

Edwards opened my mind and showed me Christ in the Old Testament like nothing I had read in my life. More than that, he unveiled to me the depths of the Father's cup of wrath which Jesus prayed about in the Garden of Gethsemane and engulfed on the cross. His sermon, "Christ's Agony," caused a theological revolution in my life.

Let's look more deeply now into the revival under Jonathan Edwards, for there is much to learn from this amazing man. Edwards is not only a brilliant theologian, he was a revival theologian. Martyn Lloyd-Jones said that Edwards is "preeminently the theologian of Revival, the theologian of experience, or as some have put it 'the theologian of the heart.'"[11] Iain Murray says that Edwards is "being read today as he has not been read for over a century and in more countries than ever before. Such a recovery of truth has commonly been a forerunner of revival."[12]

AMERICA'S FIRST GREAT AWAKENING

America's First Great Awakening broke over New England in the 1740s like a "thunderbolt rushing out of a clear sky."[13] People had been reading Edwards' *A Faithful Narrative of Surprising Conversions*, which described the revival that broke out in his church in 1734. (We looked at this first revival under Edwards in a previous chapter.) Now a deep spiritual hunger pervaded the land. A spirit of prayer was filling the churches and people everywhere experienced concern for their souls.

In his own church, Edwards had preached his thirty sermons on *The History of the Work of Redemption*, and the Holy Spirit had begun pouring out again. Hearing that a young preacher named George Whitefield from England would be visiting in Georgia, Edwards invited him to come over and preach in his church.

Traveling by horseback through the forest of New England, this twenty-five-year-old Englishman caught a ferry across the river to Northampton in October of 1740 to preach in the church of the esteemed Jonathan

Edwards. When he stood, trembling with fear in Edwards' pulpit, suddenly the Spirit of God blew in and took over. Whitefield wrote in his journal, "I began with fear and trembling, but God assisted me. Few eyes were dry in the assembly....It seemed as if a time of refreshing was come from the presence of the Lord."[14]

When he preached the next day, Whitefield wrote that "Mr. Edwards wept during the whole time," and the power of God poured out graciously.[15] Mrs. Edwards wrote her brother, telling him that Whitefield preaches "with a heart all aglow with love, and pours out a torrent of eloquence which is almost unthinkable."[16]

Now America's First Great Awakening burst into flames throughout New England. Biographer Perry Miller said that New England was like a "powder keg," and though Edwards lit the fuse, George Whitefield blew the flame all across the land.[17]

But it wasn't just young Whitefield who preached with holy fire. When Edwards preached, the same fire burned; for though some today try to paint him as a stiff old Puritan preacher who read his sermons, there is no proof of this. The primary impression he made was that he spoke like a man standing in the presence of God.[18] "He was the most eloquent man I ever heard," said a doctor who heard him preach.[19]

In May of 1741, near the conclusion of a sermon, several persons were so affected by the glory of God that they could not contain the "visible effects upon their bodies." Edwards said that the young people and children "appeared to be overcome with a sense of the greatness and glory of divine things, and with adoration, love, joy, and praise, and compassion to others." Many others were "overcome with distress about their sinful and miserable estate and condition so that the whole room was full of nothing but outcries, fainting, and the like."[20] Others in the town heard of this and were drawn to the church. They were overpowered in a similar manner.[21]

In his *Thoughts on Revival*, Edwards describes even more about the manifestations of the Spirit, emphasizing the impression on the heart as being far more important than "bodily effects." He writes that people have been caught up in "views of the glory of divine perfections and Christ's excellencies; so that the soul has been as it were perfectly overwhelmed and swallowed up with light and love."[22] His own beloved wife was in a trancelike state for seventeen days. She would try to get up, but every time she heard the name of Jesus she fell back into the glory.[23]

When Edwards preached his fiercely convicting sermon, "Sinners in the Hands of an Angry God" in Enfield, a nearby town, before he could finish people were bowed down in conviction of sin. An eye-witness said, "A great moaning erupted as people cried out for salvation."[24] The power of God upon the people was described as astonishing; but these same cries for salvation under the convicting power of God were prevalent all over New England as the Great Awakening spread like a forest fire.

All revivals have their critics, and Edwards was severely criticized by Charles Chauncy, a famous Boston pastor of his day. Chauncy described Edwards' meetings as being filled with confusion, some screaming, some praying, others singing or lying prostrate on the floor. He warned of "roarings, trembling, and the strangest bodily effects," which "proved the work could not be of God."[25] Interestingly, when Iain Murray traced Charles Chauncy's influence in history, he found that Chauncy's work eventually evolved into Unitarianism and Universalism. On the other hand, Jonathan Edwards' work has inspired evangelical Christians for centuries.[26]

Of course, Edwards never encouraged fanaticism, or "enthusiasm," as it was called in his day. But neither did he oppose the "bodily effects" or manifestations, about which he wrote this profoundly affirming word:

> Now if such things are enthusiasm and the fruits of a distempered brain, let my brain be evermore possessed of that happy distemper! If this be distraction, I pray God that the world of mankind may be all seized with this benign, meek, beneficent, beatific, glorious distraction![27]

Because I had saturated myself in many of Edwards' greatest works, his words concerning revival impacted me deeply. He warned that one must never join the opposition by speaking against revival and thereby risk speaking against God Himself. He wrote, "Therefore, how heinous will it be in the sight of God, if, when a work of that nature is begun, we appear unbelieving, slow, backward, and disaffected."[28] "Let us all be hence warned by no means to oppose, or do anything in the least to clog or hinder the work; but, on the contrary, do our utmost to promote it."[29]

Let me tell you an interesting story about George Whitefield, the young Englishman who helped spread revival through America's Great Awakening. When he saw manifestations occurring in his meetings, he shut them down. But his friend, Lady Huntingdon, whom he greatly respected, gave him some sound advice. She said, "You are making a mistake. Don't be wiser than God!"[30]

And though many today cast dispersion on revival, Edwards said, "This is what Jesus Christ, our great Redeemer and head of the church, did so much desire and set his heart upon, from all eternity, and for which he did and suffered so much, offering up strong crying and tears, and his precious blood, to obtain it; surely his disciples and members should also earnestly seek it, and be much in prayer for it."[31]

Just reading about this Great Awakening of revival in America made my heart yearn for such an outpouring of God again. As I drank deeply from Edwards' well of knowledge, my thirst became insatiable. Though I was initially put off by the manifestations I saw in current revivals, once I looked into the revivals of church history, especially the revivals of Jonathan Edwards, I saw that manifestations always take place in revivals.

The way I see it now is this—if God can shake a mountain: "the whole mountain trembled violently" (Exod. 19:18); if He can shake the threshold of a massive temple: "at the sound of their voices, the door posts and thresholds shook" (Isa. 6:4); and if He can shake an upper room: "After they prayed the place where they were meeting was shaken" (Acts 4:31); then it's nothing for Him to shake a human body.

Of course, we don't seek manifestations, we seek Christ; so whether or not one shakes or falls is irrelevant. What matters, said Edwards, is do we love God and people and the Bible more, and are we being "weaned from the world"?[32] The question is not whether your body shakes; the question is—does your heart shake? Does your heart tremble over the cross of Jesus Christ? Has God set your theology ablaze and has your heart been undone by a revelation of the Lamb? This is what endures.

A LATTER DAY OF GLORY

When Scottish ministers began reading about the revival in America, they asked Edwards to write a treatise on the importance of prayer in revival. In his *Humble Attempt,* he wrote the following:

> We may infer that it is a very suitable thing and well-pleasing to God for many people in different parts of the world, by express agreement, to come into a visible union in extraordinary, speedy, fervent, and constant prayer, for those great effusions of the Holy Spirit, which shall bring on that advancement of Christ's church and kingdom, that God has so often promised shall be in the latter ages of the world.[33]

And today, though thick darkness is covering the land, the time to pray for "those great effusions of the Holy Spirit" has come, for we are living in great days in this country. This tremendous outpouring of the Holy Spirit to gather in a harvest of souls is the revival for which we've been believing.

Edwards described these days as a "Latter Day of Glory."[34] He said that God has "had it much on his heart, from all eternity, to glorify his dear and only begotten Son; and there are some special seasons that he appoints to that end." This will be when God "comes forth with omnipotent power to fulfill his promise and oath" to His Son. And these are "times of remarkable pouring out of his Spirit to advance his kingdom; such a day is a day of his power."[35]

I believe we are in that "day of his power!" I am convinced that we have come to the "Latter Day of Glory!" This is why we need to lay aside our doubts and pray more earnestly than ever. Edwards compared this "Latter Day of Glory" to the fulfillment of the feast of tabernacles. Just as Passover fulfilled "the purchase of redemption by Jesus Christ"; and just as Pentecost fulfilled "the outpouring of the Holy Spirit in the church age"; the feast of tabernacles, also called the feast of ingathering of the fruit harvest, will be fulfilled by the ingathering of a harvest of souls from the earth.[36]

This will also be a time of great shakings in the world, but this coming of the kingdom of Christ on earth is what Jesus labored to bring about in

His work of redemption on the cross. This is the summation of Christ's monumental sacrifice. He drank the Father's cup of eternal wrath to bring about this great cause. Ultimately it is to pour out upon the earth a glorious revival to prepare for Him a bride.[37]

SOUND DOCTRINE THAT BURNS

The reason we've looked at America's First Great Awakening under Jonathan Edwards is because he epitomizes sound doctrine coupled with the fire of revival. Edwards exemplifies a man filled with theology ablaze. Oh, this is what we need!

When Jesus revealed Himself in the Old Testament Scriptures to the two men on the road to Emmaus, they later said, "Were not our hearts burning within us while he talked with us on the road and opened the Scriptures to us?" (Luke 24:32). John Stott explains, "It was when they glimpsed new vistas of truth that the fires began to burn. It is still truth—Christ-centered, biblical truth—which sets the heart on fire."[38]

Martyn Lloyd-Jones said that we need "Logic on fire! Eloquent reason!...Theology on fire and a theology which does not take fire, I maintain, is a defective theology."[39] Stott writes the following:

> Some preachers serve out excellent theology from the pulpit, but it seems to have come out of the freezer. There is no warmth, no glow, no fire. Other pulpits catch fire all right, and threaten to set the church ablaze, but precious little theology goes with it. It is the combination which is almost irresistible in its power, namely theology on fire, passionate truth, eloquent reason.[40]

This book is a plea for sound doctrine that burns. It is a cry for depth and truth. It implores the church to once again return to the blood of the Lamb and honor the Father's cup which Jesus quenched in our place. Again, in theology this is called "penal substitution," but I've chosen to use the family term Jesus Himself used, namely the Father's cup.

And so, with the apostle Paul, this book is a cry to return to "sound doctrine that conforms to the glorious gospel of the blessed God" (1 Tim. 1:10). It is an earnest appeal for passion and fire to burn in the midst of strong biblical truth. It sounds a clarion call for theology ablaze. This comes from having your heart pierced and undone by a revelation of the Lamb.

Chapter 19 Endnotes

1. Allen Hood, *The Excellencies of Christ*, 98. Derek Prince came to this same conclusion which he states on his CD "The Cross at the Center" (Derek Prince Ministries, Charlotte, NC).
2. Derek Prince, "The Cross at the Center" CD teaching, Derek Prince Ministries, Charlotte, NC.
3. Andrew Murray, *The Cross of Christ* (London, UK: Marshall, Morgan, and Scott, Ltd, 1989), 17.
4. Selwyn Hughes, *Revival, Times of Refreshing* (Eastbourne, UK: Kingsway Publications, 1990), 35.
5. You can find a (slightly edited) copy of Jonathan Edwards' sermon "Christ's Agony," which first awakened me to the Father's cup, in the appendix of my book *The Unquenchable Flame*. It can be ordered from your local bookstore, Amazon.com, or our website: www.gloryofthelamb.com.
6. Lewis Drummond, *Spurgeon, The Prince of Preachers*, 643.
7. John Piper, *Supremacy of God in Preaching*, 67–68.
8. This pastor was Dr. Stephen Mansfield who has authored many New York Times Best Selling books on great leaders of our times.
9. John Piper, *Supremacy of God in Preaching*, 68.
10. Ibid., 14–15.
11. D. Martyn Lloyd-Jones, *The Puritans* (Westchester, PA: Banner of Truth Trust, 1987), 361.
12. Iain H. Murray, *Jonathan Edwards, A New Biography* (Carlisle, PA: The Banner of Truth Trust, 1987), 454, 472.
13. Iain H. Murray, *A New Biography*, 55.
14. George Whitefield, *Whitefield's Journal* (Edinburgh: The Banner of Truth Trust, 1978), 476.
15. Ibid.
16. Sarah Pierrepont Edwards, cited in Iain H. Murray, *A New Biography*, 162.
17. Perry Miller, cited in Iain H. Murray, *A New Biography*, 158.
18. Ibid., 175.
19. Sereno Dwight, compiler of Edwards' Memoirs, said "he was an instructive...animated and most powerful and impressive preacher... and through the blessing of God, one of the most successful preachers since the days of the apostles." Dwight once asked Dr. West, who actually heard Edwards preach, if he was an eloquent preacher. West

said that he was "the most eloquent man I ever heard." He told how Mr. Edwards could present a truth with such "overwhelming weight of argument, and with such intenseness of feeling" that his whole soul was thrown into every part of his delivery, keeping the people riveted, from beginning to end" (Sereno Dwight, *Memoirs of Jonathan Edwards: The Works of Jonathan Edwards*, vol. 1 [Banner of Truth Trust, 1995], cxc.

20. Jonathan Edwards, *Revival in Northampton in 1740–1742: The Works of Jonathan Edwards*, 149–150.
21. Edwards writes, "The months of August and September were the most remarkable of any this year for appearances of the conviction and conversion of sinners, and great reviving, quickening, and comforts of professors, and for extraordinary external effects of these things. It was a very frequent thing to see a house full of outcries, fainting, convulsions, and such like, both with distress, and also with admiration and joy" (Jonathan Edwards, *Revival in Northampton in 1740–1742*, 151).
22. Jonathan Edwards, *Thoughts on Revival: The Works of Jonathan Edwards*, 376.
23. He glowingly described the experiences of people who trembled, cried out, wept profusely, leapt for joy, fainted with love sickness, swooned (falling under the power), and were swallowed by the glory of God like a mote in a ray of sunshine (Ibid., 378–379).
24. Iain Murray, *A New Biography*, 169.
25. Charles Chauncy, *Seasonable Thoughts on the State of Religion in New England* (Boston, MA: Rogers and Fowle, 1743), 6.
26. Iain Murray, *A New Biography*, 454.
27. Jonathan Edwards, *Thoughts on Revival*, 387.
28. Ibid., 388.
29. Jonathan Edwards, *Distinguishing Marks of a Work of the Spirit: Jonathan Edwards on Revival* (Edinburgh: Banner of Truth Trust, 1995), 135.
30. Dutch Sheets, *The River of God*, 179; cited from Michael Brown, *From Holy Laughter to Holy Fire*.
31. Jonathan Edwards, *An Humble Attempt to Promote Explicit Agreement and Visible Union of God's People, in Extraordinary Prayer for the Revival of Religion and the Advancement of Christ's Kingdom on Earth: The Works of Jonathan Edwards*, vol. 2 (Banner of Truth Trust, 1995), 282, 289.
32. Jonathan Edwards, *Distinguishing Marks of a Work of the Spirit* (a brief summary of whole book).
33. Jonathan Edwards, *An Humble Attempt*, 282, 289. Edwards also compared this earth flooding revival to the streaming out of Ezekiel's river,

which flows from the sanctuary, toward the east, till it runs into the Dead Sea, healing the waters. He said this represents "the conversion of the world to the true religion (Christianity) in the latter days" (286).

34. Edwards described this "latter day of glory" as a time in which the earth would be filled with the glory of the Lord as waters cover the seas. Edwards said this would be a time "wherein God's people should not only once see the light of God's glory, as Moses, or see it once a year with the high priest, but should dwell and walk continually in it, and it should be their daily light." He adds: "The future promised advancement of the Kingdom of Christ is an event unspeakably happy and glorious. The Scriptures speak of it as a time wherein God and His Son Jesus Christ will be most eminently glorified on earth; a time wherein God, who till then had dwelt between the cherubim—and concealed himself in the holy of holies, in the secret of His tabernacle, behind the veil, in the thick darkness—should openly shine forth and all flesh should see His glory" (Jonathan Edwards, *An Humble Attempt*, 287).

35. Jonathan Edwards, "Thoughts on the Revival of Religion in New England," *The Works of President Edwards in Four Volumes*, vol. 3 (New York: Carter and Brothers, 1864), 311.

36. Jonathan Edwards, "Some Thoughts Concerning the Present Revival of Religion in New England and the Way it Ought to be Acknowledged and Promoted," *The Works of Jonathan Edwards*, vol. 1 (Edinburgh: Banner of Truth Trust, 1995), 383–384. Edwards said that during this time, the visible kingdom of Satan will be overthrown and the kingdom of Christ will spread "throughout the whole habitable globe." Now Christ shall become "the desire of all nations" (Hag. 2:7), for all the ends of the earth shall look to Christ "and be saved" (Isa. 45:22). "And the kingdom and This will be a time of great light and revelation of God as "the kingdom of this world has become the dominion and the greatness of the kingdom under the whole heaven, shall be given to the people of the most high God" (Dan. 7:27). "So great shall be the increase of knowledge in this time," said Edwards, "that heaven shall be as it were opened to the church of God on earth" (Jonathan Edwards, *The History of the Work of Redemption*, 609).

37. Jonathan Edwards, *An Humble Attempt*, 288.

38. John R. W. Stott, *Between Two Worlds: The Art of Biblical Preaching in the Twentieth Century* (Grand Rapids, MI: William B. Eerdman's Publishing Company, 1982), 286.

39. D. Martyn Lloyd-Jones, *Preaching and Preachers* (Grand Rapids, MI: Zondervan Publishing House, 1971), 97.

40. John R. W. Stott, *Between Two Worlds*, 286.

Chapter 20

PREACHING *with* FIRE

The High Calling of Preaching Christ and Him Crucified

F LAMES LEAPT FROM the roof of the pastor's home in Epworth, England. Susanna and Samuel Wesley desperately rounded up their children and counted them, but one was missing. Little five-year-old John was still in the burning house. Susanna broke into a loud sob. She had already lost ten of her nineteen children before they reached the age of two, and she couldn't bear to lose her beloved little John.

Just then a neighbor spotted the child, as the boy looked helplessly out the upstairs window. The house was about to burst into uncontrollable flames; but, acting quickly, the neighbors made a chain, climbing on each other's shoulders. Finally the top man was able to reach out and gather the boy into his arms. Immediately, even as they lowered little John to safety, the whole house exploded into flames, shooting sparks into the midnight sky.

For the rest of his life, John Wesley referred to himself as "a brand plucked out of the burning" (Zech. 3:2). Because of this near death experience, he always believed that God had a special calling on his life, a destiny he must fulfill.[1]

Years later his heart was "strangely warmed" in a Moravian meeting on Aldersgate Street in London. A few months later, he wandered along a cobbled pathway at Oxford, reading Jonathan Edwards' *A Faithful Narrative of Surprising Conversions*. This was Edwards' thrilling account of the revival at Northampton, just before America's First Great Awakening.[2]

Edwards' inspiring descriptions of revival stirred Wesley's heart, causing him to pray for God to bring revival to England as well. He began joining with his friends and praying earnestly for revival. One night, as Wesley and sixty others prayed all night, suddenly the power of God swept in and broke over all of them. Many of them cried out and others were knocked to the floor by God's power.[3]

These proper Englishmen were undone by the presence of God; and from that time on, Wesley began seeing mighty manifestations of God's power. Often while Wesley preached, people would be seized with conviction, crying out in pain and sinking to the ground, "thunderstruck," as he put it. Sometimes a "violent trembling" would grip the people.[4]

Wesley's revivals didn't burn for a few years and then smoke out like most revivals today. They lasted for fifty years![5] His biographer A. Skevington Wood in *The Burning Heart* gives us the secret to Wesley's unquenchable flames of revival. The heart of John Wesley's gospel, said Wood, "is to be found at the cross." This was his "consuming pre-occupation," the atonement his "burning focus of faith." Indeed, "It was with the *kerygma* of the cross that he set out to reach Britain for Christ."[6]

Like the apostle Paul, John Wesley "was prepared to strip his message of all that was peripheral and to know nothing among his hearers except Jesus Christ and him crucified."[7] In fact, Wesley once said, "Give me a hundred men who fear nothing but God, hate nothing but sin and are determined to know nothing among men but *Jesus Christ and Him crucified*, and I will set the world on fire with them."[8]

AMERICA ABLAZE

This is what we need! Where are the preachers like John Wesley who will lift up the torch of the cross until their entire nation is set ablaze? Where are those like the Moravians, who will cry, "May the Lamb who was slain receive the reward of His suffering!"[9] until the gospel spreads around the world? Where are those like Evan Roberts, only twenty-six years old, who will preach "Calvary's love and a love for Calvary" until an entire nation is changed as in Wales in 1905? Where are those like Jonathan Edwards, who will describe the Father's cup with such intensity that people will groan for mercy and a Great Awakening will result?[10]

We need prophets like John the Baptist who will cry, "Behold the Lamb of God!" until the church is "baptized in the Holy Spirit and fire" (John 1:29; Luke 3:16). We need preachers like Peter who will preach the gospel with such power that people are "cut to the heart" (Acts 2:35). We need apostles like Paul, who will resolve to "preach Christ and him crucified" (1 Cor. 1:23), until the whole world is turned upside down.[11] We need visionaries like John who will look into heaven until they see the slain Lamb on the throne (Rev. 5:6), then will reveal Him down on earth.

We need revivalists like British evangelist Nathan Morris who will proclaim the glory of the gospel until revival fire falls and miracles explode. Nathan cries, "There is no message but the cross of Jesus Christ!" and a hunger for the cross is stirring in this land, for Nathan has struck a raw nerve in the body of Christ. People realize this is what has been missing. At last the time has come for the Lamb to be glorified in this nation.

We need thousands of revivalists like Nathan and John Kilpatrick who will sweep this land with the gospel. We need men and women who burn and blaze for the gospel and will never give up preaching the blood of the Lamb. We need an army of young revivalists who will brandish the sword of the cross and drive the blade of the gospel into tender hearts.[12]

Won't you join us in this great cause? This is not just another Charismatic bandwagon to jump on. This is not just one more stream in the body of Christ. We are talking about the Son of God—God's eternal Lamb! He deserves the reward of His suffering. We simply cannot give up until there is a paradigm shift in the church. It must be a theological revolution—a return to theology ablaze. A reformation which is driven by a rediscovery of the glory of the gospel of Jesus Christ. A resurrection of the cross which is founded on a revelation of the Lamb.

FINDING YOUR PREACHING VOICE

But you say—I'm not a preacher. I can't stand before people and speak. Neither could Moses or Gideon, but God used them to lead a whole nation. You see, once God consumes your heart with a melting revelation of the Lamb, He will change you into a different person. Once the cross penetrates your soul and fills your heart, you will become pregnant with a message.

I wish you could have seen our interns preaching in a prison in South Carolina. Most of these young girls and guys, in their early twenties or late teens, had quiet personalities. They weren't your typical "preacher type." But they had a message burning and bubbling inside. As they looked out on these muscle-bound, tattooed, macho men, they weren't intimidated because they couldn't hold back the message imploding in their hearts. Then, when they opened their mouths, inflamed by passion, the words burst out of their soul-hot lips and pierced the hearts of big strong men. I watched many of the inmates wiping away tears, and some of them shaking under conviction. This is what John Piper calls "blood earnest preaching."[13]

Victor was so shy he couldn't speak a clear sentence in my systematic theology class. Let me tell you what happened. After he read about the Father's cup and the Lord pierced his heart, which I told you about in section two, I asked him to preach to a youth group from Texas. As we worshiped in the prayer garden, Victor slipped up to me and said, "Dr. Sandy, I don't have a message. I just don't have anything to say." I knew he was quite shy but he had a tremendous prayer life, often shaking the walls of the camp with his passionate prayers. So I said, "Don't worry. Just get up and pray with all your heart; then when you touch heaven in prayer, preach from that high place." That's exactly what he did, and the kids were so gripped by his message of the cross that most of them ran up to the front of the prayer garden and threw themselves on their faces in the dirt, repenting and crying out to God. Today Victor preaches the cross in crusades all over Mexico where hundreds are healed and thousands saved.

Sophie was a shy, quiet teenager. She had never spoken on a microphone, but she had an earnest heart to learn. She didn't really find her preaching voice in her first year at our internship, but she left with a message surging in her heart. When she was invited to Africa, she found herself exploding with the message of the cross, preaching in slums and garbage dumps and leading many to the Lord. By the time she returned to the camp the second year, she had found her preaching voice and was preaching with powerful passion. Now she preaches in crusades in Kenya and people are undone by this message of the cross pouring from this twenty-four-year-old white girl from England.

Mary has become a peerless preacher, whose sermons blaze with passion and biblical truth. She has learned to get hold of a passage in Scripture, then to grapple with it and wrestle in prayer over it until she feels it burning and trembling in her spirit. Then she releases the passion of her heart; and as people listen, their own hearts begin to tremble and burn. When I hear her preach, I feel like my heart is being nailed to the back of my chair.

Stephanie was painfully shy when I had her as a student at BRSM. But when she joined our internship, she asked God to do a fresh piercing in her heart. One summer afternoon, she wept and wept on the floor of our chapel, as her heart was utterly undone by the cup, the cry, the sacrifice of the Lamb. When she got off that floor, she was a preacher! She couldn't help it. Her heart, like the veil in the temple, had been ripped open by the hand of God and the message of the Lamb now poured out. Now when she ministers, the piercing cry of Jesus bursts from her lips and the presence of God fills the room.[14]

But preaching with fire is not just for the young. Mark was fifty-five and his wife Cathy was sixty-eight when they came to our internship. They already had a national healing ministry with the Healing Rooms and a pastoral ministry with Patricia King on the Internet; but when they read *The Unquenchable Flame* book, they knew they had to get here and get this message.

They didn't come with the typical prideful attitude that says, "I already know all there is to know about the cross." And though many told them they were making a mistake, they forged ahead and came with desperately hungry hearts. When they left a month later, they were exploding with the message of the Lamb. Now the miracles have increased amazingly and Cathy has become a preaching fireball. She told me, "I would never ever speak at our conferences. I let Mark do all the preaching, but now I can't help it! I'm burning inside with a message."

How then do you find your own preaching voice? What I tell our students is this—you must let the message of the cross consume you. Then saturate yourself in the Bible and let the Spirit of Truth burn and blaze in your spirit. He will highlight the verse or passage of Scripture that He wants you to preach. He will show you. The way you will know is that your spirit will surge with the verse and the message.

Your sermon is like a baby, gestating and growing in a mother's womb. Hold it inside and ponder it in your heart, like Jesus' mother Mary. Don't even talk about it prematurely because you don't want to birth the baby too soon. And when the time to preach comes, I suggest to our students that they begin speaking in a low key tone. Then suddenly, as soon as the door in your spirit opens, let the message burst forth with passion. Pour your whole spirit, soul, and body behind your red-hot words.

It's like the time Jeannette, a fifty-five-year-old Canadian woman, exploded with her preaching voice in our second preaching class. She got up to give her ten minute sermon on the cross and suddenly the Holy Spirit fell on her. Her sermon flowed out of her with a tremendous, roaring power. I heard it; and I'm not kidding you, she was like a house afire as she exploded with the message of the cross. She later admitted she too was shocked but thrilled to find her preaching voice. Some time later, she stood to preach in an outdoor campaign in Africa. Suddenly her preaching voice came back and she erupted in the same power. One of the pastors asked, "How can a woman preach like that?" and they asked her to return and preach a weeklong revival campaign.

This is what happens when you find your preaching voice. It begins by being saturated in the work of Christ on the cross. But never forget, above all, to soak your sermon in prayer. Cry out to God in private for your hearers. Ask the Holy Spirit to attend your words and open their hearts. If you will, God will confirm His word with the power of His presence. With heaven sent fire!

But you might ask—won't I appear fanatical? Maybe, but who are you trying to please? The people or God? I assure you, people are bored with dry, lifeless sermons. They want genuine passion. Spurgeon said, "It is dreadful work to listen to a sermon, and feel all the while as if you were sitting out in a snowstorm, or dwelling in a house of ice, clear but cold, orderly but killing."[15] That's why he pleaded for "much heavenly fire," and said that "even fanaticism is to be preferred to indifference."[16] He cried, "Give us more of the speech which comes of a burning heart as lava comes of a volcanic overflow."[17]

So I urge you, let the gospel go in deep. Let it surge and seethe within you until it does a deep work in your soul. Let it crucify your heart, until your selfish ambitions are nailed to the cross, for it's not about your fame; it's His fame. John Watson said, "The chief effect of every sermon should be to unveil Christ, and the chief art of the preacher to conceal himself."[18]

Remember, when the priests mocked and battered Jesus, He "remained silent" (Matt 26:63). "As a sheep before her shearers is silent, so he did not open his mouth" (Isa. 53:7). The Lamb of God was silent, but now it's no longer time for silence! Once the gospel has done its crucifying work in your heart, "shout it from the rooftops" and be a voice for the Lamb to your generation. Let the gospel explode from your lips, as Spurgeon said, like hot lava from the volcano of a ruptured heart. From a heart that's been broken open and spilled out with love for the Lamb. And if the Spirit of God attends your words, people will be undone by a revelation of the Lamb.

Preaching with Fire in Africa

I know I've said a lot about Kenya in this book, but it's because this country has been like a model of what can happen in a nation if preachers get hold of this message of the Father's cup. Our purpose has not been to build a big ministry for ourselves. I'm sure by now you know my heart—my passion is to give away this message of the Lamb and to raise up others to spread the message. So please let me tell you more of this story of what happened to the pastors when they grasped hold of this truth.

As I've said, when we brought this teaching of the cross to the pastors in Kenya, they hit the floor, weeping in sorrowful repentance. As mentioned earlier, they had told me they'd only been teaching demonology and prosperity, concepts gleaned from the West. But when they heard about the Father's cup and the cry of dereliction and all that Jesus did on the cross, they were completely undone by a revelation of the Lamb.[19]

Pastor Zacheaus cried out, "God forgive us! God forgive us! We have neglected the cup! We have forgotten the cross! God forgive us!" They lay out on the floor, weeping and sobbing until there were no more tears. Then we sent them out to the streets, the slums, and the villages. They preached with a passion like I have never seen in my life. They wept and roared and cried out the gospel in English with translation in Swahili. Pastor Newton said, "I almost wailed as I preached because the fire is so deep in me. I feel like I'm pregnant!"

Someone might argue, but the gospel doesn't need to be "wailed." No, it doesn't; but please know this—it is clearly scriptural. Paul wrote, "We preach [*kēryssō*] Christ crucified" (1 Cor. 1:23), and *kēryssō* means "to preach, discharge, herald, cry out."[20] It's like the old town crier who brought a message from the king, crying out, "Hear ye, hear ye, hear ye!" It's like Abraham, an African college student, who came to our school and then went out with his *Glory of the Lamb* book in one hand and a megaphone in the other, preaching the gospel as loudly as he could in the streets. When you have a message boiling inside, you cannot help but discharge it with great passion.

Pastor Allan, who is only in his early twenties, said, "This message of the cross has got power and that's why I cannot hold it in me." In a crusade he held under a tent in the village, after leading hundreds to the Lord and seeing many instantly healed, he said, "On the last night of the crusade, it was so amazing. Something came like a blowing wind and all the people in the tent got fire. The fire was so real!" In another crusade, he and Pastor Newton began preaching the gospel with such fire, people thought they were burning. As they were being saved and healed and delivered, they cried out, "I am burning! I am on fire!"

I'm telling you, the fruit that resulted from the message of the cross through these young Kenyan pastors thrilled my heart. Twenty-one-year-old Judy preached the gospel in a church, and one man said to her, "Young girl, this message you are preaching—it is true. Kenya is dying because of sin! They need this gospel!"

Pastor Tobias, a more seasoned pastor, said, "My preaching has been transformed by the message of the cross and the cup! It put something in my spirit!" Pastor Zachy said, "As I preached about the cup, some in the crowd burst out in loud cries, and God gave them a revelation of the Lamb!" "Brethren," urged Pastor Joseph, "we must make sure that not just Kenya, but all of Africa receives the glory of the Lamb!"

Pastor Joseph, a former street boy, said, "When I took my courses in Bible college, the cross of Christ was never mentioned. Now I burn to tell about the fire of the cross! I know I will set my church ablaze and all of Kenya!"

Pastor Manase said, "Until this week I had no power in my preaching, but after I received this message of the cross, I felt myself trembling as I preached on the streets, and I preached with power!" Pastor George said, "I could preach before but not like this. Now power comes out when I preach the cross. Souls are saved and people are slain by the message. This is real fire and it will save all of Kenya!"

Pastor Lillian said, "Yesterday I saw so much fire on everyone, and I wanted to know if it was real. When I came to the altar, the fire of God came on me. *It is real! It is real! It is real!*" Her husband, Edmond, wrote me after the school and said that he preached about the Father's wrath falling on Jesus and people began weeping loudly. Then he roared out the cry of dereliction and the sobbing became so loud he had to stop and wait for the crying to die down. When he finally came to the cry of victory, "*Tetelestia!*" the whole place erupted with revival fire.

Pastor Wickenol said, "When I came here I was crying to God, 'Do it in me!' Then I embraced the cross, repenting for never feeling Christ's pain. I opened my heart to receive the cross. Jesus came and began to squeeze my heart. Now I have the cup message in my life, and I feel fire!"

These young men and women were excellent preachers before they ever came to our Kenya Ablaze for the Lamb school, but they didn't have a message. Once they learned about the Father's cup which Jesus engulfed on the cross, they exploded with preaching like I've never heard in my life. But the key is simply this—the message of the cross, pouring from blazing hearts and burning lips, flowing like molten lava into desperate souls. Oh, if only more people will get hold of this message, the results will be world changing!

This is a good example of what I mean by theology ablaze. These pastors already were preaching with passion. They had heat but no light. They had a little fire but weak theology. Once they became gripped with all their hearts by the cross and the sound doctrine of the Father's cup of wrath, the light of truth and the heat of passion blazed in flames of revival.

Do You Sizzle?

John Stott tells the story about W. E. Sangster, a wise British pastor, interviewing a nervous young man for the ministry. The young man said, "I think you should know that I'm not the sort of person who would ever set the River Thames on fire." "My dear young brother," said Sangster, "I'm not interested to know if you could set the Thames on fire. What I want to know is this: if I picked you up by the scruff of your neck and dropped you into the Thames, would it sizzle?"[21]

In other words, was this young man so burning with the Spirit of Truth that, like a hot pan sizzling when it hits cold water, he would cause cold hearts to sizzle? As Stott said, "Fire in preaching depends on fire in the preacher."[22]

G. Campbell Morgan, who preached at the renowned Westminster Chapel in London, said that the three essentials for a sermon are "truth, clarity, and passion."[23] To receive truth means to saturate your sermon with Scripture. This doesn't mean asking people to turn to every verse in your message. It means "oozing Scripture," as Piper says,[24] letting the Bible pour out of you naturally. John Stott, a masterful preacher himself, encourages us, in both the preparation and delivery of the sermon, to let the Spirit of Truth have His way. "Then the light and the fire, the truth and the passion will be reunited."[25]

Not only does this result in theology ablaze, but preaching with fire. Oh, this is what we must have! We need a revelation of the Lamb that burns. In Paul's day, the mad emperor Nero illumined his garden parties by hanging Christians upside down and lighting their hair on fire. If these Christians were willing to burn for the Lamb, then how much more should we let our preaching burn for the Lamb?

Even more, Jesus went through the fire of God's wrath for us. The least we can do is let our hearts burn and our spirits blaze as we preach "Christ and Him crucified." John Wesley was a great example of this. Again, when people asked why he drew such a huge crowd when he preached, he simply said, "Well, you see, when you set yourself on fire, people will come and watch you burn!"

I often illustrate this point in my classes by soaking a rolled up paper towel in cooking oil, then setting it aflame. The fire burns on for at least ten minutes while I continue calling out for men and women to burn for Jesus. One day, however, I held up the torch in Queen's College at Cambridge University in England, and suddenly the smoke alarms set off! Proper English people were a bit shocked; but I cried out, "It's about time the alarm sounded in England!" Lifting higher the torch, I shouted, "It's time to catch this place on fire for the Lamb!"

Yes, Jesus said, "I have a fire to bring on this earth, and how I wish it were already kindled!" (Luke 12:49). He spoke of the mighty fires of revival, a great conflagration which He wants to spread across this earth. This spiritual blaze must be ignited in human hearts and sustained by a revelation of the Lamb.

So where are those in America and the Western church who will sink their roots into sound biblical theology until they are preaching and teaching with fire? Will you be one? Will you embrace the glory of the cross until God sets your church ablaze? Will you rise up and preach the Lamb with passion and power? Will you preach with such theological truth and blazing passion that the hearts of your hearers are undone and ultimately your nation is set ablaze by a revelation of the Lamb?

CHAPTER 20 ENDNOTES

1. Wesley struggled with a lack of assurance over his own salvation. But one night, after returning to England from a failed mission to America, he attended a Moravian meeting in London. The Moravians had been an inspiration to him while on the boat and in America. They had a deep relationship with Christ and spoke often of bringing the Lamb who was slain the reward of His suffering. At the meeting one of the Moravian leaders read the preface to Martin Luther's commentary on Romans. Suddenly, John Wesley said, "I felt my heart strangely warmed," and he knew, because at last his spirit bore witness, that he was saved.

2. John Wesley, *The Journal of the Rev. John Wesley in 4 Volumes*, vol. 1 (London: J.M. Dent & Co., n.d.), 158.

3. Wesley wrote about this experience in his journal. He said, "About three in the morning, as we were continuing instant in prayer, the power of God came mightily upon us, insomuch that many cried out for exceeding joy, and many fell to the ground. As soon as we were recovered a little from that awe and amazement at the presence of His majesty, we broke out with one voice, *'We praise Thee O God; we acknowledge Thee to be the Lord'*" (Robert Southey, *The Life of Wesley: The Rise and Progress of Methodism* [London: George Bell and Sons, 1890], 137.

4. While preaching at Newgate, God bore witness to His word: "Immediately one, and another and another, sank to the earth; they dropped on every side as thunderstruck." A physician, who suspected these manifestations were fraudulent, came to observe. Suddenly, one of his patients fell to the ground, trembling "till great drops of sweat ran down her face, and all her bones shook." He slipped up close to

watch and "when both her body and soul were healed in a moment, he acknowledged the finger of God" (Robert Southey, *The Life of Wesley*, 147).

5. For Wesley it was the fruit of changed lives that proved this was true revival. These were, said Wesley, "my living witnesses." He described the habitual drunkard as now "temperate in all things; the whore-monger now flees fornication; he that stole now steals no more but works with his hands; he that cursed or swore, perhaps at every sentence, has now learned to serve the Lord with fear" (*The Letters of the Rev. John Wesley*, vol. II, 290. To the Bishop of London, 11th June, 1747; quoted in A. Skevington Wood, *The Burning Heart* [Minneapolis, MN: Bethany Fellowship, 1967], 179).

6. Ibid., 237.

7. Ibid.

8. John Wesley, quoted in "The Haystack Effect," *Prayer Magazine*, Autumn 2005, (4:9).

9. See John R. W. Stott, *The Cross of Christ*, 293.

10. Jonathan Edwards' sermon, "Sinners in the Hands of an Angry God," was instrumental in America's First Great Awakening.

11. In *The Majesty of God* Stuart Greaves writes, "It is crucial that the revelation of the knowledge of God found in Christ Jesus be the premier focus and top priority of our lives. Jesus, the Lamb of God, shining in all His thunder and glory holds the central attention of multitudes above" (Stuart Greaves, *The Existence and Majesty of God*, 13).

12. See our website: www.gloryofthelamb.com and learn about our Revivalists of the Cross and Unquenchable Flame Internships as well as our new training school, Behold the Lamb School of Revival.

13. John Piper, *The Supremacy of God in Preaching*, 54.

14. I must, however, say to budding young preachers—please don't run out flailing your sword in the air, like Peter in the garden, cutting off ears and discrediting the gospel. If you are dying to preach, then you need to sit down and be quiet for awhile. You aren't ready. This is not about you preaching for the sake of preaching. It's about the sacred and holy gospel of Christ. So please stop dreaming about changing your church and your pastor. Look for the lost, the hungry, the poor, the broken—like Jesus and Paul and John Wesley did—and preach to them the gospel.

15. Charles H. Spurgeon, cited in John Stott, *Between Two Worlds*, 283.

16. Ibid.

17. Ibid.

18. Leslie J. Tizard, *Preaching—The Art of Communication* (George Allen & Unwin, 1958), 40–41; cited in John Stott, *Between Two Worlds*, 325.

19. See our website: www.gloryofthelamb.com for videos of these African pastors repenting.
20. *The Hebrew-Greek Key Study Bible*, "New Testament Lexical Aids," Spiros Zodhiates, ed. (Chattanooga, TN: AMG Publishers, 1996), 1641.
21. John Stott, *Between Two Worlds*, 285.
22. Ibid.
23. Ibid., 284.
24. John Piper, *The Supremacy of God in Preaching*, 88.
25. John Stott, *Between Two Worlds*, 286.

Chapter 21

JEWISH HEARTS UNDONE

A Revelation of the Lamb for Israel

S ONYA WORKED AS a seamstress in a store in New York City. She did her work efficiently, never speaking to anyone. Often, after work, she turned off the lights in her apartment and crawled into bed, desperately trying to escape the torment, which often erupted in violent nightmares. Here's the rest of the story:

As a Jewish refugee from Germany, the Gestapo had arrested Sonya's husband and son. She never saw them again. Even her sister and two children had been forced into slave labor. Frightened and alone, Sonya had been smuggled to America. Memories of her past had been locked away in the silent vault of her heart.

One day, however, she came face to face with her past. Sitting alone in a cafeteria, a familiar voice said, "Sonya..." It was Mrs. Stein, who was on the refugee assistance committee which had helped Sonya find her job and small apartment. "We have two children from Germany," she began. "They've been through so much. The girl is ten; the boy is seven. They need a home. I thought maybe you needed someone, too."

Sonya shook her head and snapped, "I cannot." The girl and boy, ten and seven, were the same ages that her niece and nephew would have been. They would be morbid reminders of the family she lost.

"Will you at least think about it, Sonya? I'll come back tomorrow and you can give me your answer then."

"There's no need. I cannot take them," Sonya said rigidly, keeping her head down until the woman left. As soon as work ended, she rushed home, turned off the lights and threw herself in bed. The mention of those children had stirred the memories so tightly locked within. The ache throbbed with physical pain against the door of her heart. Finally, the storm burst and she cried for the first time since leaving Germany.

She stumbled to the closet, sobbing, and dragged out the photographs of her family. She tearfully unwrapped the picture of her husband, her son, and her sister, placing them on the dresser. It hurt to look at them but it also brought relief. She thought of the good times, mingled with memories of suffering. She knew for the sake of her lost family that she must start living again. She must begin to reach out and carry on for them.

Kneeling by her bed, she prayed for the first time in years. "I want to come alive again!" she wept. "I don't know how but I'm hoping you can help me. Amen." She fell asleep and for the first time since she lost her family, she slept peacefully through the night. When she awoke, she knew what she must do. She would take the children. It would be her first step in reaching out.

At the cafeteria she found Mrs. Stein and nervously told her she would take the children. Though it would be crowded, she would try to make a home for them. "Good!" Mrs. Stein smiled. "I'll bring them tonight."

After work, Sonya hurried home and began baking the traditional pastries, which she hadn't made in so many years. Soon the knock on the door came. Sonya opened the door and, as she looked into the sad eyes of the children, her heart twisted. There was something strangely familiar about them.

"Sonya, this is Liese and Karl," said Mrs. Stein. Sonya's stomach lurched. These were the same names of her niece and nephew. The painful memories came pounding back with a cruel thud.

"Is something wrong?" asked Mrs. Stein, puzzled by her reaction. The girl, Liese, lifted her sad dark eyes and searched

Sonya's face. Then suddenly, Karl gave a piercing wail. "Karl, are you alright?" asked Mrs. Stein.

The boy pointed a trembling finger toward the three pictures Sonya had set out the night before. He ran toward the dresser, grabbing the picture of Sonya's sister. Holding it to his heart, he cried—"Mama!"[1]

REPENTING FOR FORMER WOUNDS

I share this story to help us feel a little of the pain Jewish people have experienced, for before we can heal we must feel what they have suffered. The huge divide between Jewish people and Christians is beginning to heal because of all the acts of repentance for Jewish suffering.

But, you protest, I love Jewish people. I didn't do this to them. From a Jewish perspective, however, the Crusaders burned innocent Jews under the sign of a cross. Then tragically, Martin Luther, who led the Protestant Reformation, wrote a book in his later years called *About the Jews and Their Lies* in which he said, "They are thirsty bloodhounds and murderers of all Christendom." He told how they were often accused of poisoning water and wells, stealing children and hacking them apart "in order to cool their temper secretly with Christian blood."[2]

Luther lived in Germany, and his writing had a towering influence on German thinking. Paul Johnson, in *A History of the Jews*, said that Luther's book "was the first work of anti-Semitism and a giant step forward on the road to the Holocaust."[3]

Finally, Adolf Hitler, with his bent cross called a swastika, began to mount his "final solution" of the Jewish problem. He had rabbis' heads sawed off in front of their families, thousands of innocent Jewish people thrown into human graves in Poland, and millions of Jewish people taken in cattle cars to the death camps.[4]

Never will I forget what I felt when I stood gazing at the ovens which cremated Jewish bodies in a concentration camp in Germany. A spirit of morbidity still hung in the air. The chill was appalling.

Here at this death camp, German soldiers herded the weak, sick, elderly, young, and pregnant ones into the gas chamber, under the pretense of being showered for lice. Steel doors slammed behind the naked masses who stood under the false shower heads. Then SS-guards poured zyklon-B pellets in through special vents in the roof, releasing gas into the chamber. People coughed and choked, then fainted and in twenty minutes lay dead in piles. What was their crime? Their only crime was—they were Jews.[5]

Sadly, because Hitler claimed he was wiping out Jews for the sake of Christ and because, through the centuries, many so-called Christians have accused Jewish people of being "Christ killers," many Jewish people blame Christians for these atrocities. Stan Telchin said, "Jewish people have heard about…and experienced every imaginable evil act that one person can inflict on another, and these were done in the name of Jesus!"[6] As Michael Brown titled his brilliant book—*Our Hands Are Stained with Blood!*[7]

German nun, Basilea Schlink, asked, "How are the Jews to believe in Jesus? Have we not ourselves blindfolded them? They cannot see Jesus because of our conduct. They cannot believe in Him because in our lives we have not presented to them the image of Jesus; rather we have shown them the image of mercilessness."[8]

Because barbaric acts against Jewish people were carried out by people who called themselves Christians, Christ and His cross are considered the cause of much of their suffering. This is why it will take acts of genuine repentance to God and to Jewish people to begin to heal the rift between us. John Dawson calls this "Identificational Repentance" in his book *Healing America's Wounds.*[9]

I saw the power of identifying with Jewish pain one day while flying in from a prayer journey in Jakarta, Indonesia. Sitting next to me on the plane was a lovely Jewish lady. I politely tried to make conversation with her, but she refused to respond. After a while, I whispered a prayer, took a deep breath and said, "Excuse me, Ma'am, but I am a Christian from America and I wanted to tell you how deeply sorry I am for the way you were called a 'Christ-killer' when you were young."

She looked at me in shock, and to my surprise she blurted, "Oh, yes, it was horrible!" She began pouring her heart out to me about all the anti-Semitism she had experienced, telling me many stories of persecution in her childhood. I listened in rapt attention, my heart aching, and then I asked, "Has anyone ever repented to you for these terrible words?" She said, "N-no…" With tears in my eyes, I sincerely repented for each incident she had described, and her own eyes filled with tears. By identifying with her pain and repenting for her suffering, her heart seemed to open to me.

So I took the risk and said, "Jewish people didn't kill Jesus Christ. Neither did the Romans. God did! It was His plan from before the creation of the world for His Son to come into this world as a Jewish man and then lay down His life as a Lamb. That's why God shows us lambs all through the Old Testament."

She looked at me quizzically and began asking many questions, showing deep interest. This opened up a stream of conversation about Christ becoming God's Passover Lamb. Then suddenly she looked up and saw a man coming toward her, scowling. "Oh, that's the man I live with. I can't talk about this around him, but I have a sister who is a Messianic Jew and I am going to visit her. I'm going to talk with her and look more deeply into these things."

Several years ago Peter Wagner led hundreds of Christians on a "Reconciliation Walk" from Germany to Jerusalem, retracing the steps of the Crusades. Through Germany, the Balkans, Turkey, Syria, Lebanon, and into Israel, Christians repented to Jews and Muslims for the atrocities committed under the sign of the cross over 900 years ago. Wagner said, "There is nothing more powerful than true, sincere repentance in opening the way for the light of the glory of Christ to shine where it has previously been resisted."[10]

In one of my classes at the Brownsville Revival School of Ministry (BRSM), we were looking at the wounds of Jewish people. Davida was a Messianic Jew, and she began sharing her story. She told of always feeling inferior because she was Jewish. Her father, a medical doctor, told her stories of being abused, persecuted, and labeled a "dirty Jew." She grew up believing that being Jewish was shameful rather than a privilege.

As we listened, we were all broken by her story. We gathered around her and wept with her. We poured warm water into a tub and gently washed her feet, our tears dripping into the water. We "stood in the gap" for the people who had falsely accused her and her father. With sincere emotion we cried, "Davida, we are sorry. We were so wrong!" As we identified with the sins of her persecutors, the results were powerful.

Davida wept and wept, and when finally we dried her feet, the Lord began to minister to her heart. I held a little mirror in front of her and asked her to say into her own eyes, "Davida, I forgive you for being Jewish—just like Jesus!" Suddenly, those words broke over her heart and she realized—"Hallelujah! I'm Jewish, just like Jesus!" The Holy Spirit flooded her with deep healing and she's never been the same.

One day, Chris, one of my students, stood outside the Brownsville church in the crowd that had gathered for revival, when he started talking to a young Jewish man. Suddenly the spirit of repentance hit Chris, and he fell to his knees sobbing at the Jewish man's feet. "Oh, please forgive me! Forgive us for all the terrible things Christians have done to you and your people!" The man was overwhelmed. "No one has ever said that to me before," he said, tears filling his eyes.

At a prayer meeting in Pensacola, a Jewish rabbi spoke briefly. Suddenly, the spirit of repentance came upon my friend Kurt Kamikowa, another teacher at BRSM. In front of the crowd, he fell to his knees and crawled across the platform to the feet of the Jewish rabbi. The people looked on spellbound. Then with sobbing grief, Kurt poured out his tears of repentance for the sins of the church against Jewish people. The rabbi was visibly touched and the whole crowd melted.

JEWISH HATRED OF THE CROSS

Thank God for these sincere efforts of reconciliation, but still the hatred toward Christ and even toward God runs deep in many Jewish hearts. "After Auschwitz," said Richard Rubenstein, "It is impossible to believe in God."[11] Said Elie Wiesel, remembering the night he was separated from his mother and sister in the death camps as a boy, "Never shall I forget those flames which consumed my faith forever."[12]

Rabbi Israel Shahak says that still today pious Jewish people, if they see a cross or a crucifix, they spit on it. With the rise of anti-Semitism, they are discreet about it, often spitting on their own chests as a sign of disgust toward the cross. Many Jewish schools even object to the "+" sign being used in math, replacing it with an inverted "T."[13]

Messianic Jew, David Stern, who wrote a Jewish version of the Old and New Testaments, called *The Complete Jewish Bible*, said:

> To many Christians the cross represents all they hold dear...
> but for centuries Jews were done to death under the sign of the
> cross by persons claiming to be followers of the Jewish Messiah.
> Therefore to me, the cross symbolizes persecution of the Jews.
> As a Messianic Jew, still feeling the pain on behalf of my people,
> I do not have it in me to represent my New Testament faith by
> a cross.[14]

In Stern's Jewish New Testament, he uses the term "execution stake"
or "crucifixion stick," but never "the cross." How can this be? If Jesus
engulfed the Father's cup of wrath on the cross, and if Paul said, "I glory
only in the cross," how can we take the cross out of our message to
Jewish people?

What do we do? Do we just wring our hands and retreat from sharing
the gospel with Jewish people? Do we muzzle our mouths and give them
a watered-down, wishy-washy, lukewarm gospel, which is no gospel at
all? What hope is left if we have to deny the cross of Christ? The answer
to this question is fathomless.

We cannot approach Jewish people with "the cross," but we can give
them a revelation of the Lamb!

A REVELATION OF THE LAMB

Jewish people cannot receive the message of the cross, but the message of
the Lamb is their Hebrew heritage. The scarlet thread of bloody lambs
weaves throughout their entire history. So tell them about a God who
gave Himself as a sacrificial Lamb before the creation of the world. Tell
them about Abel's lamb, accepted by God because it showed His Son
pouring out blood as a Lamb. Show them Abraham's son, called to
become a burnt offering, because he pictured Christ the Lamb.

Reveal to them the Passover Lamb, lifted on a pole because it displayed Christ, our Passover Lamb. Unveil to them Jesus as the scapegoat
on Yom Kippur, bearing the curse of God upon Himself and removing
that curse from us. Unfold to them the meaning of Isaiah 53 as the
Suffering Servant was "led like a lamb to the slaughter" (53:7). These are
their Scriptures, so show them Christ the Lamb in the Old Testament.

Help them see the pierced Lamb of God because the Bible says, "And they will look on me, the one they have pierced, and they will mourn for him as one mourns for an only child" (Zech. 12:10). Jonathan Edwards says that when this verse is fulfilled, "then shall the house of Israel be saved."[15] As Spurgeon said, "The conversion of the Jews will come from a sight of their crucified Messiah."[16] And when this happens, it will be worldwide revival.[17]

Now do you see why, from the beginning of this book to the end, we have unveiled Christ as the Lamb? We have beheld the Lamb of God from glory to glory, from eternity past to eternity future. One reason we have continually tried to unveil the Lamb through eternal history is for this very end—to prepare you to unveil a revelation of the Lamb to a Jewish person.

Let God use you in this grand eternal plan of redemption. Show Jewish people why Jesus was born in Bethlehem, where lambs were born for the sole purpose of being slain in Jerusalem. Disclose to them why God chose lowly shepherds to attend His birth, for shepherds always attend the birth of lambs. Bring to light why He was placed in a manger, an animal feeding trough, which was a fitting place for a lamb. Yes, lambs are the heritage of their Jewish faith. God planned it this way in the eternal covenant of redemption before the creation of the world.

So remind them of their Jewish prophet John the Baptist, pointing to Jesus and proclaiming: "Behold the Lamb who takes away the sin of the world!" In that moment of colossal disclosure, he shook the whole land as he unveiled a revelation of the Lamb to all Israel.

That's what you too are called to do—cause them to behold Jesus as the Lamb. Reveal to them how every detail of His crucifixion fulfilled different aspects of their sacrificial lambs. Just as the sin offering was always taken outside the city, Jesus was crucified outside the city gates. Just as a lamb was examined before dawn, Jesus was examined before dawn and found faultless. Just as the lamb for the burnt offering was cut and flayed in pieces, Jesus was cut and flayed in pieces by a Roman scourge. Just as the lamb for the burnt offering was cast down on the altar at the third hour or nine o'clock in the morning, Jesus was cast down on the altar at Calvary at nine o'clock in the morning.

Lay bare before their eyes the Passover Lamb skinned and then lifted up on the pole and roasted over the fires of God's wrath. Roar out the cry of dereliction, "My God, my God, why have you forsaken me?" Thunder this cry from your visceral being so they can feel the quaking in their own hearts and the veil that covers them will begin to tear. Only God can rip the veil that covers their hearts, like the veil in the temple which He tore in two from top to bottom. But He uses vessels like you, so don't hold back.

Let them see His precious blood, pouring down to wash, not just cover, but wash away all sin. Let them understand that every drop of that precious blood of the Lamb is the fulfillment of the blood streaming out through the Old Testament sacrifices. Help them see that the reason their sacrificial system no longer exists is because their Messiah—the ultimate Lamb of God—has been sacrificed.

But let them see that He rose from a Jewish grave in Jerusalem. He ascended from the Mount of Olives just outside Jerusalem. He entered again the courts of heaven and was glorified in the presence of His Father. Tell them the story of Pentecost, when Christ, their Messiah, sent down the Holy Spirit on 120 Jewish people in an upper room. Then tell about the 3,000 Jewish people who were "cut to the heart" and saved (Acts 2:37) when they heard Peter's heart-piercing sermon. Help them understand Saul, persecuting Christians, until the lightning of God struck him from heaven and he heard Jesus say in essence, "When you persecute these Christians, you are persecuting Me!"

But when you tell the story, tell it with love bleeding from your heart. Tell it with tears dripping down your face. Let them feel the warmth of your heart as you pour out this amazing story.

DIP EVERY WORD IN LOVE

An old Gentile carpenter lived in the remote mountains of a Romanian village, but he had begged God not to let him die until he led a Jewish person to Christ. He had said, "Lord I'm old, and sick, and I can't get out of this little village. Please bring a Jewish person here to this place in the mountains."

Richard Wurmbrand was a young Jewish atheist who cared nothing about God. One day he found himself visiting the village, later admitting he felt strangely drawn there. When the carpenter heard about this Jewish man, he was overjoyed. He and his wife began praying for

Wurmbrand earnestly, reaching out to him and pouring out love and kindness to him. Wurmbrand had never experienced such love from a Gentile Christian.

Fervently the old carpenter continued to pray for his conversion; then one day he gave him a Bible. Wurmbrand had read the Bible before, but not like this. He said, "The Bible he gave me was not so much in words but in flames of love fired by his prayers. I could barely read it. I could only weep over it." Soon Richard Wurmbrand and his wife believed on the Lord Jesus Christ as their Messiah, and though many persecutions followed, he has been a hero to the suffering church throughout the world.[18]

Like this old Gentile carpenter, I urge you also to pray fervently for Jewish people. And when you are able to tell them about your Jesus, soak every word with love. Dip every thought in tears. Let them feel your deep, deep sorrow over the suffering of Jewish people through the centuries. Repent with godly grief for the anti-Semitic barbs and cruelty they still experience. Then from your own pierced and humble heart, pour out the message of the Lamb.

This is why, all through this book, we've been calling you to behold the Lamb until your own heart is undone. For once the veil over your heart melts, you can be used by God to help melt other veils.

It's just like the prophet said to Mary, "A sword will pierce even your own soul—to the end that the thoughts from many hearts may be revealed [*apokalyptō*]" (Luke 2:35, NAS). As we've seen, *apokalyptō* means an "unveiling of revelation." In other words, those with a revelation of the Lamb can give that revelation to others. Those with pierced hearts can be used by God to pierce other hearts. According to the prophet, the purpose of the piercing is so that others can receive an "unveiling of revelation."

We have a large flag of Israel hanging from the ceiling of our chapel. Almost every day as I pray, I stretch my hand toward that flag and cry out for Israel. I ask God to pierce the veil that covers Jewish hearts. I ask Him for a revelation of the Lamb for Jewish people everywhere.

Maybe you haven't had a strong theology concerning Israel, but I can assure you—the church has not replaced Israel. This is called "Replacement Theology," and it is false. In fact, Jesus' own flesh was the veil, torn in two to remove the divide between Gentiles and Jews: He "made both groups into one, and broke down the barrier of the dividing wall." He did this "that he might make the two into one new man...and might reconcile them to God through the cross" (Eph. 2:14–16).

So won't you begin to pray earnestly for a revelation of the Lamb for Israel? Then ask the Holy Spirit to give you divine appointments with Jewish people. When it happens, pour out your heart in love and brokenness until—through your own pierced open heart—they can feel the glory of the gospel burning out to them. Let love and truth spill from your lips until they begin to soften and warm and finally you will see a Jewish heart undone by a revelation of the Lamb.

CHAPTER 21 ENDNOTES

1. Cynthia Mercati, "She Didn't Pray for a Miracle," in Jack Canfield, Mark Victor Hansen, Rabbi Dov Peretz Elkins, *Chicken Soup for the Jewish Soul*, 2–6.
2. Martin Luther, *About the Jews and Their Lies*; cited in Raul Hilberg, *The Destruction of the European Jews* (Chicago: Quadrangle Books, 1961), 9.
3. Will Durrant, *The Story of Civilization*, vol. 6 *The Reformation* (New York: MJF Books, 11957); cited in Stan Telchin, *Abandoned: What is God's Will for the Jewish People and the Church?* (Grand Rapids, MI: Chosen Books, 1997), 71.
4. Martin Rosenbaum, the only survivor in his family, described his heart ache as he parted forever from those he loved: "It is impossible to describe the agony of those few moments before we parted. I will never forget the wise eyes of my father and the tears of my mother when we embraced for the last time. In my wildest dreams I would never have imagined that I was parting from my whole family forever, never to see them again" (Martin Rosenblum, quoted in Martin Gilbert, *The Holocaust, A History of the Jews During the Second World War*, 444; recited in Michael Brown, *Our Hands Are Stained with Blood*, 178).
5. Though many Jewish people say, "After Auschwitz, how can we talk about God?" Jürgen Moltmann says, "After Auschwitz, how can we not talk about God?" God Himself was in the death camps, "suffering with the martyred and the murdered" (Jürgen Moltmann, *The Source of Life: The Holy Spirit and the Theology of Life*; cited in Mick Stringer, "Our Cries in His Cry: Suffering and The Crucified God," 10).

6. Stan Telchin, *Abandoned!* (Grand Rapids, MI: Chosen Books, 1981), 52.
7. Michael Brown, *Our Hands Are Stained with Blood.*
8. Basilea Schlink, *Israel, My Chosen People: A German Confession before God and the Jews* (Old Tappan, NJ: Fleming H. Revell, 1987); cited in Michael Brown, *Our Hands Are Stained with Blood,* 206.
9. John Dawson, *Healing America's Wounds* (Ventura, CA: Regal Publications, 1996).
10. C. Peter Wagner, *Prayer Track News* 8:3 (July–September 1999): 1.
11. Richard Rubenstein, quoted in John R. W. Stott, *The Cross of Christ,* 334.
12. Elie Wiesel, *Night,* 45.
13. Rabbi Israel Shahak, "Jewish Hatred Toward Christians," 1.
14. David Stern, *Jewish New Testament Commentary* (Messianic Jewish Publishers, 1992), 40–41.
15. Edwards wrote, "When this day comes, the thick veil that blinds their eyes shall be removed (2 3:16); and divine grace shall melt and renew their hard hearts, 'and they shall look on him whom they have pierced, and they shall mourn for him, as one mourneth for his only son and shall be in bitterness, as one that is in bitterness for his first born' (Zech. 12:10). And then shall the house of Israel be saved: the Jews in all their dispersions shall cast away their old infidelity and shall wonderfully have their hearts changed....and shall flow together to the blessed Jesus, penitently, humbly and joyfully owning him as their glorious King and only Saviour, and shall with all their hearts, as with one heart and voice, declare his praises unto the nations" (Jonathan Edwards, *The History of the Work of Redemption,* 312–123).
16. Spurgeon, "How Hearts Are Softened" *Spurgeon's Expository Encyclopedia,* vol. 8, 380.
17. The Apostle Paul, a Jew of the highest descent, said "all Israel will be saved" (Rom. 11:26), and when Jewish people receive their Messiah, it will be "life from the dead" to the church (Rom. 11:15). A revelation of the Lamb must come to God's people in order to enter into that great day of worldwide revival. Jonathan Edwards said, "Nothing is more certainly foretold than this national conversion of the Jews is in the 11th chapter of Romans." Edwards says that this is why God has miraculously preserved His people, through bloodshed and persecution for thousands of years. "Though we do not know the time in which this conversion of the nation of Israel will come to pass; yet this much we may determine by scripture, that it will be before the glory of the Gentile part of the church shall be fully accomplished; because it is said, that their coming in shall be life from the dead to the Gentiles

(Rom. 11:12, 15)" (Jonathan Edwards, *The History of the Work of Redemption*, 27).

18. This story is told in Richard Wurmbrand's book, *Tortured for Christ*, and on the website: www.gracealoneca.com/sitebuildertortured for Christ.pdf.

Chapter 22

THE LAMB'S REWARD

Living for the Greatest Purpose on Earth

MY FATHER WAS a great man. He gave from his resources to help poor children who had no means of receiving proper medical care. I used to hear him tell stories, with tears in his eyes, about little children who now could hear with hearing aids, who now could see with glasses, or who had received vital operations which saved their lives. He received many civic awards for his philanthropic deeds. I deeply admired him for his heart of mercy for children; but sadly, he never had a personal relationship with God through Jesus Christ.

One day, I was praying earnestly for his salvation when my mother called with the tragic news that he was in intensive care dying. I immediately got my children out of school and rushed to his side in Abilene, Texas. When I got there, he lay in a coma, completely unconscious. Hoping he could hear me, I asked, "Daddy, do you want to go to heaven and be with Jesus?" To my shock, he whispered, "Uh huh!"

All my life I had tried to share Jesus with my parents but was always rudely rebuffed. Now in this state of brokenness at the end of his life, he seemed receptive. *But no, that couldn't be,* I thought. *He's in a coma and doctors say he is dying.*

Then I asked him again and he nodded his head. With my heart in my throat, I asked him to follow me in a prayer to repent of his sins and receive the Lord. When I finished, I looked at his face and saw a huge tear dripping down his cheek. It was like a sign to me that he really had repented and turned to the Lord.

A few days later he came out of the coma; and every time I saw him, he wanted me to pray with him and talk to him about the Lord. He only lived a few more weeks, but I believe he is with Jesus, in spite of the fact that he lived without Him his whole life. And yet, how tragic it is when all one offers to Christ is the last few weeks of life.

John Piper tells about an old man in his father's church who finally got saved. He sat on the pew, his face in his hands, sobbing, "I wasted it! I wasted it! I wasted it!" Piper said, "When I heard my dad tell that story....I felt with every fiber of my being, *I will not waste it!* You only get one crack at life!"[1]

Oh, I know how he feels. Life is too short to waste, but how do we live with real purpose? How do we make a difference in this world? Piper explains:

> The people that make a durable difference in the world are not the people who have mastered many things, but who have been mastered by one great thing. If you want your life to count, if you want the ripple effect of the pebbles you drop to become waves that reach the ends of the earth and roll on into eternity... you have to know a few great, majestic, unchanging, obvious, simple, glorious things—one great all-embracing thing—and be set on fire by them.[2]

That one great thing is the cross of Jesus Christ, as Piper says, "A cross-centered, cross-exalting, cross-saturated life is a God glorifying life—the only God glorifying life. All others are wasted."[3] He continues, "Life is wasted if we do not grasp the glory of the cross, cherish it for the treasure that it is, and cleave to it as the highest price of every pleasure and the deepest comfort in every pain." Then he cries with passion, "May the one thing that you cherish, the one thing that you rejoice in and exult over, be the cross of Jesus Christ!"[4]

Now for almost thirty years, I have lived my life to pour this passion for the cross into the next generation. To help illustrate the importance of living for life's greatest purpose, I sometimes tell this story. Holding up a rose and plucking out the petals, I tell the students that each petal represents the years of your life.

When Abby was a child, the voice of the Holy Spirit came to her saying, "Abby, don't waste your life. Come to me now, with all your heart, and live for the Glory of the Lamb." Abby protested, "But Lord, I'm so young, please wait until I'm a little older and can really know what I'm doing."

So the years passed (and I continued to pick off the petals, dropping them to the ground), and finally the Lord returned and said, "Abby, don't waste your life. Come to me now, with all your heart, and live for the Glory of the Lamb." "But Lord, I'm a teenager now and all I really care about is my friends, and my boyfriend, and the fun we have together. Wait until I'm a little older (and the petals continued to fall).

When Abby was in her mid twenties, the Lord returned, and said, "Abby, don't waste your life. Come to me now, with all your heart, and live for the Glory of the Lamb." "But Lord, I'm engaged to be married, and I have to prepare this wedding, and I'm far too busy. Please give me a little more time." Ten years passed and finally the Lord returned, saying, "Abby, don't waste your life. Come to me now, with all your heart, and live for the Glory of the Lamb." But Abby refused, excusing herself because now she had two children and one more on the way.

The years passed and the petals fell. Abby's children grew up and moved away, her husband died, and finally the Lord returned when she was in her late seventies. He whispered, "Abby, don't waste your life. Come to me now, with all your heart, and live for the Glory of the Lamb." "Yes, Lord," she softly replied. "I want to give my life to you now. Here, take it and use it for your glory."

I held out the stubble of what was left of the rose, now emptied of its beautiful petals. It was a dramatic picture of giving to the Lord the residue of a wasted life.[5]

I was a bit like Abby in that story. Even after giving my life to Christ and being filled with the Holy Spirit, I didn't seem to have much passion for Jesus. I wanted to live a life of purpose, but the years were quickly passing and I hadn't quite found a passion for which I could burn.

Then one day, as I told you in the beginning of this book, I had an encounter with the cross that changed everything. The fire of God came upon me and I resolved, like the apostle Paul, "to know only Christ and him crucified" (1 Cor. 2:2). As John Piper says, "Life is wasted when we do not live for the glory of God....Christ is the glory of God. His blood soaked cross is the blazing center of that glory."[6]

At last I had found that "blazing center." And like the Moravians, I soon discovered that living to bring Jesus, the Lamb who was slain, the reward of His suffering is the greatest purpose on earth.

IF YOU ARE YOUNG

Perhaps you are young and have the rest of your life in front of you. If so, then now is the time to set your sights on Christ, asking, "Lord, how can I bring you the reward of your suffering with my life?" Let me tell you what happened to twenty-three-year-old Sophie which showed her how to bring Jesus His reward:

> A soft little knock came on the door of the office at the orphanage in Ramba, Kenya. A scrawny little eight-year-old boy with HIV came in quietly. His head was down, and he was crying pitifully because he was so hungry. Earlier that day Sophie and Pastor Newton had prayed for God to provide food for the orphans. They had completely run out of food and the children were hungry.
>
> Sophie had given almost all the money she brought with her, only saving enough to keep her comfortably fed on her trip back to England. But that little bit of money can go a long way in poverty stricken Kenya. Now, as she looked at the little boy, tears dripping down his face because he was so hungry, conviction stabbed her heart.
>
> She ran to the church, an open air tabernacle at the orphanage, and fell to her knees. She sobbed and sobbed before God in gut-wrenching repentance. "Oh, God, I'm so sorry! Please forgive me for my selfishness, for my greediness! Change my life, Lord, and help me to turn and give everything I have to help these orphans!"

When she finally got off the floor, she was never the same. She has dedicated her life to giving everything to help the poor. She lives above all for the Lamb, but this is her way of bringing Him the reward of His suffering. Now she has started a ministry to help the orphans, and her work is exploding as she spreads the message of the Lamb and His mercy to the suffering children.[7]

So I urge you to expand your horizons and get a higher vision for your life. Don't just coast along aimlessly, but let one single motive compel you. Let it become your consuming passion. As Misty Edwards says, "You were designed for God. You will live aimless until you find Him as your purpose."[8]

If you are young and on the threshold of your life, lift your vision upwards and live for His reward. If you are older, come grasp a fresh vision to impel you for the rest of your years. Come up higher. Gaze upon Jesus until your heart bursts into flames of love and the wind spreads the blaze out to others. Like Paul, let the cross—"the blazing center of God's glory"—be your highest glory: "God forbid that I should glory, save in the cross of the Lord Jesus Christ" (Gal. 6:14).

IF YOU ARE OLDER

But what about those of us over fifty? Oh, this is where it gets exciting! Piper points out a stunning truth for those of us who are a bit older. He says, "What a tragedy it is in America that every year billions of dollars are invested yearly to lure us to waste our lives. It's called retirement!"[9]

You know how the allurement goes: "You've worked for it; now take life easy and enjoy what you've worked to attain!" But Jesus warned about a rich man who said, "I'll say to myself, 'you have plenty of good things laid up for many years. Take life easy.'" In other words, "You've earned it. Now relax and enjoy yourself!" But God said to the rich man, "You fool! This very night your life will be demanded from you. Then who will get what you have prepared for yourself?" (Luke 12:16–19).

John Piper reminds us that two-thirds of the world is sinking in poverty and sickness, with children dying and people suffering, while we have the means to help them. But we choose to spend our last years taking "life easy." Think about it. Thousands of retired Christians run from conference to conference, getting spiritually and physically fatter, while the rest of the world is starving, spiritually and physically.

Dear one reading these pages, I'm calling you to rise up, find the greatest purpose in life, and *never retire*! You cannot control the length of your life, but you can control the depth of your life. Jesus said, "Whoever wants to save his life will lose it, but whoever loses his life for my sake and the gospel will save it" (Mark 8:35). We may not always feel physically able, but He is able. Let's give Him our best years, our "golden years," laying up our treasures in heaven where moth and rust do not corrupt.

I am in my late sixties, and it's difficult sometimes to push my body to go to Africa or Asia or Europe or wherever I travel to bring the message of the Lamb. But I refuse to be governed by how I feel. God gives me the strength, and though it's not easy, it's worth it to bring the worthy One His reward. Besides, I'd rather burn out than rust out!

Let me tell you about some amazing people who have found the secret of living for the Lamb's reward. In their later years, Rod and Michelle from England have adopted five adult children in Kisumu, Kenya, and now they do everything they can to raise money and provide education for these young adults who are dirt poor but beautiful and intelligent. They are trying to raise funds to build an orphanage and provide soybeans for the hungry. What a great way to add purpose to one's life!

Ian and Jeannette, in midlife, traveled with us to Kenya; and when they saw a little seven-year-old boy at an orphanage having to father his four brothers and sisters because his parents had died of AIDS, their hearts went out to him. They saw how these children had to walk miles just to get water and food, so they dug deeply into their resources and had a well dug and a field plowed for crops. They later built a school for the children, and continued to help support the orphanage. This has brought amazing relief to the children of this orphanage, but it has also brought great meaning to Ian and Jeannette's lives.

A seventy-five-year-old little blind lady often sat outside a boys' school with her Bible open. When a student would approach her, she would ask him to read for an old blind woman an underlined verse in the Bible. He would read: "For God so loved the world that he gave his one and only Son, that whoever believes in him shall not perish but have eternal life" (John 3:16). Then she would ask, "Do you know what this means?" Almost always the door opened for her to share the gospel, and she led many young men to the Lord—while seventy-five and blind!

So please don't say, "I'm too old!" Be creative, like that seventy-year-old blind lady. You can spend the last years of your life bringing Jesus the reward of His suffering. I often remind our older students that Joshua was eighty years old when he led the young generation into the Promised Land. Truth is—this generation starves for older people who will love them, lead them, mentor them, and impart wisdom into their lives. We have so much to give to these younger guys. They cannot spread the Lamb through the world without us.[10]

Arthur Blessitt exemplifies one who was creative in his effort to share the cross with the lost. For forty years he carried a wooden cross over his shoulder, walking through every nation of this world.[11] He faced a firing squad in Nicaragua, near stoning in Morocco, and was imprisoned two dozen times. He even walked with his son through the streets of Beirut as bombs exploded all around them.[12] Everywhere he went, he found that people either love the cross or hate it passionately.[13] The responses were simply amazing, for Arthur Blessitt had found the greatest purpose in life—lifting up the cross and bringing souls to the Lamb.

Cathy was in her late sixties, and though she was an ordained pastor with a powerful healing ministry, she came to our Unquenchable Flame Internship to look more deeply at the cross. She was so impacted that she later told me, "Now when I preach, I tell the people, 'We've been deceived! We've been lied to! The church doesn't tell us about the cross, and until we understand what Jesus did when He drank the Father's cup of eternal wrath, we will never see the victory God has for us!'" One day, after she had preached a burning sermon on the Father's cup, a very godly eighty-year-old gentleman, who walks in the presence of God, came up to her. With flashing eyes he said, "No one ever told me about the cup. This changes everything for me!"

After our one month internship on the Gulf Coast, twenty-three-year-old Collin was asked to share what he had learned with a local ministry school. As he stood to speak to this group of older adults, suddenly, his heart began to pound so hard it took his breath away. Finally he managed to utter, "I...received...a...revelation of the cross!" Then he burst into tears and fell over sobbing.

As he wept, the whole room filled with the glory of God. People all over the classroom got on their faces and cried out to God. Because of this powerful testimony, spoken with only seven words, Collin's dad and many older adults are coming to our internship and getting set ablaze for the Lamb.[14] I am so thankful because the two generations simply must come together to spread a revelation of the Lamb.

I've watched Hazel and Nicky blossom as they've started reaching out to the orphans and the poor in Africa. I used to hurt for Hazel because I could see that she, like many of us, now in her late sixties, was beginning to feel useless and discouraged with her life. Her family depended on her to care for all the aging relatives, and she hardly had a life of her own. Then she rose up, wrote a few missionary support letters, went to Africa with us, and now she is helping the poor and the orphans and giving to young pastors as they preach the gospel in Africa. Now Hazel absolutely glows! She shines with the inner confidence that she is living to bring Jesus the reward of His suffering.

Nicky also pours out her life and her resources to help the poor and the orphans in Kenya. She stands alongside her daughter Sophie, encouraging her, helping raise money for the orphans, and ministering to them at the orphanage. One day she met a street boy, a young man who was saved but had been chased out of his church because his pastor was jealous of him. Nicky reached out to Joseph, helped raise money for his education in Bible college, and now he is a pastor.[15] Nicky has found the deep satisfaction of knowing she is bringing Jesus His reward.

DON'T FORGET THE CHILDREN

Let me encourage you—when you think about bringing Him His reward—please don't forget the children. God is breathing on children today in unprecedented ways. I discovered this myself one day in Africa. Along with our team, I had taught the pastors every day in our Kenya Ablaze for the Lamb School. We had preached in their churches, ministered for hours, prayed for the sick, and preached in small crusades. When the school was over, I was utterly spent, exhausted from pouring out.

We were staying at Gideon's Army Orphanage, where 140 precious orphans had given up their beds so that we would have a place to sleep. I hate to say this, but I was too tired for the children. One evening, however, I sat outside resting and watching the children play. Suddenly a group of teenagers surrounded me and began plying me with questions. I half-heartedly responded because I was so tired. One thirteen-year-old's question captured me. She said, "Dr. Sandy, how can I be filled with the Holy Spirit?"

I saw her deep hunger, so we slipped over to the church where I began briefly telling them about the cross and the Holy Spirit. They were so hungry, and within moments the Holy Spirit came down and all of them lay on the concrete floor, overflowing in the language of the Spirit. I never said anything about praying in tongues or falling under the power of God. And they knew nothing about it, except perhaps what they might have heard from adults. I was amazed. Ministry is usually tiring. I did nothing. The Holy Spirit swept in and flooded down on these children with ease and power.

The next night I heard these same kids weeping and wailing in prayer in the little church. My heart was irresistibly drawn, and when I walked in, more teenagers began asking for the Holy Spirit. The same thing happened. They fell to the floor weeping in tongues as the wind of the Spirit rushed down upon them. The next night all the orphans gathered and began crying out to God; and the same teens who had received the night before, laid their hands on the younger children. Soon they too were all on the floor, weeping before God, filled with the Holy Spirit and praying in a new prayer language.

Oh, I tell you, watching a little five-year-old boy with tears spilling down his cheeks, as he rocks back and forth praying in the Holy Spirit, is a beautiful sight. This was the highlight of my time in Africa. It's great to see pastors grab hold of the message of the cross, knowing they will spread the message throughout their land. But what I saw happen among the children showed me that God has indeed targeted these little ones to carry revival throughout the earth. They are His reward.

You Tell Them

So regardless of your age, find something you can do to bring Jesus His reward. And please, now that you've learned about the Father's cup and a revelation of the Lamb, tell people what Jesus has done for them. Like the godly eighty-year-old gentleman told one of our graduates after she preached on the Father's cup, he said, "No one ever told me about the cup. This changes everything for me!"

"No one ever told me" is what I hear everywhere I go, especially from the young. But even those of us who are older, if we've heard about the wrath, haven't really given it much thought. Is this how you feel? When you realize there was so much more about the cross and the cup and the core of our Christian faith, do you find yourself thinking—"Why didn't anyone tell me?"

If this is how you feel, then I charge you, in the name of Jesus Christ— you tell them! You write the books! You paint the pictures! You compose the songs! You develop the videos! You create the dramas! You teach the classes! You preach the sermons! You give time to a third world nation and tell them what Jesus did for them!

And when you tell them, turn people's ears into eyes. Paul said, "Before your very eyes Jesus Christ was clearly portrayed [*prographō*] as crucified" (Gal. 3:1). The Greek *prographō* means "to paint a picture and lift it up on a public placard before peoples' eyes. John Stott said, "One of the greatest arts or gifts in preaching is to turn people's ears into eyes, and to make them see what we are talking about."[16]

So whether by preaching or painting or writing or singing, let people see His blood trickling down His face. Let them almost feel the whip and thorns, the spikes and the spear, mutilating His flesh. Let them almost sense the molten hot lava of the Father's cup roaring down on Him. Let them hear His cries rending the heavens and tearing the Father's heart. Let them sense the anguish breaking open His heart. Let them feel the emotion, the passion, the glory. Tell them the story until people's hearts are undone by a revelation of the Lamb.

I AM NOT MY OWN

A popular young man on campus got saved and started handing out tracts on his college campus and crying out, "Jesus saves!" One day his friends pulled him into the library and said, "You are ruining your life! You are ruining your reputation and your career!" In tears the young man cried, "Did He shed His blood for me? If He shed His blood for me, I have no choice now. I am not my own anymore!"[17]

This sums it all up. Why should I live for His reward? Because He shed His blood for me! "You are bought with a price, do not become slaves of men" (1 Cor. 7:23). Because He drank the Father's cup for me, He is worthy of my whole life! Because He took the punishment of hell for me, He is my greatest purpose in life.

Why should I live for His reward? Because He cried the cry of forsakenness, I will never ever forsake Him! Why should I live for His reward? Because His heart ruptured open and every drop of His sacred blood rushed out! Why should I live for His reward? Because he breathes His Spirit on me and I can do no other. I must live for His reward because my heart and my whole spiritual and theological perspective have been undone by a revelation of the Lamb!

CHAPTER 22 ENDNOTES

1. John Piper, "Don't Waste Your Life," Presentation to Campus Crusade for Christ, December 29, 2003, A Crossway Video Production.
2. John Piper, *Don't Waste Your Life*, 44.
3. Ibid., 59.
4. Ibid., 48–49.
5. I heard this story at Camp Mystic, before I was saved; and through the years I've always remembered it. For fourteen years of my young life, I attended this wonderful girls' camp with many Godly influences, in the hill country of Texas. I was about twelve when I heard a counselor tell this story. It had a profound influence on me and I have never forgotten it.
6. John Piper, *Don't Waste Your Life*, 32, 59
7. Sophie and her mother Nicky's ministry to the poor and the orphans is called Awaken Love: www.awakenlove.org.
8. Misty Edwards in a message at IHOP "One Thing Conference," January, 2012.
9. John Piper, *Don't Waste Your Life*, 32, 59.
10. Again, please don't think you're too old. It's not time for you to be "out to pasture," watching young ones burn for the Lamb. You do have to let God fan again the flame within you so that you too will burn. But then, turn and reach out to the younger ones. They long for your fellowship and your encouragement, and you can be like a beacon to them, leading the way as together we bring the Lamb the reward of

His suffering. (We offer short, ten day internships as well as a ministry training school for older adults: www.gloryofthelamb.com).

11. In South Africa bombs had just exploded in the city, when a woman rushed up to Blessitt and cried, "What is this?...I have been sick for years. I just went to the doctor today. I was walking along the pedestrian walk right there in great pain. Suddenly, I was completely healed. I have no pain! I stopped, looked around, and I saw that cross! What is happening?" Blessitt explained the mission of the cross and led her in a prayer to receive the Lord. For the next twenty-one days people gathered in a park as hundreds were healed, with thousands saved. Soon people from all over Johannesburg, blacks and whites alike, were kneeling around the cross, crying, hugging, and washing one another's feet. What made it so amazing was that this was when Apartheid still racially divided the land. "These explosions of love, hope, and unity were a powerful response to the explosions of violence tearing South Africa apart," said Blessitt. "My goal in life is to invite people to the cross," he says. "The cross is the sign of the love of God in sending Jesus" (Arthur Blessitt, *The Cross* [Colorado Springs: Authentic Publishing, 2009], 108, 122–123).

12. A general in war-torn Barundi shouted, "Don't you know it's dangerous here!" Blessitt said, "Yes, I know, but the cross is needed in the places of suffering and death and hurt." While carrying the cross through Estonia, people ran up and kissed the wooden beams. In Okinawa, while praying with six young men, he looked up and saw groups of young people lining up, wanting to hear about Jesus and be near the cross (Arthur Blessitt, *The Cross*, 75).

13. A man from Sri Lanka ran up to Blessitt, pointing to the twelve-foot cross which he carried through this predominantly Buddhist, Hindu, and Muslim nation. "I was sick and dying one night," the Sri Lankan said excitedly, "but a man came to me and said I should follow Him. Afterward, I was immediately well." He continued, "Passing a store one day I saw a picture of Him. He was hanging on a big cross like this." Blessitt gave the man a Bible, explained to him who Jesus is, and led him in a prayer to receive the Lord. "As we talked to other people in Sri Lanka," said Blessitt, "we didn't talk about Christianity or Buddhism or Islam or Hinduism. We talked about Jesus." One day, while carrying the cross up a mountain in Israel, an Israeli army bus stopped and invited him to come on the bus. After he talked about the cross and the love of Jesus, concluding with a prayer, the Jewish people burst into applause. They rushed off the bus and grabbed the cross, lifting it high and taking pictures (Arthur Blessitt, *The Cross*, 100).

14. This same thing happened to Collin's dad, Mark, and the others. They all looked into the cup until their hearts were undone. Then when Mark was asked to tell what happened to him in the ministry school, he, too, burst into tears and the glory filled the room.

15. Nicky has found what Jesus meant when He said, "Enter in through the narrow gate [the cross], for wide is the gate and broad is the road that leads to destruction, and many enter through it. But small is the gate and narrow the road that leads to life, and only a few find it" (Matt 7:13–14).

16. John Stott, *The Cross of Christ*, 343. Paul's whole world revolved around "Christ and him crucified" (1 Cor. 2:2). He said, "God forbid that I should glory [*kauchaomai*], save in the cross of the Lord Jesus Christ" (Gal. 6:14). The Greek word *kauchaomai* means "to trust in, boast in, revel in, rejoice in, live for," points out John Stott. Paul's message was the cross: "I preach Christ crucified" (1 Cor. 1:23) (Stott, *The Cross of Christ*, 349). To Paul the cross was the apex, the zenith, the colossus of all time. It was the pinnacle of redemption. The mountain peak of creation. The hinge of all history. The heart of all heaven. This is what drove Paul over land and sea, in spite of incredible hardships, to preach the gospel of Christ. "Paul's whole world was in orbit around the cross." It filled Paul's "vision, illumined his life, warmed his spirit. He 'gloried' in it," says John Stott. He was driven by Christ's love displayed on the cross. It consumed him and gave him a clear sighted focus for ministry.

17. Paul Washer, "Crushing Christ," a sermon on www.sermonaudio.com.

Chapter 23

FOREVER UNDONE

The Mystery of the Father's Heart Unveiled

WAVES CRASH AGAINST the rocks, splashing the old apostle John with icy spray. As he sits on a cliff overlooking the Aegean Sea, he watches the rising sun cast orange folds across the waters. Lines of age chisel his face. His white hair tosses in the breeze as he closes his eyes to pray. Worship spills from his lips and tears flood his eyes, clinging to his lashes.

He has been banished to this island for "the word of God and the testimony of Jesus" (Rev. 1:9), but he hardly notices his chains. Even as sunlight swallows up the light of the stars, the sweet presence of God swallows up the pain of his persecution.

As he worships, he feels the warmth of the Holy Spirit envelop him like a blanket. Suddenly the heat increases and a deep trembling begins somewhere in his innermost being. He looks up as heaven opens and he hears a voice proclaiming, "Behold the Lion of the tribe of Judah!" (Rev. 5:4).

John peers into the throne room and what he sees takes his breath away. The glory of God floods the room like rainbows of splendor. And there, standing before the throne, he sees, not a lion, but a slain Lamb: "Then I saw a Lamb, looking as though it had been slain, standing in the center of the throne" (Rev. 5:6).

Instantly he knows it is Jesus. The reason he looks like a freshly slaughtered lamb is because He still bears wounds from His sacrifice. The wounds carve into His flesh, shining like glorious gems. I can imagine that, in that moment of divine inspiration, John was completely undone by a revelation of the Lamb.

I'm sure John fell to his knees sobbing, "My Jesus! My Savior! My Adonai!" I can picture him reaching out a shaking hand, longing to touch the wound in His feet. Then finally, he pulls out a scroll and begins writing. Twenty-nine times he describes the Lamb of God in the Book of Revelation. He knows this vision must be recorded so that others can behold the Lamb.

He looks back up at Jesus, standing like a shining orb, lighting all heaven with His glory. He suddenly becomes aware of choirs of angels surrounding the Lamb and giving Him glory. The theme of these heavenly worshipers is the same: "You are worthy...because you were slain, and with your blood you purchased men for God" (Rev. 5:9). Angelic beings, numbering "ten thousand times ten thousands and thousands of thousands" are "saying in a loud voice 'Deserving is the Lamb, Who was sacrificed, to receive all the power and riches and wisdom and might and honor and majesty (glory and splendor) and blessing!'" (5:12, AMP).

With trembling hand and blazing heart, tears swimming in his eyes, John writes what he sees. Nothing means more to him than seeing Jesus receive the glory He deserves for what He suffered as the Lamb. In fact, he knows that when at last Jesus receives the glory He deserves from His bride —heaven will at last kiss earth.

CLOTHED IN HUMILITY

Now the Father looks down on this earth, searching for a bride for His Son. She must be one who loves Him as He loves Him and is clothed in true humility. "Those who aspire to go higher in God, need to learn to go deeper in humility," said Judson Cornwall in *Forbidden Glory*.[1]

I want to tell you about a dream I've never forgotten which I had over thirty years ago. It was my first night at a Christian university, which also had a Christian television program. In the dream I saw Jesus standing behind a huge red velvet curtain, weeping profusely. He said simply, "My people have made my church a *stage*."

Ever since then my heart aches whenever I hear ministers and worship leaders refer to the platform in a church as a "stage." This is where preaching the gospel and worshiping the Lamb take place, but a "stage" implies a place of performance. I also wince when I hear preachers refer to the people as "the audience," because again that implies a performance. Maybe that seems extreme but I saw Jesus weeping over it.

So may we lay aside our need to be seen, our need to perform, and the pride that causes us to be crippled by fear of others. May we draw near to Jesus, not looking down on ourselves, but looking up to Him. As Judson Cornwall said, "True humility is not looking down on yourself, but looking up to Christ."[2] May we come like little children, focusing on Him and learning from His humility. As Paul said,

> Your attitude should be the same as that of Christ Jesus: Who being in very nature God, did not consider equality with God something to be grasped, but made himself nothing, taking the very nature of a servant....And being found in appearance as a man, he humbled himself and became obedient to death—even death on a cross.
>
> —PHILIPPIANS 2:5–8

May we learn from our Lord's humility, but may we also learn from the angels. Though millions of angelic beings are beautiful beyond description, they never draw attention to themselves. Lucifer and one-third of the angels did that once before, and we know what became of them: "How you have fallen from heaven O morning star, son of the dawn....You said in your heart, I will ascend to heaven; I will raise my throne above the stars of God" (Isa. 14:12–13).

Now in the courts above, where angelic beings focus continually on the Lamb, they bow and fervently cry, "Deserving is the Lamb, Who was sacrificed, to receive all the power and riches and wisdom and might and honor and majesty (glory, splendor) and blessing!" (Rev. 5:12, AMP).

Look especially at the seraphs who burn the most brightly: "Above him were seraphs, each with six wings: With two wings they covered their faces, with two they covered their feet, and with two they were flying" (Isa. 6:2).

These glorious creatures cover their faces with two of their wings so they can hardly be seen. They even cover their feet with two more of their wings, for they don't want their spectacular brilliance to draw attention away from the Lord. He is the one who paid the price at Calvary, and He alone deserves all the adoration and glory.

Yes, if we can get out of the way, God wants to use us to bring glory to His Son. He wants to use us to bring Him the reward of His suffering as a Lamb. Can you believe it? That He would allow us to be part of bringing glory to His Son on earth staggers our human senses. But He delights in using common people. He loves to slip in quietly through lowly mangers, swaddled in rags of meekness, worshiped by humble shepherds. That's why God will have a bride for His Son who is clothed in humility, just like her humble Bridegroom Lamb.

BEHOLDING THE LAMB IN HEAVEN

Lift your gaze back up to heaven now, and look through John's eyes. Remember, the Book of Revelation is a window into heaven. It shows us the central focus of eternity. It gives us a revelation of the Lamb.

Focus again on the crowd of heavenly beings that surround the Lamb of God. Notice their reactions. So undone are the twenty-four elders when they gaze on His undimmed splendor, all they can do is fall on their faces and cast their crowns at His nail-scarred feet. Angels are so undone that all they can do is cry, "Worthy is the Lamb!" Seraphim are so undone that all they can do is cover their eyes and whisper, "Holy, holy, holy!"

As you gaze on the brilliance of the Son, with unveiled eyes look once more upon the glory streaming from every wound in His flesh. See the hands and feet, which ached from iron spikes driven through them, now beaming with light rays of splendor. See that hole in His side now rushing with rivers of glory. Draw up close and immerse yourself in these shining pools.

Now focus your gaze directly on His face, once coated with blood and human spit, now beaming like a trillion suns. See His head and His hair, once drenched in His own blood, now gleaming white like snow. Look into His eyes, once bloodshot and bulging with tears, now burning with tears of fire. See His lips, once cracked and battered and bruised, now smiling brightly, splashing all heaven with glory. See the risen Lamb, shining in beauty and splendor, as eternity explodes with His light.

When Father Beholds Him

Now once again remember, if this is what John sees, and if this is what the angels and elders and seraphs see, above all else, this is what the Father sees. He sees His Son—wounded and blazing in glory. Yet every glimpse at His Son, looking like a slain Lamb, reminds Him of His profound sacrifice.

It reminds Him how Jesus left His side in glory, then took our place and hung like a bleeding Lamb on a cross. It brings to His memory His Son's mangled limbs and body, coated with blood and tears. It causes Him to remember His Son writhing under the horror of His cup of wrath. It makes Him recall His Son's split lips and raw tongue as He bellowed the cry of the ages, "My God, why have You forsaken Me?" It stirs up His feelings as He watched His Son's heart rupture and every precious drop of His sacred blood roll out. Now as the Father looks at His wounded Son, I'm sure His heart is continually undone.

So let your heart fill with the Father's longings. Like a stethoscope, let your sensitive spirit pick up the heartbeat of the Father for His Son. Let His passion for His Beloved flood your own heart. Sense His feelings until your own heart trembles with His tremblings.

This is indeed the mystery of the Father's heart unveiled. It probes into the secret chambers of God's tender feelings for His Son. It taps into the sacred emotions of God loving God. It senses the throbbing of His pulse beat as He looks upon His Son and adores. It dares to absorb the warm atmosphere of divine love that fills the Triune Godhead. It reveals the greatest love story of all time.

The Father's Love Story

The apostle John looked into heaven and saw a company of people who "follow the Lamb wherever He goes" (Rev. 14:4). This is what we've been trying to do in this book. From before the world's foundation, through the unveiling of His glory at creation, all through the Bible, to the garden of tears, to the mount of crucifixion, to His resurrection and ascension into heaven, to His glorification and exaltation on the throne, to the day when He pours out a revelation of the Lamb to the nations.

From glory to glory, from Alpha to Omega, from eternity to eternity, we have tried to "follow the Lamb wherever He goes."

Yes, long before God tumbled worlds into space and fashioned the body of a man, the Father turned to His Son. As He gazed at the uncreated glory of His Beloved, He said,

> *Son, I want a family. I want to give You a bride, but it will require a fathomless sacrifice. You must lay down Your life as a lamb.*

This is God's grand love story. God told the story of His love all through the pages of the Old Testament, but this was only a preview. Then He dramatized it on two stakes of wood. He portrayed it on a platform called Calvary. He painted it on His own Son's flesh.

He illumined it as He rose from the grave. He orchestrated it with choirs of worshiping angels when He ascended. He placed it in the museum of eternity and immortalized it by causing His human flesh to perpetually shine. This visage of the wounded One on the throne, with glory bleeding from every wound, ever reminds us of God's eternal love story.

Yes, this is the greatest love story of all time. It's the story of a Father's love for His Son and the Son's love for His bride. It's the story of the Holy Spirit preparing a bride who will love the Son as the Father loves Him.

FOR THE HONOR OF YOUR SON

The church now stands at a watershed moment in human history. It's a critical juncture in time, as darkness creeps over the land and seeks to enter the church. Even popular teachings threaten to blind us from what Paul said was "of first importance" (1 Cor. 15:3), which is the gospel of Jesus Christ.

We must tune our ears above the din of the crowd, not being distracted from the pierced One on the throne by the latest and greatest revelation. We must lift our vision to higher heights. We must feel the heartbeat of the Father as He looks down from heaven. It is time to hear His cry, from the depths of His being, as He bellows to His church:

This is My Son! He will be honored in My church on earth as He is honored in heaven! He will receive what He deserves for giving His life as your Lamb!

May we kneel before Him and echo, with our whole heart, this cry of the Father's heart.

Oh Father, this is Your Son! For Your Son's sake, bring the church back to the cross. For Your Son's sake, pour revival fire upon Your people. For Your Son's sake, breathe Your wind upon the fire and spread revival through the whole earth!

Give a revelation of the Lamb to Israel for Your Son's sake! Do it for Him, Father! For Your Son's sake, bring Him the bride who loves Him as He deserves! Bring the nations to the Lamb for Your Son's sake! Set America ablaze with revival for Your Son's sake! Let His blood be honored and His cross be lifted—for Your Son's sake! Let Him receive the reward of His sufferings as a Lamb! It's all for Jesus! All for Your Beloved Son! All for the sake of the Lamb!

Now may you live your life for this high calling—to bring Jesus, the Lamb who was slain, the reward of His suffering. Then, when at last you see Him face to face, you won't turn your eyes away in shame. You'll look Him full in the face as He unfolds to you revelation after revelation of Himself. And as He continually unveils His wonder before your adoring gaze, your heart will be eternally undone by a revelation of the Lamb!

CHAPTER 23 ENDNOTES

1. Judson Cornwall, *Forbidden Glory: Portraits of Pride* (Hagerstown, MD: McDougal Publishing, 2001), 225.
2. Ibid.

ACKNOWLEDGMENTS

I WANT TO THANK all the African pastors who so voraciously read the prepublication of this book at our Kenya Ablaze School of Revival. Your hunger for truth moves me deeply, and your passion to spread the fire of the cross through Africa inspires us all. I especially want to express my love and gratitude to Mary and Kevin Wells for your insightful comments in the preparation of this book. And finally I want to thank all whose hearts have been undone by a revelation of the Lamb and who are burning to bring Jesus His reward.

ABOUT *the* AUTHOR

D R. SANDY'S HEART burns to bring Jesus, the Lamb who was slain, the reward of His suffering. She is a theology professor, leading "Unquenchable Flame" and "Revivalists of the Cross" Internships at a beautiful camp on the Gulf Coast. She teaches in Bible colleges and churches and ministers with a team of "young revivalists" throughout America, England, Kenya, and East Africa, as well as Canada, Hong Kong, and Germany. She has written thirteen other books. She earned her PhD at Fuller Theological Seminary in Pasadena, California.

BEHOLD *the* LAMB SCHOOL *of* REVIVAL

Equipping Revivalists of the Cross

I<small>F YOU ARE</small> hungry for revival, longing for a move of God that is grounded in solid biblical theology, Behold the Lamb School of Revival welcomes you. Through classes, prayer and worship, and ministry opportunities, you will find your preaching voice, you will be impacted by a cry for justice for the poor, and you will receive impartations of genuine revival fire. Join students from all over the world—Germany, England, Scotland, Mexico, South Africa, and more—to behold the Lamb of God. You will emerge from this school as a Revivalist of the Cross, burning to bring Jesus the reward of His suffering as a Lamb.

Mission: To equip and send leaders who will make "Christ and Him crucified" (1 Cor. 2:2) central, ultimately spreading the fire of the Cross through the world and preparing a bride for the Lamb.

CLASSES OFFERED:

Glory of the Lamb: Unveiling the glory of Christ through the Bible

Theology Ablaze: Digging into the theology of the cross

Cry for Justice: Become compelled with God's compassion for the poor and suffering children

The Lamb's Heart: Developing the character of Christ.

Missions/Evangelism: Learn mission principles and have opportunities to minister in rehabs and an international mission trip.

The Blood Cries: Hear the stories of racial pain and help bring reconciliation with races.

Supernatural Ministry Training: Grow in the prophetic, signs and wonders, and miracles.

Revival History: Discover revival secrets from the Moravians, Wesleys, Edwards, and others.

S.O.A.R: Advanced Ministry Training

Finding Your Preaching Voice: Learn to preach with anointing and fire.

Anointed Writing: Learn skills in writing and how to make your writing burn.

Hands on ministry: You will not just be sitting in classes but you will have many opportunities for hands on ministry such as praying in fire tunnels, praying on the America Ablaze prayer team, and ministering in rehabs and on mission trips. There will also be a Mission Practicum in your second trimester.

CONTACT US

WEB SITE:
www.gloryofthelamb.com

E-MAIL:
drsandy.aam@gmail.com OR hmmmary@hotmail.com

LOCATION:
Dr. Sandy Kirk
America Ablaze Ministries 12251
County Rd 91
Lillian, AL 36549
(on the Gulf Coast of Alabama)

TELEPHONE:
251-962-7172 OR 251-979-9068

Unquenchable Flame Internships

Calling Revivalists of the Cross

Come be part of a one-month or twelve-day Internship at America Ablaze Ministries on the Gulf Coast where you will receive a deep impartation of the Cross and the Fire of Revival.

What to expect

- Be undone by the depths of the Cross.
- Receive impartations of revival fire.
- Find your preaching voice.
- Develop fervent prayer.
- Attend Church of His Presence and Bay of the Holy Spirit Revival.

Where?

- Join us on our beautiful ministry grounds on the Gulf Coast in Lillian, Alabama.

When?

- Spring or Fall for twelve days and summer for one month

Who?

- All ages are welcome.

For more info or to apply:

- Go to www.gloryofthelamb.com

- Or email hmmmary@hotmail.com or drsandy.aam@gmail.com

OTHER BOOKS *by the* AUTHOR

The Pierced Generation

Bethlehem's Lamb

The Unquenchable Flame

Glory of the Lamb

Rivers of Glory

The Cry of a Fatherless Generation

The Pain

The Masterpiece

Theology Ablaze

A Revelation of the Lamb for America

The Pain in an African Heart

America Ablaze

Would Jesus Eat His Vegetables? (children's book)

Order from our Web site: www.gloryofthelamb.com

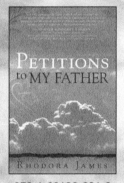

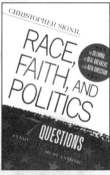